The
NEAL A.
MAXWELL
Quote Book

The NEAL A. MAXWELL Quote Book

EDITED BY

CORY H. MAXWELL

BOOKCRAFT
Salt Lake City, Utah

Library of Congress Catalog Card Number: 97-68806

ISBN 1-57008-325-8

Third Printing, 1997

Printed in the United States of America

Contents

PREFACE

For many years I have wanted to prepare a book containing insights from my father, Elder Neal A. Maxwell. I am blessed to know him both as a wise father who loves his family (and loves to spend time with them) and as one of the Lord's anointed who has an abiding love of the restored gospel of Jesus Christ, a keen intellect, and a marvelous facility with language. His ability to coin a phrase that teaches or reaffirms a gospel principle in a succinct and memorable way is widely known. The scope of his understanding and the diversity and clarity of his insights are striking, and he has the requisite courage and charity to say things that will "comfort the afflicted and afflict the comfortable."

Elder Bruce C. Hafen recalls sitting in the Tabernacle when Elder Maxwell gave one of his first general conference talks. "His speaking style was so provocative that it left the brethren among whom I sat visibly breathless. They were not accustomed to such phrases as 'The living of one protective principle of the gospel is better than a thousand compensatory governmental programs—which are, so often, like "straightening deck chairs on the Titanic."' Or, 'Hearts "set so much upon the things of this world" are hearts *so set* they must first be broken.'" Elder Hafen goes on to note that Elder Maxwell's books and addresses "are nearly all laced with verbal imagery, metaphors, and alliteration. These poetic devices and his sense of the well-turned phrase often make his language closer to poetry than to prose. For instance, 'Let us have integrity and not write checks with our tongues which our conduct cannot cash.' Consider also: 'The home lies at the headwaters of the stream of civilization and we must keep it happy and pure' rather than putting all our efforts into reducing the 'downstream pollution.' The LDS educators who heard him will always remember his thoughtful response to the issue of balancing one's Church and professional interests: 'The LDS scholar has his citizenship in the Kingdom, but carries his passport into the professional world—not the other way around.'" ("Elder Neal A. Maxwell: An Understanding Heart," *Ensign*, February 1982, pp. 9–10.)

I have spoken with Elder Maxwell a number of times over the years about a quote book, and five or six years ago began reviewing his talks and books. I have worked in earnest over the last two years preparing this manuscript. The task has been both challenging and rewarding. Because I have heard Elder Maxwell speak to numerous gatherings and have read his books and articles, I knew from the outset that this would be a daunting task. Once I really became immersed in the project, I realized that it was even more intimidating than I had expected.

The body of work from which I had to draw (just in terms of books, articles for magazines, and talks for which complete transcripts exist) would comprise, estimating conservatively, some 5,000 pages. I have read the twenty-five books written by Elder Maxwell (as well as chapters he has contributed to several other books) and over a hundred of his articles and talks. Transcripts of some of these talks are not widely available because they were given in private or informal settings. In this undertaking I have been aided by work performed by Hoyt W. Brewster, Jr. Prior to his call to preside over the Netherlands Amsterdam Mission, he was the managing director of the Priesthood Department for the Church and had occasion to work with Elder Maxwell. Brother Brewster has long had a keen interest in Elder Maxwell's books and sermons, and assembled numerous quotes, organizing them topically, out of a desire to be helpful to Elder Maxwell and his family. Brother Brewster's efforts have made it possible to release this book much earlier than otherwise would have been possible.

Deciding which quotes to include in a work such as this is naturally a subjective process. While I have attempted to include those quotes that I felt were the most important, incisive, and memorable expressions of gospel principles, another compiler would undoubtedly have included some quotes that I have not. Some readers will likely be disappointed to learn that a favorite quote of theirs is not found here. I hope I have been successful in finding "most of the best" and in conveying a sense of the keenness of Elder Maxwell's insights and his boundless love for the fulness of the gospel. Though some duplication is almost unavoidable—and perhaps is even advisable to round out a particular topic—I have tried to keep such repetitions to a minimum.

The excerpts included do *not* reflect the frequency with which Elder Maxwell has quoted from the scriptures, nor do they show the great frequency with which he has shared ideas derived from his reading of the writings of prophets and of other leaders and thinkers. It seemed advisable, given the limitations of space, to give preference to Elder Maxwell's insights and his contribution to our understanding of the gospel. Obviously, short excerpts also do not give a sense of continuity or illustrate Elder Maxwell's development of a theme.

As to source citations, most references are given in shortened form in the text, and full bibliographic details for all sources are provided at the back of the book. A list of abbreviations used for book titles appears in the preliminary pages. It should also be noted that page numbers have not been included in references to talks not formally published.

Many people have helped make this work a reality and have offered invaluable suggestions and counsel. I appreciate the secretaries who have worked for Elder Maxwell over the years, particularly Susan Jackson, his secretary of fourteen years, for helping to gather copies of his talks and other material written by him. I am grateful to George Bickerstaff for his wise and conscientious editorial assistance on this manuscript (and on others he has edited for Elder Maxwell in recent years), and to Jana Erickson for her thoughtful and capable oversight of the design of this book. I am indebted to Jan Jensen for assisting in numerous ways to ensure that work on the manuscript proceeded as quickly and efficiently as possible and for helping to tie up loose ends. I appreciate the careful attention to detail given by Garry Garff and Janna Nielsen as final preparations were made to send the book to press.

My wife, Karen, has not only encouraged me to complete this project but also reviewed drafts of the manuscript and offered many helpful suggestions. I could not have done it without her support. I'm also grateful to my children, who have been willing to put up with my tendency, while working on this project, to be preoccupied or inaccessible.

Finally, I am grateful to Elder Maxwell for allowing this work to be published and for "paying the price" to become an effective teacher of and powerful advocate for the gospel of Jesus Christ. For

Elder Maxwell, speaking or writing about the gospel is not merely an intellectual pursuit. His teachings are borne of the perspective that understanding and applying the principles of the gospel is the very purpose of our experience on earth—that bringing our behavior in line with gospel standards is serious business. Elder Henry B. Eyring has observed: "Many of us have felt the special calling and power of Elder Neal A. Maxwell. There is no doubt that in focusing the light of the gospel on others, to illuminate their lives and help them contribute more, Elder Maxwell has been illuminated and changed by that light himself." ("Elder Neal A. Maxwell: Pursuing 'A More Excellent Way,'" *Ensign*, January 1987, p. 11.) I hope readers will find this representative sample of his work as thought-provoking and inspiring as I have.

CORY H. MAXWELL

Salt Lake City, Utah
May 1997

From the Author

In the course of my ministry, I hope to have provided some useful commentary about the restored gospel and Church. Even so, I have a concern about being quoted too frequently; therefore, producing a quote book seems paradoxical. Yet, if it is to be done, the time has come in my ministry when such a selected compilation can best be undertaken.

I am grateful to have an able and devoted son, Cory, who has done the compiling.

A significant number of "new" quotes, not previously published, is included. Slight editing of a few earlier quotes has been done for improved punctuation or for a better rendering of a phrase.

The topical organization of the book should be a convenience for readers even though, of course, topics overlap. While no cross-referencing of related topics and quotes has been done, the extensive subject index should supply the required access.

With all its limitations, the book comes to the reader with my love and with my sincere hope that it may be of some value and of some convenience.

ELDER NEAL A. MAXWELL

Salt Lake City, Utah
May 1997

ABBREVIATIONS USED

Abbreviation	Book Title
As I Am	Even As I Am
Believe	That Ye May Believe
Choose	A Time to Choose
Deposition	Deposition of a Disciple
Endure	If Thou Endure It Well
Excellent	". . . A More Excellent Way"
Experience	All These Things Shall Give Thee Experience
Faith	Lord, Increase Our Faith
Flood	A Wonderful Flood of Light
Heart	Of One Heart
Look Back	Look Back at Sodom
Meek	Meek and Lowly
Men and Women	Men and Women of Christ
My Family	That My Family Should Partake
Not My Will	"Not My Will, But Thine"
Notwithstanding	Notwithstanding My Weakness
Power	"For the Power Is in Them . . ." Mormon Musings
Precious Things	Plain and Precious Things
Press Forward	Wherefore, Ye Must Press Forward
Prove	We Will Prove Them Herewith
Really Are	Things As They Really Are
Sermons	Sermons Not Spoken
Small Moment	"But for a Small Moment"
Smallest Part	The Smallest Part
We Talk of Christ	We Talk of Christ, We Rejoice in Christ

ABILITY

God does not begin by asking us about our ability, but only about our availability, and if we then prove our dependability, he will increase our capability! ("It's Service, Not Status, That Counts," p. 7.)

The large attributes, those that cover the most ground, are almost always developed incrementally—by small steps, small decisions, and small initiatives. These attributes and talents we bring with us from the premortal world were most likely developed there in the same way. Yet upon seeing someone with highly developed cardinal attributes, we may respond that "he was born that way." Whatever the case, so far as the mortal life is concerned, it is what we do with these qualities that matters. (*Endure*, p. 35.)

ABORTION

Abortion, which has increased enormously, causes one to ask, "Have we strayed so far from God's second great commandment—love thy neighbor—that a baby in a womb no longer qualifies to be loved—at least as a mother's neighbor?" (*Ensign*, May 1993, p. 76.)

If the nearly one-and-a-half million babies aborted in America each year could, somehow, vote, chameleon candidates would find fresh reasons to be concerned about abortion, whereas now they are unconcerned. (Dictated December 1996.)

When we don't like to face up to hard facts, we use soft words. We do not speak about killing a baby within the womb, but about "termination of potential life." Words are often multiplied to try to cover dark deeds. (*Really Are*, p. 55.)

ACCOUNTABILITY

Pilate's hands were never dirtier than just after he had washed them. (*Ensign*, November 1974, p. 13.)

The scriptural line, "Nevertheless thou mayest choose for thyself," remains a true and fixed reality of mortality. After all we can do, people remain free to choose for themselves even when we err. (Dictated December 1996.)

I wish we could all sense how often our little pebble of poor performance helps to start, or to sustain, an avalanche. (*Deposition*, p. 90.)

Commendable generosity in one thing does not reduce our accountability for smallness of soul in another. Remember "one thing thou lackest" (Mark 10:21). (*Flood*, p. 104.)

Faith is never lost without leaving a valid record of its past presence. Its tracings, like it or not, show the bounds of previous belief and tell of our present accountability. These tracings will disclose what we once knew, when we knew it, and how we behaved in reference to it. No present rationalizations can erase past realizations. (*Faith*, p. 28.)

ACTIVATION

This work of reactivation often involves group study and socials, but, essentially, it is done a soul at a time, quietly and with dignity. It is done less "by the numbers" and more "by the Spirit." It is less technique than genuine caring, more extending a helping hand than writing new handbooks. (*Ensign*, May 1982, p. 37.)

Organized love is better than generalized concern. (*Ensign*, May 1982, p. 37.)

Never underestimate the power of privately extending a simple, loving, but direct challenge. Though it may not be reciprocated, such love is never wasted. (*Ensign*, May 1982, p. 37.)

Once one leaves the porch and comes inside the Church, then one not only hears the music more clearly—he becomes a part of it. (*Ensign*, November 1974, p. 13.)

Significantly . . . Church members did not become inactive while crossing the plains, when the sense of belonging and being needed was so profound. (*Ensign*, May 1982, p. 37.)

It is easier to find and to help "the one" when the "ninety and nine" are securely together. (*Deposition*, p. 35.)

So often what parched and thirsty people need is to be nourished by the drinking of true doctrines and to be revived by the food of fellowship. Giving genuine companionship to the malnourished mortals who have known so little love and so few friends is as vital as food for the starving. (*Experience*, p. 55.)

Early identification—in the home and in Church settings—of the deep, unmet needs of members can often result in an opportunity to move against habits that are still manageable and in chances for love to be effective while the personality is still partially plastic. We have heard and rejoiced in the stories of gallant members who have been rescued "downstream" by the various organizational "fish out" parties; what we have not heard about are how many individuals who might have been leaders were swept beyond our reach by youthful habits or attitudes which hardened under the full gaze of some of us who might have intervened intelligently while there was still time. (*Excellent*, pp. 52–53.)

ADVERSITY

We should not complain about our own life's not being a rose garden when we remember who wore the crown of thorns. (*Ensign*, May 1987, p. 72.)

How can there be later magnification without our enduring some present deprivation? The enlarging of the soul requires not only some remodeling, but some excavating. . . . How could there be refining fires without our enduring some heat? (*Ensign*, May 1990, p. 34.)

A good friend, who knows whereof he speaks, has observed of trials, "If it's fair, it is not a true trial!" That is, without the added presence of some inexplicableness and some irony and injustice, the experience may not stretch us or lift us sufficiently. The crucifixion of Christ was clearly the greatest injustice in human history, but the Savior bore up under it with majesty and indescribable valor. (*Experience*, p. 31.)

For the faithful, our finest hours are sometimes during or just following our darkest hours. (*Ensign*, May 1984, p. 22.)

Only the Lord can compare crosses, but all crosses are easier to carry when we keep moving. (*Ensign*, November 1976, p. 14.)

How can it rain on the just and the unjust alike without occasionally raining on our personal parade? (See Matthew 5:45.) (*Ensign*, November 1989, p. 84.)

Real storm fronts do pass turbulently through our lives, but they do not last forever. We can learn the important difference between passing, local cloud cover, and general darkness. (*Faith*, p. 43.)

One of the most powerful and searching questions ever asked of all of us in our sufferings hangs in time and space before us: "The Son of Man hath descended below them all. Art thou greater than he?" (D&C 122:8.) (*Ensign*, May 1990, p. 35.)

Adversity can increase faith or instead can cause the troubling roots of bitterness to spring up. (*Ensign*, May 1991, p. 88.)

One's life . . . cannot be both faith-filled and stress-free. (*Ensign*, May 1991, p. 88.)

How can you and I really expect to glide naively through life as if to say, "Lord, give me experience, but not grief, not sorrow, not pain, not opposition, not betrayal, and certainly not to be forsaken. Keep from me, Lord, all those experiences which made Thee what Thou art! Then let me come and dwell with Thee and fully share Thy joy!" (*Ensign*, May 1991, p. 88.)

Deprivation may prepare us for further consecration, though we shudder at the thought. If we are too easily contented, God may administer a dose of divine discontent. (*Ensign*, November 1992, p. 66.)

Daily hope is vital, since the "Winter Quarters" of our lives are not immediately adjacent to our promised land either. An arduous trek still awaits, but hope spurs weary disciples on. (*Ensign*, November 1994, p. 36.)

While boulders surely block our way, loose gravel slows discipleship, too. Even a small stone can become a stumbling block. (*Ensign*, May 1994, p. 66.)

Like his Master, the true believer loves his life but is willing to lay it down *or* to see it slip slowly away through affliction. If he is given a "thorn in the flesh," he does not demand to see the rose garden. ("'True Believers in Christ,'" p. 139.)

The storm fronts that come into our lives will not last forever. We can surmount the drifts of difficulties and we can hold out if we maintain our perspective and faith. . . . Just as we know there is a sun just beyond today's cloud cover, so we must not doubt the continued, watchful, and tutoring presence of *The Son* in spite of the stormy seasons in our lives. (*As I Am*, pp. 102–3.)

The harrowing of the soul can be like the harrowing of the soil; to increase the yield, things are turned upside down. (*Men and Women*, p. 72.)

We cannot expect to live in a time when "men's hearts shall fail them" (D&C 45:26) without expecting the faithful to have a few fibrillations of their own! (*Believe*, p. 76.)

There is a clear and obvious difference between being "given" a "thorn in the flesh," as Paul was, and willfully impaling ourselves on the spears of sin. In the former circumstance, the afflicted may ask "Why?"—but in the latter situation that is not a useful question to address to anyone but ourselves. (*Experience*, p. 32.)

Bad breaks . . . need not break a good man; they may with God's help even make him better! (*Experience*, pp. 40–41.)

The thermostat on the furnace of affliction will not have been set too high for us—though clearly we may think so at the time. Our God is a refining God who has been tempering soul-steel for a very long time. He knows when the right edge has been put upon our excellence but also when there is more in us than we have yet given. (*Experience*, p. 46.)

You are all familiar with Olympic high-divers. They get scored on their dives according to the degree of difficulty. And you and I see people who are deprived in various ways performing so well in the midst of deep difficulty. . . . I think of the scripture, "Where much is given, much is required," (D&C 82:3) and wonder if there is a sub-scripture that "Where less is given, some nevertheless return so very much. . . ." In [a sermon the Prophet Joseph] rendered a verse in the Book of Hebrews differently. Paul said, "[God] is a rewarder of them that diligently seek him." (Hebrews 11:6). The Prophet Joseph rendered it, "God is a *revealer* to them that diligently seek him. . . ." I salute all of those through whom the works of God are manifest in the midst of their deprivations. . . . I remind us all that we should submit to Him in the degrees of difficulty that are given to us and rejoice in those who then do so well. On judgment day when all those who have been faithful will hear the words "Well done, thou good and faithful servant" (Matthew 25:23), perhaps there will be one addendum to some who have in their extraordinary deprivation done so very well—"Especially well done, thou good and faithful servant." (Talk given January 13, 1995.)

Some will ask, what of those circumstances when individuals appear to be no more than a surviving vegetable, unable to express themselves, not able to serve? We are not equipped to answer fully such questions. We should not assume, however, that just because something is unexplainable by us it is unexplainable. Meanwhile we see in such a situation opportunities for service, even when the one being served may not know of the service. (*Not My Will*, p. 124.)

The sobering indication "All these things shall give thee experience, and shall be for thy good" (D&C 122:7) tells us that while we are doctrinally rich, we are usually experience poor. God's plan is designed to correct the latter deficiency; one's soul shivers, however, as one contemplates the implications. (*Faith*, pp. 34–35.)

God said He would structure mortality to be a proving and testing experience (see Abraham 3:25; Mosiah 23:21). Clearly He has kept His promise and has carried out His divine intent. Therefore adversity must be part of the pattern rather than always an aberration. Therefore even our fiery trials, as Peter said, should not be thought of as being "some strange thing" (1 Peter 4:12). Hence throughout the varying lengths of our lives there is rolling relevance contained in the counsel to endure it well. (*Endure*, p. 2.)

Though God always meters out life's challenges so that they don't exceed our ability to cope, there may be times and seasons, mightn't there, when from our standpoint we feel we are encountering a fire-hydrant's torrent of tribulation? (*We Talk of Christ*, p. 70.)

If we are faithful the day will come when those deserving pioneers and ancestors, whom we rightly praise for having overcome the adversities in their wilderness trek, will praise today's faithful for having made their way successfully through a desert of despair and for having passed through a cultural wilderness, while still keeping the faith. (*Endure*, p. 28.)

Adequacy in the first estate may merely have ensured a stern second estate with more duties and no immunities! Additional tutoring and suffering appears to be the pattern for the Lord's most apt pupils. (See Mosiah 3:19; 1 Peter 4:19.) Our existence, therefore, is a continuum matched by God's stretching curriculum. (*Ensign*, November 1985, p. 17.)

Sometimes we must "take the heat," even if we are not certain the thermostat of trial will soon be turned down. (*Experience*, p. 48.)

Perhaps the greatest trial to descend upon modern disciples will not be military or political bondage but environmental bondage in which we are forced to live in a wicked world with evil ever present around us. (*Press Forward*, p. 54.)

Trials and tribulations tend to squeeze the artificiality out of us, leaving the essence of what we really are and clarifying what we *really* yearn for. (*Really Are*, p. 89.)

Exceptional souls are not developed . . . by being made exceptions to the challenges that are common to mankind. (*Prove*, p. 116.)

We undergo afflictions such as are "common to man" (1 Corinthians 10:13). Additionally, God will deliberately give us further lessons and experience which take us beyond the curriculum common to man and on into uncommon graduate studies or even postdoctoral discipleship. (*Not My Will*, p. 4.)

In the isometrics of individual development God may try us where we are the weakest (see Ether 12:27). One understandably may wince while exploring the implications of that hard teaching. (*Faith*, p. 35.)

A few individuals may appear to have no trials at all—which, if it were so, would be a trial in itself. If, as do trees, our souls had rings to measure the years of greatest personal growth, the wide rings would likely reflect the years of greatest moisture—but from tears, not rainfall. (*Endure*, p. 94.)

AFFLUENCE

Affluence is usually no friend of spirituality, and, oh, how we hope that teaching is not true—and, oh, how our teeth chatter when the chills of experience tell us it is true! (*Choose*, p. 33.)

Adversity does not always produce appreciation, but affluence rarely does. (*Look Back*, p. 11.)

AGENCY

The Lord knows how true individual development requires a setting of agency and opportunity. There is no other way. (*Ensign*, May 1983, p. 11.)

When God brought before us His plan of salvation, Jesus was there, volunteering meekly and humbly, "Here am I, send me" (Abraham 3:27), saying, "Father thy will be done, and the glory be thine forever" (Moses 4:2). The Father, ever anxious that all be free to choose, even gave Lucifer opportunity to campaign. (*Ensign*, November 1987, p. 32.)

We [should] allow for the agency of others (including our children) *before* we assess our adequacy. Often our deliberate best is less effectual because of someone else's worst. (*Deposition*, p. 29.)

Agency in its fullest sense requires the individual to be in command of himself, for one who is a prisoner of his bad impulses cannot really choose; another truth about "things as they are," therefore, is that we either control our bad impulses or they control us. (*Smallest Part*, pp. 10–11.)

God leaves us free. He is deeply committed to our moral agency and to letting people make mistakes if they choose to. And war is the reflection of how institutions fail and of the corruption of individuals. And yet, God leaves us mortals free to make decisions. Sometimes God intervenes as in the Noachian flood, or in Sodom and Gomorrah, but not always. And so needless and terrible tragedies occur because of leaders' and people's misuse of their freedom. (*Searching for God in America*, p. 124.)

Some seek to brush aside conscience, refusing to hear its voice. But that deflection is, in itself, an act of choice. . . . Like it or not, therefore, reality requires that we acknowledge our responsibility for our desires. (*Ensign*, November 1996, p. 21.)

God gives us breath to blaspheme as well as to praise him. Because he is a loving Father, he gives us muscles to smile or to sneer. (*Deposition*, p. 96.)

Agency is essential to perfectibility, and meekness is essential to the wise use of agency and to our recovery when we've misused agency. (*Precious Things*, p. 53.)

When we are unduly impatient . . . we are in effect trying to hasten an outcome when acceleration would abuse agency. (*Notwithstanding*, p. 61.)

Our agency is preserved . . . by the fact that as we approach a given moment we do not know what our response will be. Meanwhile, God has foreseen what we will do and has taken our decision into account (in composite with all others), so that His purposes are not frustrated. (*Experience*, p. 12.)

As to the questions asked—even by faithful Saints—such as, "If what is going to happen is 'all set,' why pray?," the answer is that God foresees, but He does not compromise our agency. All the outcomes are not, for our purposes, "all set." True, God's foreseeing includes our prayers, our fasting, our faith, and the results that will thereby be achieved. But until our mortal actions occur and our decisions are made, things are not "all set." (*Experience*, p. 97.)

The hard, cold fact is that how we use our moral agency does not result in a withdrawal of God's love but does determine the ways and the degrees to which a loving God can express His love of us. Only the righteous will receive His praise, His approval, and enjoy His presence. (*Endure*, p. 35.)

David fell from his appointed place because of grave errors. David's fall did not surprise the Lord, but the Lord gave David every chance, just as he did Judas. Jesus knew from the beginning who would betray him in every dispensation, and he stood ready to roll back, wherever repentance was real (as in the case of the city of Nineveh), any prophetically projected dire consequences. Not only readily but gladly! (*Deposition*, p. 43.)

ANGER

Letting off steam always produces more heat than light. (See Matthew 18:15.) (*Ensign*, November 1989, p. 84.)

God's anger is kindled not because we have harmed him but because we have harmed ourselves. (*Sermons*, p. 85.)

It is customary, even understandable, when we read of God's indignation and anger to think of it in terms of an angry mortal father and to not ponder it much more. Some even mutter about Old Testament "tribalism," mistakenly thinking of God as being personally piqued or offended at some human act of wickedness or stupidity because He has told us to behave otherwise. This is erroneous, bumper-sticker theology. Simply because we are, so often, angry at a wrong done to us, we assume the same about God's anger. (*Sermons*, p. 83.)

In the same way that aggressive, evil thoughts should not be offered a chair and invited to sit down, so anger should never be an overnight guest. (*Endure*, p. 115.)

ANXIETY

Overanxiety . . . is like pulling up the daisies to see how the roots are doing, checking up on the sentries so incessantly that they become trigger-happy, and wringing one's hands instead of folding them in prayer. (*Press Forward*, p. 63.)

It is a mistake . . . to assume that franticness is really aliveness; otherwise the just beheaded, but flopping, chicken would qualify as being intensely fulfilled. (*Really Are*, p. 3.)

Apparently it is necessary for us on occasion to be brought to a white-knuckles point of anxiety so as to be reminded, when rescued, of who our Rescuer is! (*As I Am*, p. 45.)

Conscientious people are often too anxious about being anxious. (*Deposition*, p. 69.)

Anxiety spreads, and even if our personal "wiring" can stand the voltage from our overanxiety, someone else may blow a fuse because of an overload to which we have contributed. (*Press Forward*, p. 63.)

APATHY

Ironically, if the Master is a stranger to us, then we will merely end up serving other masters. The sovereignty of these other masters is real, even if it sometimes is subtle, for they do call their cadence. Actually, "we are all enlisted" (*Hymns*, 1985, no. 250), if only in the ranks of the indifferent. (*Ensign*, November 1995, p. 22.)

APOSTASY

Is not apostasy a denial of that which was once genuinely known but which now comes to be doubted, discounted, and discarded? Neglected and unnourished, the tree of testimony is, alas, plucked up and cast out. But the tree was there, a fact to which its dried branches and roots are stark witness. (*As I Am*, p. 76.)

The Savior was also quite specific in indicating the major and usual causes behind the falling away of Church members: The cares of the world, temptations, tribulations, persecution and *fear* of persecution (Matthew 13:20–22; Mark 4:17; Luke 8:13; D&C 40:2). ("Thanksgiving for the Fulness of the Gospel Granary.")

Those who believe for a while make only a brief tour in the kingdom, though thereafter they often feel qualified to inform those who know even less about the Church; but the fact is they were really only tourists—not natives who really knew the kingdom's countryside. ("'True Believers in Christ,'" p. 135.)

A few will be deceived by defectors. Likewise, others will be offended, for sufficient unto each dispensation are the stumbling blocks thereof! A few will stumble because, in their preoccupation with the cares of the world, they do not have oil in their lamps. And again and again, those who refuse to eat their spiritual spinach will come off second when they wrestle with the world. (*Ensign*, November 1982, p. 68.)

While we usually think of apostasy solely in terms of theological deviation, we often fail to see its connections to the everyday, human condition in which the consequences of that deviation are enormous. (*Sermons*, p. 70.)

Apostasy is more than doubt; it is sometimes actual "mutiny," just as the Apostle John experienced it from Diotrephes (see 3 John 1:9–10). The defections and betrayals in the Kirtland and Nauvoo periods represented mutiny. So many people "piled on" by being disloyal to the Prophet. Not everyone was a Hyrum [Smith] or a Brigham [Young] or a Wilford [Woodruff]. (*Faith*, p. 92.)

APOSTATES

Those who turn against the Church do so to play to their own private gallery, but when, one day, the applause has died down and the cheering has stopped, they will face a smaller audience, the judgment bar of God. (*Really Are*, p. 90.)

Occasionally a member of the Church who is weak in the faith struggles with his other questions and circumstances and loses the battle. Those few members who desert the cause are abandoning an oasis to search for water in the desert. Some of them will not just wander off but will become obsessed critics occupying offices in the "great and spacious building" (1 Nephi 8:26–27; 11:35–36), that large but third-class hotel. (*Not My Will*, p. 28.)

Unlike those who wander off the straight and narrow path because of indifference, a few will actually defect. Like Lucifer, the first defector, who did not accept the rejection of his bid for ascendancy with parliamentary politeness, these, his minions, will also depart in anger. Like Lucifer, they will take all they can with them. (*Really Are*, p. xiii.)

The enemies and the critics of the Lord's work will not relent; they only regroup. Even among the flock, here and there and from time

to time, are a few wolves, wearing various styles of sheep's clothing—ironically, just before the shearing season! A few defectors
and "highminded" traitors (2 Timothy 3:4) even go directly to the
"great and spacious building" to hire on (1 Nephi 8:26). There re-
cruits are celebrated and feted until—like their predecessors—they
have faded into the dark swamps of history. (*Ensign*, May 1988, p. 9.)

Let these few departees take their brief bows in the secular spotlight; someday they will bow deeply before the throne of the
Almighty, confessing that Jesus is the Christ and that this is his
work. (*Ensign*, November 1980, p. 14.)

Defectors often cause more difficulty than disinterested disbelievers. (" 'All Hell Is Moved,' " p. 177.)

In racing marathons, one does not see the dropouts make fun of
those who continue; failed runners actually cheer on those who
continue the race, wishing they were still in it. Not so with the
marathon of discipleship in which some dropouts then make fun of
the spiritual enterprise of which they were so recently a part!
(" 'True Believers in Christ,' " p. 135.)

No attacks on the Church will be more bitter or more persistent
than those made in the Salt Lake Valley. No taunts will be more
shrill than those of apostates and excommunicants. In that valley
and in the state of Utah, Church members will be accused of the
"crime" of being a majority! Some clever defectors will imitate
their model, Satan, and will try to take others over the side with
them. Elsewhere, you will encounter the same sort of snobbery
that gave rise to "can any good thing come out of Nazareth?" (*Press
Forward*, p. 80.)

The quiet and steady decrease of faith leads to a surrendering to
the world. When that happens there are no white flags or formal,

public ceremonies marking such subjugation. The adversary cleverly does not insist on these ceremonies so long as the results are
what he desires. A few "sell out" directly, like Judas. Thirty pieces of
silver are not necessary if a little notoriety will suffice. (*Faith*, p. 6.)

A few in the Church today choose to meet their defining moments by separating themselves from the Church and its leaders.
A few set themselves up in open rebellion as a substitute light (see
2 Nephi 26:29). (*Faith*, p. 92.)

Apostles

We have been given apostles and prophets not only "for the perfecting of the Saints" but also to make sure that we are "no more
children, tossed to and fro, and carried about with every wind of
doctrine" (Ephesians 4:11–14). Apostolic watchcare over the doctrines of the kingdom, in order to keep them pure, is a very important duty. The performance of that important duty should be expected, not resented. (*Faith*, p. 96.)

It has been quite a few years now since that call [to the Council of
the Twelve] came. Yet I still feel unready and unable. You may
wonder why this calling has made me, and I expect others of the
Twelve, feel perpetually inadequate. Consider this statement about
the holy apostleship from the Prophet Joseph, as reported by
Brigham Young: "All the Priesthood, all the keys, all the gifts, all
the endowments, and everything preparatory to entering into the
presence of the Father and of the Son, are in, composed of, cir-
cumscribed by, or I might say incorporated within the circumfer-
ence of, the Apostleship. . . . Said Joseph, . . . Do you not know
that the man who receives the Apostleship, receives all the keys

that ever were, or that can be, conferred upon mortal man?" (*Believe*, p. 88.)

I thank [Christ] for his superb selection of his special witnesses and for his omniscient orchestration of their varied gifts in a symphony of salvation. (*Ensign*, May 1976, p. 27.)

The office and calling of the holy apostleship is such a sacred and special thing. No wonder its recipients feel in awe of it! No wonder, too, that the Presidents of the Church are those seasoned by years of service as Apostles. . . . These few become, successively, the presiding high priests of The Church of Jesus Christ of Latter-day Saints at that moment when the other Apostles, who hold the keys latently, place hands upon the senior's head to set him apart. (*Believe*, p. 89.)

The Twelve were warned not to "serve tables" (Acts 6:2). Serving tables would actually be so much easier and clearly more visible than is carrying certain heavy responsibilities, as Moses finally did—he would hear "every great matter" and ponder all the "hard causes" (Exodus 18:22, 26). The Twelve must do as Moses did—delegate the small causes. This can be done without their being insensitive and unaware, while still being open to consideration. The Supreme Court doesn't have to hear every case in order to effect the flow of the law. Beyond this, each Apostle can and should have circles of friendship and personal Christian service to help keep him attuned and sensitive. These can be part of his helpful sampling of conditions in the Church. (*Believe*, p. 90.)

The members' faith in the Brethren as living Apostles and prophets not only provides the needed direction but also clearly sustains those leaders in their arduous chores. There is more to it than this, however. Sustaining them also means that we realize those select men are conscious of their own imperfections; each is even grateful that the other Brethren have strengths and talents he may not have. The gratitude of the Brethren for being so sustained thus includes appreciation for members' willingness to overlook the imperfections of the overseers. The faithful realize the Apostles are working out their salvation, too, including the further development of the Christlike virtues. Serious discipleship requires us all to be "on the way to perfection" rather than thinking we are already in the arrival lounge. (*Faith*, p. 105.)

APPETITES

Pottage comes in many forms, but each mess responds to appetites—like lust, hunger, status, wealth, praise, and so forth. It is in the darkness of dimmed perceptivity that such an appetite can cause us, like Esau, to despise our birthright (Genesis 25:34) and to surrender our possibilities. Succumbing to temptation is, therefore, not the result of one's being grossly overprogrammed, but of grossly undervaluing oneself. (*Notwithstanding*, pp. 78–79.)

[Lucifer] is also deft at manipulating us mortals by pushing one desire against another, like so many tumbling dominoes. He can use one man's desire for business profits to feed another man's alcoholism; a woman's immodest dress to kindle lust in another man's shaky marriage. Evil has its own ecology, its own interlocking arrangement of appetites. Hence it is so easy to get caught in the webbing of the world. (*Really Are*, p. 7.)

To the extent that we are not willing to be led by the Lord, we will be driven by our appetites, or we will be greatly preoccupied with the lesser things of the day. (*Ensign*, November 1995, p. 22.)

ARM OF FLESH

We cannot safely trust "in the arm of flesh." Even when it is pumped full of steroids, it lacks the strength to maintain its grasp on the iron rod. Not alone does the arm of flesh finally prove anemic, but it always reaches for the wrong things (see 2 Chronicles 32:8; Jeremiah 17:5). (*Faith*, p. 87.)

ATONEMENT

The Atonement, then, was infinite in the *divineness* of the one sacrificed, in the *comprehensiveness* of its coverage, and in the *intensiveness*—incomprehensible to us—of the Savior's suffering. (*Not My Will*, p. 51.)

The cumulative weight of all mortal sins—past, present, and future—pressed upon that perfect, sinless, and sensitive Soul! All our infirmities and sicknesses were somehow, too, a part of the awful arithmetic of the Atonement. (See Alma 7:11–12; Isaiah 53:3–5; Matthew 8:17.) (*Ensign*, May 1985, p. 73.)

Mortal experience points evermore to the Atonement of Jesus Christ as the central act of all human history. The more I learn and experience, the more unselfish, stunning, and encompassing His Atonement becomes! (*Ensign*, May 1997, p. 12.)

Having bled at every pore, how red His raiment must have been in Gethsemane, how crimson that cloak! No wonder, when Christ comes in power and glory, that He will come in reminding red attire (see D&C 133:48), not only signifying the winepress of wrath but also to bring to our remembrance how He suffered for each of us in Gethsemane and on Calvary! (*Ensign*, May 1987, p. 72.)

Only He could have carried it all. I thank the Savior personally for bearing all which I added to His hemorrhaging at every pore for all of humanity in Gethsemane. I thank Him for bearing what I added to the decibels of His piercing soul-cry atop Calvary. (*Ensign*, May 1988, p. 9.)

Ironically, during the moments when in agony He was benefitting billions upon billions of mortals, He was attended by only a faithful few. (*Ensign*, November 1988, p. 33.)

His infinite atonement affected every age, every dispensation, and every person. (See 2 Nephi 9:7; 25:16.) Hence the appropriate symbolism of His bleeding at each and every pore—not just some—in order that "as in Adam all die, even so in Christ shall all be made alive." (1 Corinthians 15:22.) (*Ensign*, November 1988, p. 33.)

There will be no end to the ripples of the Resurrection resulting from the infinite Atonement. (*Ensign*, November 1988, p. 33.)

Jesus' marvelous meekness prevented any "root of bitterness" from "springing up" in Him (Hebrews 12:15). Ponder the Savior's precious words about the Atonement *after* He passed through it. There is no mention of the vinegar. No mention of the scourging. No mention of having been struck. No mention of having been spat upon. He does declare that He "suffer[ed] both body and spirit" in an exquisiteness which we simply cannot comprehend. (D&C 19:18; see also v. 15.) (*Ensign*, May 1989, p. 64.)

Diluted Christianity is not Christianity, it is a feeble attempt to have Christianity without Christ, for it denies the central service of Jesus' life—the Atonement. Those who call themselves Christians but deny the divinity of Jesus cannot seem to tolerate those of us who accept and proclaim the divinity of Christ. No one, brothers and sisters, would pay us much heed if we were merely nonsmoking, nondrinking humanists. Without acknowledging the reality of the Resurrection and the Atonement, believing in the ministry of Jesus would mean slumping into the very Sadduceeism which Jesus himself denounced. (" 'All Hell Is Moved,' " p. 177.)

Can we, even in the depths of disease, tell Him anything at all about suffering? In ways we cannot comprehend, our sicknesses and infirmities were borne by Him even before they were borne by us. The very weight of our combined sins caused Him to descend below all. We have never been, nor will we be, in depths such as He has known. Thus His atonement made perfect His empathy and His mercy and His capacity to succor us, for which we can be everlastingly grateful as He tutors us in our trials. There was no ram in the thicket at Calvary to spare Him, this Friend of Abraham and Isaac. (As I Am, pp. 116–17.)

When Jesus comes again in reminding red attire, there will be a spectacular solar display and stars will fall from their places in the heavens. What will then be evoked will not be an exclamation over the solar display. Rather, from human lips praise will flow for Jesus' loving-kindness, for His perfect goodness. Then the scriptures assure us and tell us how long we will go on praising Jesus for that atonement: "forever and ever." (Mosiah 2:24; D&C 128:23.) The one thing He will mention when He comes again in majesty and power will have nothing to do with how He suffered in the scourging, nothing to do with the vinegar and gall or any of those things. Instead, His voice will be heard to say, "I have trodden the winepress alone, and none was with me" (Isaiah 63:3). Incredible aloneness lay at the heart of the Great Atonement, and Jesus endured it, because He let His will be swallowed up in the will of the Father. (" 'Build Up My Church,' 'Establish the [Lord's] Righteousness.' ")

Being sinless Himself, Jesus could not have suffered for personal sin nor known what such agony is—*unless* He took upon Him our sins, not only to redeem us and to save us, but also in order that He might know how "according to the flesh . . . to succor his people according to their infirmities." (Alma 7:12.) (*Experience*, p. 35.)

Jesus' daily mortal experiences and His ministry, to be sure, acquainted Him by observation with a sample of human sicknesses, grief, pains, sorrows, and infirmities which are "common to man" (1 Corinthians 10:13). But the agonies of the Atonement were infinite and first-hand! Since not all human sorrow and pain is connected to sin, the full intensiveness of the Atonement involved bearing our pains, infirmities, and sicknesses, as well as our sins. Whatever our sufferings, we can safely cast our "care upon him; for he careth for [us]" (1 Peter 5:7). (*Not My Will*, p. 51.)

ATTITUDE

At the center of our agency is our freedom to form a healthy attitude toward whatever circumstances we are placed in! Those, for instance, who stretch themselves in service—though laced with limiting diseases—are often the healthiest among us. The Spirit *can* drive the flesh beyond where the body first agrees to go! (*Deposition*, pp. 30–31.)

We are justified in being of good cheer for ultimate reasons—reasons to be distinguished, however, from proximate circumstances. If, for instance, our attitude towards life depends upon the praise of men, the level of interest rates, the outcome of a particular election or athletic contest, we are too much at the mercy of men and circumstances. (*Ensign*, November 1982, p. 66.)

AUTHORITY

The absence of authority is not freedom; nothing is more controlling than anarchy—in the home or in the streets. (*Excellent*, p. 10.)

[Latter-day Saints] are . . . part of an authoritarian organization in an age when authority, especially in religion, is an unpopular concept and when many people are reluctant to assume authority. It would be easier to go along with a de-emphasis on authority, but a divine Church cannot risk popularity at any price; neither can its members, individually. (*Excellent*, p. 9.)

BABYLON

Babylon does not give exit permits gladly. (*Ensign*, November 1988, p. 33.)

Even if we decide to leave Babylon, some of us endeavor to keep a second residence there, or we commute on weekends. (*Flood*, p. 47.)

BALANCE

As always there must be balance. The inordinate reading of the living scriptures that crowded out one's family, one's neighbors, and Christian service would be an error. One could become monastic though scholastic. Christian service to mankind could crowd out the living scriptures and become so consuming that one could forget his duties to family and to God, being a do-gooder almost as an escape from the family framework. (*Really Are*, p. 106.)

The blend of studying, serving, and praying is a powerful blend. Some try serving without the studying of the gospel and lose their moorings, even though some good is being done. Some individuals study to the exclusion of service, which could heighten guilt or desensitize. Study is not a substitute for service, nor is serving a substitute for praying. Each law to be obeyed has its own requirements. (*Deposition*, p. 34.)

How important it is to the symmetry of our souls that we interact with all the gospel principles and with all the Church programs, so that we do not become so highly specialized that, if we are deprived of one source of satisfaction, indeed we are in difficulty. It is possible to be incarcerated within the prison of one principle. We are less vulnerable if our involvements with the kingdom are across the board. We are less vulnerable if we care deeply about many principles—not simply a few. ("But for a Small Moment," p. 453.)

There have been times in my life when I have had to trim time commitments. It is somewhat like getting in debt. We can get in over our heads and find it painful to get out. Every now and then we need to examine our time as well as our dollar commitments, to make certain we can deliver on them. Generally, other people are quite understanding if we reach a time of retrenchment. (*Deposition*, p. 70.)

Naive optimism and pervasive pessimism are both to be avoided. . . . It's not an easy balance to maintain, to be asked to work away in the Ninevehs of our lives without being so conscious of the coming cataclysm that we fail to be serious citizens of our communities and nations. (*Deposition*, p. 98.)

There are even those who refuse to follow the Brethren because these individuals have overidentified with a single doctrine, principle, or practice; sadly, they exclude all other counsel, which leads to a dangerous spiritual imbalance. The difficulty with such individuals is that they have a strange sense of justification about that which they are doing. In their intensity they lack, of course, the spiritual symmetry that comes from pursuing, in a balanced way, all the commandments of God. (*Experience*, p. 111.)

BEAUTY

When we rejoice in beautiful scenery, great art, and great music, it is but the flexing of instincts acquired in another place and another time. (*Ensign*, May 1984, p. 21.)

BEHAVIOR

Sadly, there are those in the Church who try to camouflage their behavioral problems by covering up with intellectual reservations or reasons. They fool only themselves. (Dictated December 1996.)

Becoming more like Jesus in thought and behavior is not grinding and repressing, but emancipating and discovering! Unorthodoxy in behavior and intellect is just the opposite. A little pornography may not only lead to child and spouse abuse, but it slowly sucks out the marrow of self-esteem. A little tendency to gossip can lead not only to bearing serious false witness, but more often to malicious whispers which, unfortunately, "memory will warehouse as a shout" (C. S. Lewis, *The Quotable Lewis*, ed. Owen Barfield and Jerry Root [Wheaton, Ill.: Tindale Publications, 1989], p. 425). (*Ensign*, November 1992, p. 67.)

[A] few individuals let their minds seek to run far ahead of their confirming behavior. For them, exciting exploration is preferred to plodding implementation. ("The Inexhaustible Gospel," pp. 141–42.)

BELIEVERS

People who are inside the Church are in a sense inside something holy, and we can understand it, mostly. It is difficult to tell a so-called tourist more than superficial things about something he remains outside of or experiences only fleetingly. If he really wishes to know, he must come inside. Tourists seldom really savor a place even when inside! It is difficult for nonbelievers to describe the believer's world. The nonbeliever can circle a concept indefinitely—like besieging armies outside a city wall—without grasping it. (*Deposition*, p. 61.)

BLESSINGS

Small minds forget large blessings! Proud minds ceaselessly inquire of God, "What have you done for me lately?" (*Men and Women*, p. 90.)

We cannot count all our blessings every day, but we can carry over the reassuring bottom line from the last counting. (*Ensign*, May 1989, p. 64.)

If I have any entitlement to the blessings of God, it has long since been settled in the court of small claims by His generous bestowals over a lifetime. (*Ensign*, May 1997, p. 11.)

If we do not remember how "we have proved [God] in days that are past" [*Hymns*, no. 19], then the experimental evidence can be lost. Hence going through the files of faith, counting our blessings, is needed. It aids intellectual honesty and serves as an internal auditing. (*Men and Women*, pp. 102–3.)

Counting blessings as well as blemishes will show many more blessings. (*Press Forward*, p. 38.)

The developmental dues of discipleship must be paid *before* all of the blessings are received (D&C 130:20). (*Not My Will*, p. 6.)

Even when we are wise enough to count our blessings, we usually do it without also weighing them. A numerical inventory, by itself, is not sufficient. Some blessings are of extraordinary size and significance. (*Faith*, pp. 101–2.)

BOOK OF MORMON

The golden plates are history's most stunning "find" in the field of religion. (*Ensign*, May 1992, p. 38.)

Serious study of the blessed Book of Mormon admits one to a wonder world of complexity and beauty, even in the midst of the book's simple, but powerful, spiritual refrain. We are given that which we most need—yet we are athirst for more! (*Ensign*, November 1983, p. 55.)

The Book of Mormon came like a theological thunderbolt on the stage of history—to be a second witness for the divinity of Jesus Christ "to the *convincing* of the Jew and Gentile that Jesus is the Christ" (Title page, Book of Mormon). Note the word *convincing*. The Bible often initiates and helps to sustain faith in Jesus, but the Book of Mormon is the *convincer* and the *clarifier*. Isn't it ironical in this regard that there are some who still wonder if members of The Church of Jesus Christ of Latter-day Saints are Christians? ("'All Hell Is Moved,'" p. 178.)

The Gospel seeks to help us focus on those facts which have overwhelming importance, not only for this life, but for worlds to come. The relevancy and congruency of the scriptures are shown in many ways. Our Nephite predecessors could have given us their remarkable formula for cement, but instead they graphically described the glue of the Gospel which puts our lives together and gives us ingredients for the chemistry of salvation. (*Choose*, pp. 54–55.)

The doctrinal density of the Book of Mormon clearly overshadows the portion that is given over to history or to details such as the description of Nephite money. The book's structure is clearly and intentionally secondary to its substance, and its plot to its principles. (*Precious Things*, p. 14.)

As you study the Book of Mormon you will find that gospel doctrines are like diamonds with many facets. Some are hidden from our initial view. An experience can cause the glint of the gospel to illuminate a dimension of a doctrine previously unappreciated. (*Believe*, p. 50.)

Given its unique importance, it is not surprising that ever since the Book of Mormon was published in 1830, disbelievers and detractors have preferred any explanation of its coming forth to the real one! This disdain was forseen by the Lord, who consoled Joseph: "Behold, if they will not believe my words, they would not believe you, my servant, Joseph, if it were possible that you should show them all these things which I have committed unto you" (D&C 5:7). Apparently, even if skeptics had been shown the Urim and Thummim and the plates, it would not have convinced them. . . . One early enemy of the Church, E. D. Howe, mistakenly assigned authorship of the Book of Mormon to Reverend Spaulding (who died in 1816, 14 years before the Book of Mormon was published). The Spaulding "explanation" once caused such a needless stir! . . . In more recent years, another "explanation" has been advanced: Joseph Smith supposedly took his main ideas, say these critics, from the writings of one Ethan Smith, who wrote a book called *View of the Hebrews*. . . . One would no more read Ethan's book for doctrine than he would read the telephone directory in search of a plot! ("'The Gift and Power of God,'" video presentation.)

Why do we not have more disclosure concerning the process of translation of the Book of Mormon? Perhaps the full process was not disclosed because we would not be ready to understand it, even if given. Perhaps, too, the Lord wanted to leave the Book of Mormon in the realm of faith, though it is drenched with intrinsic evidence. After all, Christ instructed Mormon, who was reviewing the Savior's own teachings among the Nephites, not to record all of them on the plates because "I will try the faith of my people" (3 Nephi 26:11). Perhaps the details of translation are withheld also because we are intended to immerse ourselves in the substance of the book rather than becoming unduly concerned with the process by which we received it. (*Ensign*, January 1997, p. 41.)

The Book of Mormon will remain in the realm of faith. It has a bodyguard of scholars who now surround it and protect it from the frail attacks often made on it. But even so, it's the witness of the

Spirit that matters most and the intrinsic evidence which drenches the book itself. (*Searching for God in America*, p. 121.)

Some . . . things we know about the process of translation further qualify the Book of Mormon as a "marvelous work and a wonder." One marvel is the very rapidity with which Joseph was translating—at an estimated average rate of eight of our printed pages a day! The total translation time was about 65 working days. (See "How long did it take Joseph Smith to translate the Book of Mormon?" *Ensign*, January 1988, 47.) By comparison, one able LDS translator in Japan, surrounded by reference books, language dictionaries, and translator colleagues ready to help if needed, indicated that he considered an output of one careful, final page a day to be productive. And he was retranslating from earlier Japanese to modern Japanese! More than 50 able English scholars labored for seven years, using previous translations, to produce the King James Version of the Bible, averaging about one precious page per day. The Prophet Joseph Smith would sometimes produce 10 pages per day! (*Ensign*, January 1997, p. 39.)

Fascination with the environment in which the Book of Mormon came forth has caused some to neglect its content. Likewise, the *human-ness* of those associated with its emergence has caused neglect of the *divine-ness* of its message. (*Small Moment*, p. 23.)

Because the editing of the Book of Mormon, with its witnessing gospel of hope, occurred under divine direction, it has a focus which is essentially spiritual. Yet some will still criticize the book for not being what it was never intended to be, as if one could justifiably criticize a phone directory for lack of a plot. (*Not My Will*, pp. 29–30.)

Near the end of his ministry, with so much betrayal about him, the Prophet Joseph said to the members, "I never told you I was perfect; but there is no error in the revelations which I have taught" (*Teachings of the Prophet Joseph Smith*, sel. Joseph Fielding Smith [Salt Lake City: Deseret Book Company, 1976], p. 368). His summational statement includes the marvelous Book of Mormon. . . . Though it was not his book, Joseph was its remarkable translator. It was actually the book of prophets who had long preceded him. His intensive labors of translation let these prophets speak so eloquently for themselves—to millions of us! In fact, more printed pages of scripture have come through Joseph Smith than from any other human. (*Ensign*, January 1997, p. 41.)

The Book of Mormon will be with us "as long as the earth shall stand." We need all that time to explore it, for the book is like a vast mansion with gardens, towers, courtyards, and wings. There are rooms yet to be entered, with flaming fireplaces waiting to warm us. The rooms glimpsed so far contain further furnishings and rich detail yet to be savored, but decor dating from Eden is evident. There are panels inlaid with incredible insights, particularly insights about the great question. Yet we as Church members sometimes behave like hurried tourists, scarcely venturing beyond the entry hall. (*Not My Will*, p. 33.)

Oliver Cowdery, the most constant and involved witness to the miraculous translation, always affirmed the divinity of the process. Though later disaffected for a time from the Church, he nevertheless came humbly back. He spoke forthrightly about how he "wrote with my own pen the intire book of Mormon (save a few pages) as it fell from the Lips of the prophet" (Journal of Reuben Miller, October 1848, Archives of The Church of Jesus Christ of Latter-day Saints). Oliver would not have humbly returned to the Church at all, especially seeking no station, had there been any kind of fraud! Instead, at the approach of death, Oliver could not have been more dramatic about his testimony concerning the Book of Mormon. Oliver's half-sister, Lucy P. Young, reported: "Just before he breathed his last he asked to be raised up in bed so he could talk to the family and friends and he told them to live according to the teachings in the [B]ook of Mormon and they would meet him in

Heaven then he said lay me down and let me fall asleep in the arms of Jesus, and he fell asleep without a struggle" (Letter of Lucy Cowdery Young, 7 March 1887, Archives of The Church of Jesus Christ of Latter-day Saints). What an exit endorsement! (*Ensign*, January 1997, p. 41.)

BROTHERHOOD

Cain was *not* Abel's keeper, but he was his brother. Brother and keeper relationships are very different. The former emphasizes concerns, the latter control. (*Press Forward*, p. 88.)

BURDENS

Jesus, our Shepherd, has "marked the path and led the way, And ev'ry point defines" (*Hymns*, 1985, no. 195). His clearly defined footprints are easy to see. They are pressed distinctly and deeply into the soil of the second estate, deeply and distinctly because of the enormous weight which pressed down upon Him, including the awful burden of all of our individual sins. (*Ensign*, May 1988, p. 9.)

[Christ's] yoke, when fully and squarely placed upon us, is much lighter than the weight of sin. No burden is as heavy as the burden of the "natural man"! The annoying load of ambivalence and the hecticness of hesitation produce their own aggravations and frustrations. (*Men and Women*, p. 103.)

Happily, the commandment "Take my yoke upon you, and learn of me; for I am meek and lowly in heart" (Matthew 11:29) is a principle which carries an accompanying and compensating promise from Jesus: "and ye shall find rest unto your souls." This is a very special form of rest resulting from the shedding of certain needless burdens: fatiguing insincerity, exhausting hypocrisy, and the strength-sapping quest for recognition, praise, and power. Those of us who fall short, in one way or another, often do so because we carry such unnecessary and heavy baggage. Being overloaded, we sometimes stumble, and then we feel sorry for ourselves. ("'Meek and Lowly.'")

So it is that bearing one another's burdens in daily life consists not only in carrying the physical burdens or helping out in the obvious ways but also by bearing one another's burdens as we "put up" with each other's imperfections—repeatedly and frustratingly! As we witness, firsthand, the soul-struggles of others to develop a particular virtue, we can see how vital it is that we be more filled with loving-kindness and long-suffering. (*Faith*, p. 112.)

CANDOR

Christians can have the benefit of candor without being cutting. They can be communicative without being manipulative. (*Experience*, p. 86.)

The candlepower of candor can produce not only disclosure but *détente*, not only discovery but understanding. Usually in human affairs when we illuminate an issue it is not unlike using a flashlight, for we see better not only as to distance but also as to detail. (*Smallest Part*, p. 70.)

"Sad" experience has shown me . . . that it is just as important to know how to reprove as it is to know how to commend. . . . To be able to [be] candid when the situation calls for candor . . . has saved me and others anguish, but when I have failed in this respect, it has almost always meant that procrastination or glossing over a difficult problem simply resulted in having to face the same problem later when it was much larger and much more difficult. (*Excellent*, p. 3.)

There are simply times when the risks of candor are unacceptably high; the biting of the tongue, on occasion, can prevent the tearing of a heart. (My *Family*, p. 45.)

CAREER

The choice of a career is usually a matter of preference not principle, and preferences should not become principles under parental pressure. (*Excellent*, p. 124.)

So much of our time is ironically devoted to learning and marketing perishable skills that will soon become obsolete. It isn't just the morticians who will have a vocational crisis in the next world. ("'In Him All Things Hold Together,'" p. 104.)

CATACLYSM

Cataclysm for the people on this planet is most likely to flow from technology created by men who cannot also tame that technology because they cannot tame themselves by using the taming truths of the gospel of Jesus Christ. (*Smallest Part*, p. 5.)

CENSORSHIP

Given the choices made by some, we all end up with more protected pornography than protected children. Of course better self-restraint than censorship, but urging self-restraint on hedonists is like discouraging Dracula from hanging around the blood bank! (*Ensign*, May 1995, p. 68.)

CHARACTER

Jesus' character necessarily underwrote His remarkable atonement. Without Jesus' sublime character there could have been no sublime atonement! His character is such that He "suffered all manner of temptation," yet He gave temptations "no heed." (Alma 7:11; D&C 20:22.) ("'O, How Great the Plan of Our God.'")

Each of us will find that what we made from the ore of our experience is character, and that character, unlike so many other earthly things acquired, is portable. (*Really Are*, p. 115.)

Indifference, indolence, and indulgence do reflect the tilt of the soul and *do* immobilize the individuals involved so far as their contribution to their fellowmen is concerned. (*My Family*, p. 25.)

It is easier to be a character than to have character! (*On Becoming a Disciple-Scholar*, p. 21.)

CHASTISEMENT

God is not only there in the mildest expressions of His presence, but also in those seemingly harsh expressions. For example, when truth "cutteth . . . to the very center" (1 Nephi 16:2), this may signal that spiritual surgery is underway, painfully severing pride from the soul. (*Ensign*, November 1987, p. 31.)

Even the good can become careless without the Lord's being there to chasten. (*Ensign*, November 1987, p. 31.)

CHASTITY

Take away regard for the seventh commandment, and behold the current celebration of sex, the secular religion, with its own liturgy of lust and supporting music. Its theology focuses on self, its hereafter is now. Its chief ritual is sensation—though the irony is that it finally desensitizes its obsessed adherents, who become "past feeling" (Ephesians 4:19; Moroni 9:20). (*Men and Women*, pp. 12–13.)

As dramatic as the brave passage through the Red Sea was, those in our time who make their way through a sea of filth and still keep the seventh commandment will be even more victorious and deserving of praise. (*Believe*, p. 125.)

If we rely . . . only on contraceptives and cash—instead of conscience and chastity—we will always find ourselves dealing with harsh consequences instead of preventing misery. (*Smallest Part*, p. 31.)

A sex-saturated society cannot really feel the needs of its suffering members because, instead of developing the love that looks outward, it turns man selfishly inward. (*Choose*, p. 59.)

Surely one need not be particularly perceptive today in order to notice how the sonic boom of sexualism is sending shudders of selfishness throughout our society. (*My Family*, p. 9.)

CHEERFULNESS

Being of good cheer is the proximate preparation for ultimate joy. Being of good cheer—one day at a time—precedes that point later on when, if we live righteously, we can justifiably say what Jesus said: "Now behold, my joy is full." [3 Nephi 17:20.] (*As I Am*, p. 98.)

The gospel glow we see radiating from some—amid dark difficulties—comes from illuminated individuals who are "of good cheer"! To be cheerful when others are in despair, to keep the faith when others falter, to be true even when we feel forsaken—all of these are deeply desired outcomes during the deliberate, divine tutorials which God gives to us—because He loves us. (See Mosiah 3:19.) These learning experiences must not be misread as divine indifference. Instead, such tutorials are a part of the divine unfolding. (*Ensign*, November 1982, p. 67.)

Gospel gladness is possible even in the midst of affliction, because of the reassuring realities that pertain to our mortal circumstance. The everlastingness of certain things puts the temporariness of other things in perspective. (*As I Am*, p. 98.)

Though our trials are tiny compared to His, alas, we are often grumpy. Jesus was of good cheer because then current conditions did not alter His sources of ultimate joy. Are not our fundamental sources of joy the same as His? (*As I Am*, p. 100.)

Like freedom from death, emancipation from error is always a special reason for being of good cheer. (*As I Am*, p. 100.)

CHILDREN

A baby is a blessing—not a burden. (*Ensign*, May 1978, p. 10.)

If . . . we truly want the best for our sons and daughters, we would want for them—not status—but more *meekness, mercy, love, patience,* and *submissiveness*. (*As I Am*, p. 62.)

The great preventive forces contained in the gospel of Jesus Christ and in its premises about the nature of man and of life permit parents and children to avoid metronomic swings between coddling children too much and the tendency to push children out of the nest too soon and too harshly. (*My Family*, p. 91.)

For those either untaught or unheeding of the essential gospel truths, the lapse of faith in Christ is but one generation away! ("The Children of Christ," p. 87.)

CHILDREN OF GOD

Being the literal, premortal spirit children of the Father, each of us can, by going from grace to grace, eventually receive of the fulness of the Father, as did Jesus (see D&C 93:20). (*Flood*, p. 36.)

When we know *who* we are, then we know also much more clearly *what* we might become—and also *how* and *when*. The gospel thereby emancipates us from uncertainty as to our identity. But this precious perspective also brings with it an intensification of our personal accountability, since we know *who* we are and *why* we are here. (*Flood*, pp. 43–44.)

Inasmuch as restored knowledge teaches us we all were "in the beginning" with God and have the potential to be with Him throughout eternity, how childish it is to take advantage of another human—whether in dating, in business, in politics, or in any other area of life! (*Flood*, p. 44.)

Choices

Joshua didn't say choose you next year whom you will serve; he spoke of "this day," while there is still daylight and before the darkness becomes more and more normal. (See Joshua 24:15.) (*Ensign*, November 1974, p. 13.)

We chose not to follow Lucifer once: let us not go back on that decision now! (*As I Am*, p. 35.)

Some want to be free to choose, but to have God ever poised to rescue them. They want to call on God in their extremities, but don't want Him to interfere with their sensualities. They demand an undemanding God. Others want moral agency for humanity, but without the possibility of human misery. They desire permissiveness without the consequences of permissiveness. (*Men and Women*, p. 5.)

Life's tactical choices actually present the opportunity to exercise our moral agency. Such constitute the calisthenics of choice. The chief impediment, however, is our lack of full spiritual alignment. (*Men and Women*, p. 18.)

Wrong choices will make us less free. Furthermore, erosive error gradually makes one less and less of an individual. God and His prophets would spare us that shrinkage. (*Ensign*, November 1988, p. 32.)

CHOSEN

The designation "chosen," of course, is not just status; it confers great responsibilities upon those chosen to reach their fellowmen. God gives the picks and shovels to the "chosen" because they are willing to go to work and get callouses on their hands. They may not be the best or most capable, but they are the most available. (*Deposition*, p. 54.)

It makes sense to me that the Lord would choose out of the world those who are (or who could become) different from the world and, therefore, could lead the world to a different outcome. We must be different in order to make a difference. (*Deposition*, p. 55.)

CHRISTIANITY

Christianity is not a religion of repose—intellectually or behaviorally. (*Smallest Part*, p. 6.)

True, there are no *instant* Christians, but there are *constant* Christians! (*Ensign*, November 1976, p. 14.)

This is a gospel of grand expectations, but God's grace is sufficient for each of us if we remember that there are no *instant* Christians. (*Notwithstanding*, p. 11.)

It is the very fact that some members of the Church have spiritual health that permits them to search for the lost or to help the few who are faltering. That outcome of the Gospel is often overlooked because conspicuous goodness—doing the glamorous things—often overshadows the quiet Christianity that brings into our lives the preventive medicine that gives the relative health which permits us to help others. (*Choose*, p. 28.)

Quiet Christianity is a necessary counterpoint to the rumble of the kettle drums and the crash of cymbals of those Christian acts which are, by their very nature, visible and hard to ignore. We also need the behavioral equivalent of the flute and the violin in order to have the kind of symphony that can make a difference in mortality. (*Choose*, p. 28.)

By organizing our concern we become more involved, more effectively involved, enlarging our circles of concern. Otherwise, we might become mere "checkbook-Christians," contributing money but not involving ourselves with others, and "checkbook-Christianity" is simply monetary monasticism. (*Excellent*, p. 12.)

CHRISTMAS

God's gifts, unlike seasonal gifts, are eternal and unperishable, constituting a continuing Christmas which is never over! These infinite gifts are made possible by the "infinite atonement." (*The Christmas Scene*, p. 4.)

Yes, we still wish Christmas were more deeply felt and lasted longer, but the visibly increased goodwill nevertheless reminds us, if only briefly, of what could be *everlastingly*. For a few days, the first and second commandments are more pondered and observed. (*The Christmas Scene*, p. 2.)

The Christmas scene is so varied: frustrated fathers poring over directions written in failed English while trying to assemble toys packaged by someone who miscounted the nuts and bolts; bleary-eyed, bone-weary mothers desperately sewing after hours to finish a dress; a child neglecting an expensive gift in favor of something surprisingly simple; elegant, carefully applied wrappings being torn quickly apart as if they were an obstacle instead of part of the gift. (*The Christmas Scene*, p. 1.)

More presents were likely put under the tree than there were gifts placed in others' storehouses of self-esteem. More bright wrappings may have been scattered about than bright words of good cheer. (*The Christmas Scene*, p. 1.)

The little star of Bethlehem was not little, given all its accompanying implications. (*The Christmas Scene*, p. 2.)

He before whom a few gifts were laid in that lowly manger has spread so many gifts before us, thereby providing an unending Christmas. In fact, from Him for whom there was no room at the inn there comes to the faithful so many blessings "that there shall not be room enough to receive [them]"! (Malachi 3:10.) (*The Christmas Scene*, p. 5.)

The larger Christmas story is clearly not over. It is not solely about some other time, some other place, and some other people. It is still unfolding, and we are in it! (*The Christmas Scene*, p. 11.)

Church (LDS)

Good people still need the Church, for the best being who ever lived organized the Church—because random, individual goodness is not enough in the fight against evil. (*Ensign*, November 1974, p. 13.)

Quickly forgotten by those who are offended is the fact that the Church is "for the perfecting of the saints" (Ephesians 4:12); it is not a well-provisioned rest home for the already perfected. Likewise, unremembered by some is the reality that in the kingdom we are each other's clinical material; the Lord allows us to practice on each other, even in our imperfections. And each of us knows what it is like to be worked on by a "student" rather than a senior surgeon. Each of us, however unintentionally, has also inflicted some pain. (*Ensign*, May 1982, p. 38.)

Church membership is not passive security but continuing opportunity. (*Ensign*, May 1974, p. 112.)

It should not surprise us . . . that as the Church becomes larger and more visible we will sail in rougher waters, and that there will be more "struggling seamen" anxious to be saved and to come on board. ("'All Hell Is Moved,'" p. 176.)

As the Church comes forth out of obscurity, we will experience waves of nostalgia, at times, for such advantages as past obscurity conferred upon the Church. Visibility brings with it some stern challenges. (*Deposition*, p. 81.)

We are Christ's kingdom builders. Those who build the heavenly kingdom have always made nervous the people who are busy building worldly kingdoms. Noah's ark-building was not politically correct. ("'All Hell Is Moved,'" p. 178.)

It would be so much safer to float with the ebbing theological tides as do so many today who simply regard Jesus as a Galilean Ghandi or as a Socrates who strode in Samaria. But we know Jesus to be divine, the literal Son of the Father. We know that he established his church, and that it is not simply a church built upon doctrinal debris from other dispensations or fragments of the faith from another age. It is a church built upon the fulness of his gospel; it bears his name and is his kingdom in these latter days, a kingdom to which the good men and women of all nations, cultures, and races will be drawn. Knowing this, we are like Joseph Smith—we speak the truth because we can do no other. ("'All Hell Is Moved,'" p. 178.)

The reactions to us will vary: there will be the almost Agrippas, the puzzled Pilates, the timid Van Burens, and the stout Colonel Kanes, and, of course, there will be some scorn and some rage. But deep within the rage and the scorn, if one listens closely, are the sounds of profound pain, hushed hope, and of doubt beginning to doubt itself. ("'All Hell Is Moved,'" p. 179.)

The Church . . . is an ecclesiastical Everest. It will be seen by thoughtful men and women everywhere as the only real alternative to anarchy or to the gathering forces of anti-freedom. (Deposition, p. 49.)

There are important practices and administrative procedures in the Church today that may not have been performed in precisely parallel ways in the Church in past dispensations. However, practices and methods may vary from age to age, but the commandments are constant. (Notwithstanding, p. 20.)

Some people come in and out of the Church as if it were a theological transit lounge where they stay only briefly and then move on. But as the Savior Himself said, "My sheep hear my voice, and I know them, and they follow me." (John 10:27.) (Experience, p. 105.)

The Church does not become more true when more people join it (only more glorious in scope)—nor does it become less true when some choose to leave it. Validity has nothing to do with numbers, as the eight on the ark and the three who successfully fled Sodom testify. (*Press Forward*, p. 20.)

The Church will become, even more, the Savior's societal spearhead, the institutional rallying point for the forces of righteousness. Make no mistake about it. (*Press Forward*, p. 31.)

We need to remember that the Church is doctrine, organization, ordinances, and authority (and God be praised for these), but the Church is also *us*—people drawn together in our imperfections. We are not yet fully truthful, fully considerate, or fully free from the tendency to manipulate or from sin; we are disciples who need both loving and disciplining. Thus, when we are disappointed, it is with ourselves or other disciples, not with doctrines. (*Press Forward*, p. 35.)

The Church has done many difficult things, and from these achievements one would not wish to detract. But all the easy things the Church has had to do have been done. From now on it is high adventure! (*Press Forward*, p. 84.)

There are those Maginot-line Mormons who make the mistake of feeling unjustifiably secure, who are vulnerable on their flanks to the attacks of the world. There are also those who feel they can safely stay close to, but not in, the Church, but they will suffer the same fate as the red coal that is taken out of the bonfire and is left to itself. (*Press Forward*, p. 128.)

Our individual weaknesses will be regarded by some critics as institutional weaknesses. But, as Paul wrote, the Church is for the perfecting of the Saints (Ephesians 4:12) and, since the Church is filled with imperfect individuals, one should not expect an ecclesiastical Eden! (*We Talk of Christ*, pp. 33–34.)

The Church, like the living God who established it, is alive, aware, and functioning. It is not a museum that houses a fossilized faith; rather, it is a kinetic kingdom characterized by living faith in living disciples. (*Really Are*, p. 46.)

A living church is also one in which there is movement and action. It deals with the realities of life, rather than leaning away from them. A living church is permanently linked with the Ultimate Source of power in the universe, lest it grow cold. (*Choose*, p. 67.)

Those who wondered or made light of the question of how an obscure religion—just one of many—could be true, will learn that the way to salvation and exaltation is the same on other peopled planets; it is a gospel for the galaxies. (*Really Are*, p. 116.)

The present is a time of significant numerical and spiritual growth in the Church. We shouldn't be surprised, however, if it is also a time of some sifting. Sifting is usually self-initiated, and it is going on all the time. There are ways leading into the Church, and there are ways leading out. The influence and tug of the world is always present; but especially since the world grows more boldly wicked, this sharper defining has a greater and more visible effect on some of little faith. (*Faith*, pp. 93–94.)

Clearly the Church must neither allow its doctrines to be diluted nor its people to be diminished by compromising with the ways of the world. (*Endure*, p. 97.)

CHURCH CALLINGS

So often we feel, implicitly, that we are doing God a favor if we do his work, that we are helping him along when, in fact, our performance properly undertaken is for the welfare of our soul, not his! It is our happiness and our growth he seeks! (*Power,* p. 36.)

Some regard themselves as merely "resting" in between Church callings. But we are never in between as to this soaring call from Jesus: "What manner of men [and women] ought ye to be? Verily I say unto you, Even as I am." (3 Nephi 27:27; see Matthew 5:48; 3 Nephi 12:48.) It is never safe to rest regarding that calling! In fact, being "valiant" in one's testimony of Jesus includes striving to become more like Him in mind, heart, and attributes. (D&C 76:79.) Becoming this manner of men and women is the ultimate expression of orthodoxy! (*Ensign,* November 1992, p. 65.)

A new calling beckons us away from comfortable routines wherein the needed competencies have already been developed. (*Ensign,* November 1995, p. 24.)

Duties are not to be rejected on the basis of "I've done all that before," as if God were required to supply us with new thrills. Mortality has been described by the Lord as being like working in a vineyard—never as an afternoon at a carnival. Besides, how could we pretend to be true believers in Christ, if we shunned the chores of the kingdom? ("'True Believers in Christ,'" p. 136.)

One's task is to do more and to perform well within his callings, but it is not something else or another work he should seek. God will not judge us according to the calling of another. ("Grounded, Rooted, Established, and Settled," p. 18.)

The unmagnified calling leaves so many untouched. Someone else is sadly stranded when a calling is unmagnified: ourselves! Lucifer is not the only one who must live with what might have been. (*Deposition*, p. 95.)

The fact that the perfect Lord works through imperfect people should not obscure the divinity of the callings that come to imperfect people, any more than people could rightly disregard John the Baptist's warning counsel simply because they did not approve of his rugged diet—or dismiss the doctrines of these plain Galileans merely because they were only fishermen. (*As I Am*, p. 87.)

To be passed over can be wrongly construed as being unvalued by God or by one's colleagues. Yet in the kingdom of God to be *uncalled* is clearly not to be *unworthy*, or *unable!* (*Men and Women*, p. 102.)

Church service is not a breathlessly-brought-about roadshow followed by detached repose! (*Notwithstanding*, p. 7.)

When at times we encounter a situation in church service in which a pigeon seems to be supervising an eagle, we need to be accepting even if our evaluation seems accurate. Besides, humility keeps us from spending our time and talent wastefully in counting the plumage of our peers. (*Press Forward*, p. 49.)

Life in the Church means experiencing leaders who are not always wise, mature, and deft. In fact, some of us are as bumpy and uneven as a sackful of old doorknobs. Some of the polishing we experience is a result of grinding against each other. How vital submissiveness is in such circumstances, especially if the lubrication of love is not amply present. (*Not My Will*, p. 74.)

To magnify one's calling means seeing "with the eye of faith" the enlarged and detailed possibilities of service to one's family, flock, friends, and others. After all, the same power of God that brought into existence "worlds without number" (Moses 1:33) can surely watch over our little universes of individual experience! (*Faith*, p. 48.)

It should be clear to us with regard to various callings and assignments that just as soon as we are sustained and set apart the clock begins running toward the moment of our release. How vital it is to manage our time and talents wisely from the moment a task begins! Later, when we have devotedly invested much of ourselves in a particular calling or assignment (and especially when it has been satisfying and we have made a real difference), we may feel the release when it comes, but that, too, is part of our schooling as disciples. Being released gives us experience in patience and humility, as well as a fresh reminder of our replaceability. ("It's Service, Not Status, That Counts," p. 7.)

Commandments

Let us . . . notwithstanding our weaknesses, be reassured that the everyday keeping of the commandments and the doing of our duties is what it is all about. (*Notwithstanding*, p. 18.)

Even seeking after things which are praiseworthy or lovely is accelerated by believing all the Articles of Faith which precede article 13. Similarly, the followers of the Ten Commandments are not divided into two vast platoons—one specializing in the "thou shalts" and the other in the "thou shalt nots." (*Ensign*, November 1988, p. 31.)

To compose a symphony, to win a battle, or to save a company—each can be a commendable and worthy entry in the book of life, but these do not fully compensate for breaking the seventh commandment ["Thou shalt not commit adultery"]. In the arithmetic of heaven, several commendables do not cancel out one inexcusable! (*Ensign*, November 1988, p. 33.)

Commandment keepers, undiminished by gross sin, have so much more of themselves to give! (*Flood*, p. 97.)

All about us we see hypocrisies as between public and private behavior, as if God had issued two sets of commandments—one for indoors and another for out-of-doors. (*Endure*, p. 16.)

COMMANDMENTS OF MEN

Policies or doctrines that mirror the attitudinal majority of a given age become the commandments of men. (D&C 46:7; Matthew 15:9.) Unsurprisingly, the churches of men will inevitably preach the commandments of men, seasoned with some scripture, preferably of modern translation. (*Really Are*, p. 48.)

COMMITMENT

It is so easy to be halfhearted, but this only produces half the growth, half the blessings, and just half a life, really, with more bud than blossom. (*Ensign*, May 1985, p. 71.)

One major cause of real fatigue, little appreciated by those so afflicted, is trying to serve two masters. This is devastating double duty. (*Endure*, p. 114.)

Direction comes first, then velocity. (*Deposition*, p. 28.)

The truth is that "not yet" usually means "never." (*Ensign*, November 1974, p. 13.)

Events to transpire soon on this planet will dry up the options for the lukewarm, for the issues raised by Jesus are irrepressible issues! (*Ensign*, November 1974, p. 12.)

The winds of tribulation, which blow out some men's candles of commitment, only fan the fires of faith of . . . special men. (*Ensign*, November 1974, p. 12.)

I pledge that my little footnote on the page of the . . . history [of the Seventy] will read clearly that I wore out my life in helping to spread Jesus' gospel and helping to regulate his church. (*Ensign*, November 1976, p. 12.)

Humbly, therefore, I promise to go whithersoever I am sent, striving to speak the words He would have me say and acknowledging in the trembling of my soul that I cannot fully be His Special Witness unless my life is fully special. (*Ensign*, November 1981, p. 10.)

Suppose Enoch had demurred when called by the Lord? He would have gone on being a good person, serving the Lord part-time, living in a city which was a slum compared to the glorious City of Enoch; nor would Enoch be a part of that scene of glorious greeting yet to come. (See Moses 7:63.) (*Ensign*, May 1985, p. 72.)

Suppose Peter had not left his nets "straightway"? (See Mark 1:18.) He might have become the respected president of the local Galilean fishermen's association. But he would not have been on the Mount of Transfiguration with Jesus, Moses, and Elias and heard the voice of God. (See Matthew 17:4.) (*Ensign*, May 1985, p. 72.)

While casual members are not unrighteous, they often avoid appearing to be righteous by seeming less committed than they really are—an ironic form of hypocrisy. (*Ensign*, November 1992, p. 66.)

Satan need not get everyone to be like Cain or Judas, though he relishes such dramatic "success." He needs only to get able men like Pilate or Agrippa to see themselves as sophisticated neutrals. (*Deposition*, p. 88.)

Some would never *sell* Jesus for thirty pieces, but they would not *give* Him their all either! (*Ensign*, November 1992, p. 66.)

Some members maintain only cultural ties to the Church. Often these people have had valiant parents but they themselves live off the fruits of discipleship banked by those parents and grandparents. They make no fresh, spiritual investment; they have neither new earnings nor an inheritance to pass along to their own posterity. (*Men and Women*, p. 4.)

Weak individuals make great dominoes! ("Taking Up the Cross," p. 258.)

The cross is something we cannot shoulder and then stand still with. Of the Savior we read the following: "And he bearing his cross went forth" (John 19:17). The cross is easier to carry *if we keep moving. . . .* We must realize, finally, that we can only contemplate the cross just so long; rhetoric will not raise it. It must soon either be taken up or turned away from! ("Taking Up the Cross," pp. 259–60.)

We must put our hand to the plow and not look back, for where the eyes glance back, the heart may go also. (*Look Back*, p. 6.)

Commitment is causal, not casual, and a drifting discipleship is not real discipleship. (*Deposition*, p. 32.)

The high adventure of commitment in the kingdom is so intense, so demanding, and so unrelenting that, far from producing any kind of boredom, it more often produces a kind of combat fatigue because we are continually in the trenches of human affairs. (*Choose*, p. 11.)

Our outward involvement in spiritual things can also be illusive. One can be present at sacrament meeting but not really worship; the physical body can be there, while the mind and heart are else-where. One can accept a calling but still not magnify it, ending up by simply serving time. One can pay fast offerings unaccompanied by any personal service to needy neighbors or to the poor. We can open our checkbooks in the same way as some open their scrip-tures—more in mechanical than spiritual compliance. In church we can join in singing the hymns while being without a song in our hearts. We can take the sacrament with hand and mouth yet not be taken in mind, at least sometimes, to Gethsemane and Cal-vary. We can play artful doctrinal ping-pong in various Church classes but with minds and hearts that are less stretched than the ping-pong net. (*Men and Women*, pp. 6–7.)

Some, though decent and good, prefer the ambience of living in the general vicinity of the Lord's neighborhood. They do not really desire to go all the way home or to be "clasped in the arms of Jesus" (Mormon 5:11). (*Believe*, p. 103.)

Baptism by full immersion is best followed by full immersion in the new way of life. Disengagement from the world is best followed by being anxiously engaged in the Lord's work. Hence, there is a counterpart to pausing too long on the edge of the pool of baptism *before entering*—and that is pausing at poolside too long *on the way out*. Reactivated members who have paused on the porch of the church must not next pause in the foyer. The Holy Ghost can be our constant companion and will confirm our new course, if we so desire. He is prepared to be more than just an occasional friend. (*Press Forward*, pp. 3–4.)

Jesus suggested we take up our cross *daily*, suggesting the regularity of the commitment rather than seeing the shouldering as something that can be done in one ringing declaration. (Luke 92:23.) (*Really Are*, p. 11.)

Fair-weather followership cannot see us through life's stormy seasons. (*Not My Will*, p. 127.)

COMMUNICATION

In an age when verbal karate has some sway, we must be willing to let the gentling influence of the gospel tame the tongue—however tempting the tongue's target. So many of our soul scars are made by words—not deeds. (*Smallest Part*, p. 72.)

Geniality is a part of Christian communication, but so is accuracy. In the same way that vagueness in theology produces human misery, so vagueness in our communications produces difficulty. Evan Hill in writing about the need for accuracy said, "When we show that we care enough to be accurate, a current of warmth is generated

between people." While candor often depends upon a commitment to courage and truth, accuracy often depends upon our not
being lazy or indifferent about either issues or people. Fuzziness in
communication can mean that we simply do not have the facts,
but it can also mean that we simply do not care about the receiver
of our communication. (*Smallest Part*, pp. 72–73.)

It is difficult to say which is most dangerous—the mote in one's
eye or the moat around his "castle" that keeps out the needed communications, involving correction, counsel, or commendation.
(*Experience*, p. 80.)

Spiritual silence is a school. We may think we are sitting in that
school only waiting, but really we are witnessing those marvelous
moments of creative communication and of new commitment.
("Insights from My Life," p. 193.)

The small talk of great men and women is worthwhile. We discover so many wonders when walking carefully through another's
garden, not by crashing into it with a Mack truck. ("Insights from
My Life," p. 193.)

Trite expressions, devoid of feeling, are not particularly helpful in
inter-personal relations. How many of us have answered "Fine" to
the query "How are you?" when we were not fine at all? This is not
to suggest that we impose all our feelings and problems on others,
but rather to note the meaningless rituals we sometimes engage in
that can deaden the chances for real communication. (*Excellent*, pp.
76–77.)

So often what people need is to be enveloped in the raiment of
real response. (*Experience*, p. 55.)

If our efforts to communicate with someone are tied to their role rather than our regard for them, these efforts will not survive when that individual's role changes. If our friendship is a matter of function, what do we do when the function is changed or dissolved— cease caring? (*Experience*, p. 80.)

COMMUNITY

A person could get so caught up in making civic contributions to his community that he could lose his family. By the same token, one cannot readily save his family in an environment in decay. Thus we have obligations to contribute to the civic betterment of the communities in which we live. (*Deposition*, p. 68.)

A sister gives commendable, visible civic service. Yet even with her good image in the community, she remains a comparative stranger to Jesus' holy temples and His holy scriptures, two vital dimensions of discipleship. But she could have Christ's image in her countenance (see Alma 5:14). (*Ensign*, November 1995, p. 23.)

COMPARISONS

We [should] put our hand to the plow, looking neither back nor around, comparatively. Our gifts and opportunities differ; some are more visible and impactful. (*Deposition*, p. 30.)

Among the reasons for not comparing crosses is the fact that, first, we know so little about the weight of crosses and, second, we know even less about the bearing capacity of their owners. Someone who stumbles with seemingly little weight in one thing may have superb capacity for shouldering certain larger tasks. But the Lord insists on symmetry of soul, so it is not always the dunces who stay "after school." And whenever we think ourselves to be "above all that," we should recall that we are being tutored by Him who "descended below them all." (D&C 122:8.) (*Prove*, pp. 70–71.)

Our only valid spiritual competition is with our old selves, not with each other. (*Not My Will*, p. 70.)

COMPASSION

Compassion is important, but it can readily degenerate into the kind of pity which immobilizes us in terms of our ability to really help one another. (*Excellent*, p. 80.)

COMPLAINING

Many reject the scriptures, the moral memory of mankind, and then declare absolutely the absence of absolutes. Others reject the light of the gospel and then grump over the growing darkness. Still others cut themselves off from God and lament the loneliness of the universe. Some pursue the paths of him who openly desires mankind's misery (see 2 Nephi 2:27), and then bemoan their discontent. (*Ensign*, May 1983, p. 10.)

CONFESSION

All sins are to be confessed to the Lord, some to a Church official, some to others, and some to all of these. A few may require public confession. Confessing aids forsaking. We cannot expect to sin publicly and extensively and then expect to be rescued privately and quickly, being beaten "with only a few stripes." (See D&C 42:88–93.) (*Ensign*, November 1991, p. 31.)

Those who hold back major sins will be held back. So will those who refuse to work at repentance humbly and honestly with the Lord's appointed. The Lord will not be mocked. (*Ensign*, November 1991, p. 32.)

CONFORMITY

Though [Satan] postures as a nonconformist, my, how the adversary likes his lemmings to line up and march—toward self-destruction—to the most conforming cadence caller of them all! (*Really Are*, p. 7.)

CONSCIENCE

Conscience permits the Lord to be there, whether in early warnings or final warnings. He gives us a flash of insight or a twinge of remembrance, pulling us back from a precipice or prompting us to do good. Conscience can warn that we are only falling further behind by insisting on getting even. Conscience warns us not to sink our cleats too deeply in mortal turf, which is so dangerously artificial. (*Ensign*, November 1987, p. 32.)

Let us distinguish more clearly between divine discontent and the devil's dissonance, between dissatisfaction with self and disdain for self. We need the first and must shun the second, remembering that when conscience calls to us from the next ridge, it is not solely to scold but also to beckon. (*Deposition*, p. 29.)

Consecration

Yes, to Caesar we owe taxes. But to God, in whose image we are minted, we owe ourselves! (*Ensign*, November 1988, p. 31.)

Consecration is the only surrender which is also a victory. It brings release from the raucous, overpopulated cell block of selfishness and emancipation from the dark prison of pride. (*Ensign*, November 1992, p. 66.)

Whatever we embrace instead of Jesus and His work will keep us from qualifying to enter His kingdom and therefore from being embraced by Him. (See Mormon 6:17.) (*Ensign*, November 1992, p. 67.)

[Church members who are not fully consecrated are] the essentially "honorable" members who are skimming over the surface instead of deepening their discipleship and who are casually engaged rather than "anxiously engaged." (D&C 76:75; 58:27.) Though nominal in their participation, their reservations and hesitations inevitably show through. They may even pass through our holy temples but, alas, they do not let the holy temples pass through them. (*Ensign*, November 1992, p. 65.)

When, at last, we are truly pointed homeward, then the world's pointing fingers of scorn can better be endured. As we come to know to Whom we belong, the secular forms of belonging cease to mean very much. (*Ensign*, November 1992, p. 66.)

When we consecrate, individuality is actually enhanced, not lost. Our quirks and impurities go, but who would want to come into the Inner Court trailing such obsolete trinkets anyway? (*On Becoming a Disciple-Scholar*, p. 21.)

Increased consecration is not so much a demand for more hours of Church work as it is for more awareness of Whose work this really is! (*Ensign*, November 1992, p. 67.)

When we have an eye single to God's glory, there is no room for other consuming causes. Yes, we are to be anxiously engaged in good causes, but all good causes are actually subsets of God's great cause—to bring to pass the immortality and eternal life of man (see Moses 1:39; Moroni 7:28). (*Flood*, p. 106.)

For now, consecration may not require giving up worldly possessions so much as being less possessed by them. (*Ensign*, November 1992, p. 67.)

Consecration is not resignation or a mindless caving in. Rather, it is a deliberate expanding outward. (*Ensign*, November 1995, p. 24.)

Consecration . . . is not shoulder-shrugging acceptance, but, instead, shoulder-squaring to better bear the yoke. (*Ensign*, November 1995, p. 24.)

Consecration is . . . both a principle and a process, and it is not tied to a single moment. Instead, it is freely given, drop by drop, until the cup of consecration brims and finally runs over. (*Ensign*, November 1995, p. 24.)

CONSEQUENCES

We'd better want the consequences of what we want! (*Ensign*, November 1995, p. 23.)

Consequences come both quickly and slowly in the lives of individuals and of whole societies. Sometimes scarcely one generation passes before some consequences appear. Other consequences slumber like a silent virus, ready to take a later toll. (*Not My Will*, p. 67.)

There are no immunities from the consequences of our choices. (*Prove*, p. 83.)

It is because God loves us . . . that He seeks with such vigor and long-suffering to separate us from our sins, which He hates. He continues to care for us even when He cannot approve of us. Yet ultimately we cannot go where He is unless He fully approves of us. This outcome, however, reflects the consequences of divine justice, not His love for us, which persists. (*Endure*, p. 35.)

Consistency

As with our wasteful automobile driving habits that consume extra energy because of quick starts and stops, so it may be that with inconsistent discipleship we actually inflict costs on ourselves in the face of divine counsel. (*Men and Women*, p. 25.)

Quiet, sustained goodness is the order of heaven, not conspicuous but episodic busyness. (*Notwithstanding*, p. 5.)

The Prophet finally gave *all* that he had, but his contribution to the work of the Lord was not in a single project; it was spread over many high priority projects and also over a period of time. The paced performance of Joseph Smith brought results that were to touch millions! We, too, may be ready to give our all, but it is usually not required in one lump sum. (*Notwithstanding*, p. 5.)

When our pace exceeds our strength and means, the result is prostration instead of sustained dedication. (*Notwithstanding*, p. 6.)

A few little flowers will spring up briefly in the dry gulley through which torrents of water pass occasionally. But it is steady streams that bring thick and needed crops. In the agriculture of the soul that has to do with nurturing attributes, flash floods are no substitute for regular irrigation. (*Notwithstanding*, p. 7.)

Steady devotion is better than periodic exhaustion. . . . Even rigorousness has its rhythm. (*Notwithstanding*, p. 7.)

CONTROL

Some of us seek to control others instead of letting them grow. Controlling is, in a sense, keeping one's brother—constraining and hedging him in. Some of us want to tie people to us even if it means limiting their possibilities instead of encouraging and helping them on their way. There is great satisfaction in helping to "launch" another person who may rise to heights we ourselves may not have achieved. Real brothers are real boosters. (*Press Forward*, p. 92.)

CONVERSION

As in baptism, so in Church activity—there can be immersion without conversion! (*We Talk of Christ*, p. 139.)

The overwhelming joy of conversion or a new calling is often followed by feelings of being overwhelmed with duties and doctrines. The first joyous feelings are real and give one much-needed initial momentum. But the genuine exhilaration is soon followed by the need to perspire and to pedal. (*Press Forward*, p. xi.)

How sad that so many cannot see that to be *put out* of the secular synagogues for one's belief in Christ is the first step toward being *let in* the kingdom of God! (John 9:22.) (*Really Are*, p. 62.)

COUNSELING

We should not be candid merely to punish or to meet our own ego needs. Rather, we must do as Paul says: speak "the truth in love." (Ephesians 4:15.) And even when we must give reproof, we should, as Paul also suggested, confirm our love lest the other individual "be swallowed up with overmuch sorrow." (2 Corinthians 2:7–8.) In the Doctrine and Covenants, we are asked to "show forth an increase of love"—not the same level of love, but a visible "increase." (D&C 121:40–44.) (*Experience*, p. 75.)

Counseling delayed may be counseling denied so far as the critical moment is concerned. (*Press Forward*, p. 111.)

COURTESY

Someday the policeman will not be needed, for our love, when more developed, will make courtesy a natural matter of reflex, not a duty or protocol. (*Prove*, p. 65.)

COVENANTS

Already too many Church members have broken hearts and broken homes because of broken covenants and broken promises. Society's increasing slide towards pleasure-seeking brings our so-called civilization comparatively closer to Sodom than to Eden. (*Ensign*, November 1982, p. 68.)

To keep the commandments and to honor our covenants—whether one is a cashier at a grocery checkout counter, a neurosurgeon, an automotive mechanic, or a government official—is what matters, daily and eternally (see Luke 9:23). (*Flood*, p. 103.)

CREATION

We sing, "The stars in the heavens looked down where He lay." The on-looking universe, created by Jesus under the Father's direction, contained "worlds without number" (Moses 1:33). In that sense, Christ was cradled not only in a manger but also in the midst of His own vast creations. (*The Christmas Scene*, p. 3.)

CRITICISM OF THE CHURCH

Church members will live in this wheat-and-tares situation until the Millennium. Some real tares even masquerade as wheat, including the few eager individuals who lecture the rest of us about Church doctrines in which they no longer believe. They criticize the use of Church resources to which they no longer contribute. They condescendingly seek to counsel the Brethren whom they no longer sustain. Confrontive, except of themselves of course, they leave the Church but they cannot leave the Church alone. (*Ensign*, May 1996, p. 68.)

Church . . . leaders are cruelly caricatured by some in the world. For perspective, imagine how television's six o'clock news would have portrayed Noah as he worked on his ark day by day. Besides, attention from the adversary is merely a cruel form of commendation, if we can but stand the "praise." There is such a thing as being praised with faint damns. (*Ensign*, November 1980, p. 14.)

Why are a few members, who somewhat resemble the ancient Athenians, so eager to hear some new doubt or criticism? (See Acts 17:21.) Just as some weak members slip across a state line to gamble, a few go out of their way to have their doubts titillated. Instead of nourishing their faith, they are gambling "offshore" with their fragile faith. To the question "Will ye also go away?" these few would reply, "Oh, no, we merely want a weekend pass to go to a casino for critics or a clubhouse for cloakholders." Such easily diverted members are not disciples but fair-weather followers. (*Ensign*, November 1988, pp. 32–33.)

How handy inspired but imperfect leaders in the Church are as focal points for our frustrations, especially if circumstances require them to suffer in silence. Having confidence in leaders who keep confidences is part of sustaining them. (*Ensign*, November 1989, p. 82.)

Some murmurers seem to hope to reshape the Church to their liking by virtue of their murmuring. But why would one want to belong to a church that he could remake in his own image, when it is the Lord's image that we should come to have in our countenances? (See Alma 5:19.) The doctrines are His, brothers and sisters, not ours. The power is His to delegate, not ours to manipulate! (*Ensign*, November 1989, p. 83.)

Collectively but not perfectly, those sustained do the work to which God has called them. As with Joseph Smith, so it is for his succeeding Brethren. The operative promise persists: namely, the people of the Church will never be turned away "by the testimony of traitors." (D&C 122:3.) But the faithful know something about divine determination. They know that the Lord's purposes will finally triumph, for "there is nothing that the Lord thy God shall take in his heart to do but what he will do it." (Abraham 3:17.) (*Ensign*, May 1991, p. 91.)

Exciting exploration is preferred [by some] to plodding implementation; speculation seems more fun than consecration, and so is trying to soften the hard doctrines instead of submitting to them. Worse still, by not obeying, these few members lack real knowing. (See John 7:17.) Lacking real knowing, they cannot defend their faith and may become critics instead of defenders! A few of the latter end up in the self-reinforcing and self-congratulating Hyde Park corner of the Church, which they provincially mistake for the whole of the Church, as if London's real Hyde Park corner were Parliament, Whitehall, Buckingham Palace, and all of England combined! (*Ensign*, November 1992, p. 66.)

A little criticism of the Brethren, which seems harmless enough, may not only damage other members but can even lead to one's setting himself up as a substitute "light unto the world." (2 Nephi 26:29.) Yes, happily, some such prodigals do come back, but they usually walk alone, unaccompanied by those they once led astray! (*Ensign*, November 1992, p. 67.)

If our shortcomings as a people are occasionally highlighted, then let us strive to do better. (*Ensign*, May 1996, p. 68.)

We may never become accustomed to untrue and unjust criticism of us but we ought not to be immobilized by it. ("'All Hell Is Moved,'" p. 176.)

Some prefer to believe the worst rather than to know the truth. Still others are afraid to part the smokescreen of allegations for fear of what they will see. Yet one cannot see the Louvre by remaining in the lobby. One cannot understand the Church by remaining outside. A non-believing but fair critic of the Church, a friend of mine, once said that the Book of Mormon was the only book some critics felt they did not need to read before reviewing it. ("'All Hell Is Moved,'" p. 177.)

Some insist upon studying the Church only through the eyes of its defectors—like interviewing Judas to understand Jesus. Defectors always tell us more about themselves than about that from which they have departed. ("'All Hell Is Moved,'" p. 177.)

Some . . . patiently feed their pet peeve about the Church without realizing that such a pet will not only bite the hands of him who feeds it, but it will swallow his whole soul. Of course, we are a very imperfect people! Remember, however, that while it is possible to have an imperfect people possessed of perfect doctrines (indeed, such is necessary to change their imperfections), you will never, never see the reverse: a perfect people with imperfect doctrines. ("'All Hell Is Moved,'" p. 177.)

There are the dissenters who leave the Church, either formally or informally, but who cannot leave it alone. Usually anxious to please worldly galleries, they are critical or at least condescending towards the Brethren. They not only seek to steady the ark but also on occasion give it a hard shove! (*Men and Women*, p. 4.)

Trying to run ahead of the leaders is, in effect, trying to preempt their role as shepherds of the flock. As with the shepherds in the Middle East, prophets are to lead the flock; they do not herd the flock, nor do they merely follow it. . . . To run ahead is to say in effect that we, and not the prophets, know best, especially if we try to take some of the flock with us. (*Experience*, pp. 105, 106.)

Some chafe unduly at the carefulness in the Church. They think of themselves as being ready to go when it is being ready to follow that is the skill needed at the moment. (*Experience*, p. 106.)

There are those who reject following the Brethren because *they* wish to be the leaders. This is a mortal reflection of Lucifer's bid in the premortal world. His need for ascendancy was so great that he simply would not follow. (*Experience*, p. 110.)

We should not even be dismayed either if, in the winding-up scenes, the enemies of God attack the very foundation of the Church. Their assaults will include derision of the Prophet Joseph Smith, the Book of Mormon, and the reality of continuing revelation. These efforts will surely fail, but not before damaging some unsteady members—those who have unnecessary difficulty in following the Brethren. (*Experience*, p. 126.)

Those who stand indecisively at the foot of the gospel's gangplank, not wishing to come aboard, are, of course, not in the same circumstances as those who accept the gospel as soon as they hear it, though they hear it late in the day. Those later workers, as the Lord Himself tells us, get the same wages as those who signed on early. But those who simply mill about the dockside grumbling about the fare or questioning the seaworthiness of the vessel, instead of helping out, are those most to be pitied. (*Press Forward*, p. 5.)

The critics of the Church, who are often those within the Church, frequently say, "Why doesn't the Church do this or that?" or "Why does the Church do this or that?" Those who desire to make the greatest demands of the Church are usually those who make the fewest demands of themselves in terms of *their* discipleship. (*Press Forward*, p. 69.)

If the Church were not true, our enemies would be bored rather than threatened, and acquiescent rather than anxious. Hell is moved only when things move heavenward. (*Press Forward*, p. 81.)

Those who claim to care for the Church but who do not believe in it—the cultural Mormons—act as if the Church already belonged to history, and the Church embarrasses them, especially when it is so lively and living. Other members keep their devotions private instead of going public, for fear of being put out of the secular synagogue. (*Really Are*, p. 57.)

Those who live in homes where cutting criticism of the Church is "in the air" will find it much harder to be grounded in the gospel. (*Not My Will*, p. 63.)

As critics become more clever and enemies more numerous, let us remember and be reassured by the resurrected Jesus' promise: "My wisdom is greater than the cunning of the devil" (3 Nephi 21:10). Talk of desirable perspective! One major deprivation of the adversary is that he simply does not know the mind of Christ (1 Corinthians 2:16; see also Moses 4:6). (*Faith*, p. 96.)

DARKNESS

Misery may crave company, but darkness detests light. (*Press Forward*, p. 9.)

Men's and nations' finest hours consist of those moments when extraordinary challenge is met by extraordinary response. Hence in those darkest hours, we must light our individual candles rather than vying with others to call attention to the enveloping darkness. Our indignation about injustice should lead to illumination, for if it does not, we are only adding to the despair—and the moment of gravest danger is when there is so little light that darkness seems normal! (*Smallest Part*, p. 75.)

DEATH

Death is a mere comma, not an exclamation point! (*Ensign*, May 1983, p. 11.)

Since this life is such a brief experience, there must be regular exit routes. Some easy. Some hard. Some sudden. Others lingering. Therefore, we cannot presume, even by faith, to block all these exits, all the time, and for all people. Nor, if possessed of full, eternal perspective, would we desire so to do. (*Ensign*, May 1984, p. 22.)

Our gratitude for the gift of mortal life [should not] depend upon the manner in which we die, for surely none of us will rush eagerly forward to tell Jesus how we died! (*Ensign*, November 1983, p. 66.)

As this Easter day draws to a close, how fitting that we contemplate atoning Jesus—bending and curved in Gethsemane. His bleeding curvature transformed the grammar of death. Until Gethsemane and Calvary, death was a punctuating, rigid exclamation point! Then death, too, curved—into a mere comma! (*Ensign*, May 1994, p. 91.)

At funerals our tears are genuine, but not because of termination—rather because of interruption. Though just as wet, our tears are not of despair but are of appreciation and anticipation. Yes, for disciples, the closing of a grave is but the closing of a door which later will be flung open with rejoicing. ("'All Hell Is Moved,'" p. 181.)

We say humbly but firmly that it is the garden tomb—not life—that is empty. ("'All Hell Is Moved,'" p. 181.)

Mortality is not a conclusive and massive mausoleum, and . . . death is not extinction. (*Ensign*, May 1984, p. 21.)

As we wait with those who are dying . . . we brush against the veil, as goodbyes and greetings are said almost within earshot of each other. ("Patience," p. 219.)

On the other side of the veil, there are perhaps seventy billion people. They need the same gospel, and releases occur here to aid the Lord's work there. Each release of a righteous individual from this life is also a call to new labors. Those who have true hope understand this. Therefore, though we miss the departed righteous so much here, hundreds may feel their touch there. One day, those hundreds will thank the bereaved for gracefully forgoing the extended association with choice individuals here, in order that they could help hundreds there. In God's ecology, talent and love are never wasted. The hopeful understand this, too. (*Notwithstanding*, p. 55.)

A mortal life may need to be "shortened" by twenty years as we might view it—but if so, it may be done in order for special services to be rendered by that individual in the spirit world, services that will benefit thousands of new neighbors with whom that individual will live in all of eternity. Perhaps this reality is yet another reason and reminder why we are urged to pray only for "our daily bread," for disciples must be portable. (*Experience*, p. 99.)

Some disciples do not end their soldierly and gallant journey in a vigorous salute in a dress parade, but in halting senility or with a stroke that stretches out their days. (*Press Forward*, p. 125.)

DECISIONS

There are certain mortal moments and minutes that matter—certain hinge points in the history of each human. Some seconds are so decisive they shrink the soul, while other seconds are spent so as to stretch the soul. ("Taking Up the Cross," p. 255.)

Decisions made in the midst of fatigue are seldom the best decisions, and agreements reached between the exhausted may last only until some of the participants are revived. (*Smallest Part*, p. 48.)

It is an act of kindness for prophets to press mankind for a decision, because the absence of a decision to commit *is* a decision. (*My Family*, p. 22.)

It is very important that we not assume the perspectives of mortality in making the decisions that bear on eternity! We need the perspectives of the gospel to make decisions in the context of eternity. We need to understand we cannot do the Lord's work in the world's way. ("But for a Small Moment," p. 454.)

DECISIVENESS

Act now, so that a thousand years from now, when you look back at this moment, you can say this was a moment that mattered— this was a day of determination. (*Ensign*, November 1974, p. 13.)

How important it is not to stand by and wring our hands but to do something! (*Ensign*, May 1982, p. 37.)

A lack of decisiveness in dealing with temptation (like David's fatal view from the terrace) ties up our thought processes and prevents us from doing good with the time allotted to us. It is a free man who can dispatch devilish entreaties summarily, the better to spend his time, talent, and energy "in a good cause." The same danger exists if we allow ourselves—after true repentance—to recycle our past mistakes broodingly. (*Smallest Part*, p. 51.)

DEFIANCE

Our defiance of God is an expression of our ignorance, not of our individuality. (*Not My Will*, p. 67.)

DESIRES

What we insistently desire, over time, is what we will eventually become and what we will receive in eternity. (*Ensign*, November 1996, p. 21.)

God thus takes into merciful account not only our desires and our performance, but also the degrees of difficulty which our varied circumstances impose upon us. . . . God delights in blessing us, especially when we realize "joy in that which [we] have desired" (D&C 7:8). However, in contrast to God's merciful plan for our joy and glory, Satan "[desires] that all men might be miserable like unto himself" (2 Nephi 2:27). (*Ensign*, November 1996, p. 21.)

Mostly, brothers and sisters, we become the victims of our own wrong desires. Morever, we live in an age when many simply refuse to feel responsible for themselves. Thus, a crystal-clear understanding of the doctrines pertaining to desire is so vital because of the spreading effluent oozing out of so many unjustified excuses by so many. This is like a sludge which is sweeping society along toward "the gulf of misery and endless wo." (Helaman 5:12). Feeding the same flow is the selfish philosphy of "no fault," which is replacing the meek and apologetic "my fault." (*Ensign*, November 1996, p. 21.)

Righteous desires need to be relentless, therefore, because, said President Brigham Young, "the men and women, who desire to obtain seats in the celestial kingdom, will find that they must battle every day" (in *Journal of Discourses*, 11:14). Therefore, true Christian soldiers are more than weekend warriors. (*Ensign*, November 1996, p. 22.)

Remember, brothers and sisters, it is our own desires which determine the sizing and the attractiveness of various temptations. We set our thermostats as to temptations. (*Ensign*, November 1996, p. 22.)

Each assertion of a righteous desire, each act of service, and each act of worship, however small and incremental, adds to our spiritual momentum. Like Newton's Second Law, there is a transmitting of acceleration as well as a contagiousness associated with even small acts of goodness. (*Ensign*, November 1996, p. 22.)

President Joseph F. Smith [declared] "the education then of our desires is one of far-reaching importance to our happiness in life" (*Gospel Doctrine*, 5th ed. [1939], 297). Such education can lead to sanctification until, said President Brigham Young, "holy desires produce corresponding outward works" (in *Journal of Discourses*, 6:170). Only by educating and training our desires can they become our allies instead of our enemies! (*Ensign*, November 1996, p. 22.)

Some of our present desires, therefore, need to be diminished and then finally dissolved. . . . But dissolution of wrong desires is only part of it. For instance, what is now only a weak desire to be a better spouse, father, or mother needs to become a stronger desire, just as Abraham experienced divine discontent and desired greater happiness and knowledge (see Abraham 1:2). (*Ensign*, November 1996, p. 22.)

Brothers and sisters, a loving God will work with us, but the initiating particle of desire which ignites the spark of resolve must be our own! (*Ensign*, November 1996, p. 23.)

DESPAIR

As an ancient prophet correctly observed, sadness and badness are mutually reinforcing, for "despair cometh because of iniquity." (Moroni 10:22.) (*Ensign*, May 1983, p. 9.)

When the hopes of humans are riddled and blasted, it is usually when mortals assume that familiar formation: the circular firing squad. (*As I Am*, p. 5.)

Just as doubt, despair, and desensitization go together, so do faith, hope, and charity. The latter, however, must be carefully and constantly nurtured, whereas despair, like dandelions, needs so little encouragement to sprout and spread. Despair comes so naturally to the natural man! (*Ensign*, November 1994, p. 35.)

Destiny

His [God's] overseeing precision pertains not only to astrophysical orbits but to human orbits as well. ("'In Him All Things Hold Together,'" p. 108.)

Our planning itself often assumes that our destiny is largely in our own hands. Then come intruding events, first elbowing aside, then evicting what was anticipated and even earned. Hence, we can be offended by events as well as by people. (*Ensign*, May 1989, p. 63.)

God knows even now what the future holds for each of us. . . . The future "you" is before him now. He knows what it is he wishes to bring to pass in your life. He knows the kind of remodeling in your life and in mine that he wishes to achieve. Now, this will require us to believe in that divine design and at times to accept the truth which came to Joseph Smith wherein he was reminded that his suffering would be "but a small moment" (D&C 121:7). ("But for a Small Moment," p. 444.)

DETOURS

Detours don't have to be bad to have a bad effect—they always cost us time. They may also mean that we were not there to help a fellow traveler who needed us as he stumbled. (*Press Forward*, p. 34.)

DEVIL

He wanted glory, not growth; control, not salvation. His ascendancy meant more to him than our agency. [See Moses 4:1–4.] The devil is a despot. (*Deposition*, p. 12.)

Lucifer, who has no future, . . . desperately desires to persuade men that they have no future either. He desires "that all men might be miserable like unto himself" (2 Nephi 2:27). Misery likes company—especially ultimate misery! (*Deposition*, p. 14.)

When the adversary can get us to disbelieve in but serve him and to believe in but not serve the Lord, he has achieved a double coup. (*Deposition*, p. 11.)

Being a poor loser, Lucifer transferred his battle to this world where he displays his "wild desire to manage everything." The casualty rate in the premortal world was 33 percent [D&C 29:36–37], and Satan's harvest will be high here in the second estate. Thus what we see about us is a protracted psychodrama reenacting his power play of the premortal world. He wanted status without service, power without perfection ("I will be like the Most High"), and esteem not earned. Sodom was one of Satan's "finest" hours! (*Deposition*, p. 12.)

Let me stress that either becoming morbidly preoccupied with the devil or ignoring his reality is equally unhealthy. (*Deposition*, p. 12.)

Lucifer is permissive on most things, but not on granting passports for citizens to leave his realm. (*Deposition*, p. 12.)

There is no détente with the devil. He knows that weak individuals make great dominoes. He knows that the collapse of individuals precedes the collapse of systems. This is how he has brought down senates and civilizations; he destroys societies by destroying individuals. We must build societies by building individuals—not the reverse. (*Deposition*, p. 17.)

The adversary never uses any of his annual leave. (*Deposition*, p. 20.)

Lucifer apparently was and is multi-talented, but his memories of what might have been gnaw at him constantly. No wonder he is an incurable insomniac. (*Deposition*, p. 36.)

No one knows how to work a crowd better than the adversary. (*Flood*, p. 65.)

Lucifer did not want the responsibilities of godhood. These include shepherding and truly loving a disobedient mortal flock who are possessed of agency that will be misused, resulting in many not being saved, in many falling short of their possibilities. ("'Meek and Lowly,'" p. 29.)

How tragic it is that so many mortals are mercenaries for the adversary; that is, they do his bidding and are hired by him—bought off at such low prices. A little status, a little money, a little praise, a little fleeting fame, and they are willing to do the bidding of him who can offer all sorts of transitory "rewards," but who has no celestial currency. It is amazing how well the adversary has done; his mercenaries never seem to discover the self-destructive nature of their pay and the awful bankruptcy of their poor paymaster! (*Really Are*, p. 42.)

The adversary is much less interested in making of us physical clones than he is in converting us into behavioral clones. Truly, the stunning sameness of gross sinners ought to be enough to frighten anyone who really cares for freedom and individuality. Poor Satan—it can't be much fun being a cheerleader for a chorus of clones, but how he stays at his task! (*Really Are*, p. 43.)

The adversary seeks to lead us carefully down to hell, whereas it is the steep road of repentance which we are pledged to travel. Lucifer is an expert at giving the guided tour, studiously avoiding jarring us into spiritual sensibility during the gradual descent. He can blur the passing landscape so adroitly that we scarcely notice leaving the mountains, and then the uplands, as we are headed toward the slums and, finally, arrive at dockside on the gulf of misery. (*Not My Will*, pp. 74–75.)

Not only does God have a plan but so also does the adversary. (*Faith*, p. 41.)

The tempter's triad of tools are temptation, persecution, and tribulation (see Matthew 13:18–22). These tools will be relentlessly used upon God's flock (see Matthew 13:21; Luke 8:13). (*Endure*, p. 126.)

DILIGENCE

The Lord wants us to be *diligent* but *prudent*. We are not to give our cross a hurried heft merely to see if we can lift it and then put it down—we are to carry it for the balance of our lives. (*Notwithstanding*, p. 4.)

DISABILITIES

There are clearly special cases of individuals in mortality who have special limitations in life, which conditions we mortals cannot now fully fathom. For all we now know, the seeming limitations may have been an agreed-upon spur to achievement—a "thorn in the flesh." Like him who was blind from birth, some come to bring glory to God (John 9:1–3). We must be exceedingly careful about imputing either wrong causes or wrong rewards to all in such circumstances. They are in the Lord's hands, and he loves them perfectly. Indeed, some of those who have required much waiting upon in this life may be waited upon again by the rest of us in the next world—but for the highest of reasons. ("Meeting the Challenges of Today," p. 153.)

DISAPPOINTMENT

Our transitory disappointments are real, but the missing letter from home is not really comparable to the delivered message from heaven, the good news of the gospel. Today's unmet hunger for a few more friends must not be allowed to obscure the marvelous reality of the forever friendship of Jesus for each of us. Do not let uncertainty about how others seem to feel about you this week get in the way of how God has always felt about you . . . and always will. Proximate problems need not, and must not, undercut ultimate realities. ("'All Hell Is Moved,'" p. 180.)

Disappointments can also be blessings in disguise. This is especially so when we envy those who got what we have wanted. The sailors on the port-bound U.S.S. *Enterprise* were slowed by heavy seas and a malfunctioning escort destroyer, the U.S.S. *Dunlap*. Hence the *Enterprise* would not make Pearl Harbor, after all, as scheduled, for the weekend of December 7, 1941. Eighteen planes, however, were permitted to take off and proceed to Hawaii. Some left behind must have envied those "lucky" pilots! However, those unfortunate planes arrived during the attack of Pearl Harbor, and six were shot down. Envy is usually as uninformed as it is insistent. (*Faith*, p. 118.)

Because there cannot be immunities from disappointments, how we handle them is a reflection of how much daily faith we have in Heavenly Father's plan of salvation. Besides, how can we possibly take Jesus' yoke upon us and learn of Him without experiencing what it is like, for example, to do good with good motives, only to have others respond badly and unappreciatively? (*Faith*, p. 118.)

DISASTER

We must all work in the Ninevehs of our lives, doing all we can, even though we may have a sense of impending disaster. We should not desert our post nor can we indulge ourselves in the luxury of wanting disaster, for our goal is salvation, not vindication! (*Choose*, p. 10.)

DISCERNMENT

We cannot become like Jesus, attribute by attribute, if we display hesitancy as to our purity, or if we are undiscerning between joy and pleasure. Lust is no more like love than itching is to joy, or talkativeness to wisdom, or indulgence to compassion, or passivity to patience. (*Ensign*, February 1986, p. 19.)

DISCIPLESHIP

Disciples, like diamonds, are developed in a process of time and heavy pressures, and both the disciple and the diamond reflect and magnify the light that comes through them. (*Press Forward*, p. 125.)

Real disciples absorb the fiery darts of the adversary by holding aloft the quenching shield of faith with one hand, while holding to the iron rod with the other (see Ephesians 6:16; 1 Nephi 15:24; D&C 27:17). There should be no mistaking; it will take both hands! (*Ensign*, May 1987, p. 70.)

What finally matters, brothers and sisters, is what we have become. There will be no puffed vitas circulating in the next world.

They stay here—in the files. What we will take with us—to the degree we have developed them—will be the cardinal qualities that Jesus has perfected; these are eternal and portable. ("Out of the Best Faculty," p. 48.)

For a disciple of Jesus Christ, academic scholarship is a form of worship. It is actually another dimension of consecration. Hence one who seeks to be a disciple-scholar will take both scholarship and discipleship seriously; and, likewise, gospel covenants. For the disciple-scholar, the first and second great commandments frame and prioritize life. How else could one worship God with all of one's heart, might, _mind_, and strength? (Luke 10:27.) (_On Becoming a Disciple-Scholar_, p. 7.)

Some give of their time yet withhold themselves, being present without giving of their presence and going through the superficial motions of membership instead of the deep emotions of consecrated discipleship. (_Ensign_, May 1987, p. 70.)

Maintaining Church membership on our own terms . . . is not true discipleship. (_Ensign_, May 1987, p. 70.)

Each day we decide the degree of our discipleship. Each day we answer the question, "Who's on the Lord's side? Who?" (_Ensign_, May 1992, p. 39.)

Each of us is an innkeeper, and we decide if there is room for Jesus. (_Searching for God in America_, p. 129.)

Being settled keeps us from responding to every little ripple of dissent as if it were a tidal wave. We are to be disciples, not oscillators, like a "reed shaken in the wind" (Matthew 11:7). More members need the immense relief and peace which can come from being "settled" without which those individuals will be like "the troubled sea, when it cannot rest" (Isaiah 57:20). (*Ensign*, November 1992, p. 67.)

Dull disciples will not light the way nor draw people to the kingdom. ("'All Hell Is Moved,'" p. 180.)

Discipleship . . . means being drawn by seemingly small and routine duties toward the fulfillment of the two great and most challenging commandments [Matthew 22:35–40]. ("'True Believers in Christ,'" p. 135.)

It is not enough for us to have once been close to the Savior. (So was Sidney Rigdon.) Alma said, if we have once "felt to sing the song of redeeming love," can we "feel so now?" (Alma 5:26.) Dutiful discipleship creates many happy memories, but it does not make nostalgia a substitute for fresh achievement. ("'True Believers in Christ,'" p. 136.)

The sooner we are on the way to serious discipleship, the sooner the needed spiritual and personal reinforcements and intellectual reassurances will come to us personally. If one chooses to live out his life without God, however, it will be as if he had been sentenced to remain a permanent resident in an airport transit lounge—consigned there, briefly and expectantly, to mingle with the ever-changing, lonely crowds. Somehow, in that forlorn situation, even being granted a cot and a hotplate in the corner of the transit lounge would not ease either the sense of anomie or futility. (*On Becoming a Disciple-Scholar*, p. 19.)

One common characteristic of the honorable but slack is their disdain for the seemingly unexciting duties of discipleship, such as daily prayer, regular reading of the scriptures, attendance at a sacrament meeting, paying a full tithe, and participating in the holy temples. Such disdain is especially dangerous in today's world of raging relativism and of belching sensualism, a world in which, if many utter the name of Deity at all, it is only as verbal punctuation or as an expression of exclamation, not adoration! (*Ensign*, November 1992, p. 66.)

In opting for discipleship, we have nothing to fear but the disapproval of the natural man and his like-minded, preoccupied friends—with their pointing fingers. (*On Becoming a Disciple-Scholar*, p. 22.)

As the disciple enriches his relationship with the Lord, he is apt to have periodic "public relations" problems with others, being misrepresented and misunderstood. He or she will have to "take it" at times. Meekness, therefore, is a key to deepening discipleship. ("'Meek and Lowly,'" p. 54.)

Even articulate discipleship has its side of silent certitude! ("'Meek and Lowly,'" p. 57.)

While it is no longer necessary . . . to find a geographic Zion, the same uncomplaining dedication will be required of those who pursue discipleship. (*Smallest Part*, p. 78.)

Discipleship in our day, as in all eras, has as a goal not our being different from other men, but our need to be more like God. (*Choose*, p. 16.)

Having found the only passage, we should behave tolerantly and lovingly, and willingly serve as guides for other wanderers. There will be bitter irony if the guides follow the meandering multitudes, for to follow them is really to fail them. Leaving our sector is a special kind of desertion. (*Choose*, p. 19.)

Disciples are not perfect, but, having chosen the Christian course, they are put together with principle rather than being a bundle of appetites. (*Choose*, pp. 44–45.)

If we are serious about our discipleship, Jesus will eventually request each of us to do those very things which are most difficult for us to do. (*Choose*, p. 46.)

It is a mistake to assume that the disciple must merely be filled with anxiety for mankind or with holy—but abstract—compassion. He must increase his competence as well as his concern. (*Choose*, p. 83.)

We usually think of balancing our discipleship in words and deeds by stressing more *doing* and less *talking*. We are to be "doers of the word," lest we be hypocrites. Spiritual symmetry requires, however, that "doers" also be willing to be declarative, as was valiant Stephen [Acts 6 and 7]. (*As I Am*, p. 97.)

Much more burdening than that avoidable fatigue . . . is the burden of personal frailties. Almost all of us as members [of the Church] fail to lighten our load for the long and arduous journey of discipleship. We fail to put off the childish things—not the tinker toys, but the temper tantrums; not training pants, but pride. We remain unnecessarily burdened by things which clearly should and can be jettisoned. (*Men and Women*, pp. 3–4.)

The dues of discipleship are high indeed, and how much we can *take* so often determines how much we can then *give!* (*Notwithstanding*, p. 63.)

The costs of discipleship are not paid just once, therefore, at the front end and then all is done. The dues of discipleship continue and are on an ascending scale. (*Press Forward*, p. 33.)

The justice of God permits no special deal for disciples. We must subdue our selfishness; we must endure the pain of prioritizing. We must cope with the variables of the second estate. There can be no later outcry by the nonbelievers that they were ultimately deprived of an *equal chance* to believe and to follow. For disciples there is no spiritual equivalent to the "prime rate" or the "most-favored nation" clause. (*Press Forward*, p. 68.)

On occasion, sadly, competent disciples will not be chosen for certain professional chores of the world because their peers will see them as being incapacitated to perform fully because they are disciples. The only Roman "club" to which early Christians obtained admittance was the Colosseum, and, unfortunately, other guests—four-legged and hungry—had been invited too. (*Really Are*, p. 14.)

Discipleship is not simply surviving and enduring; discipleship is a pressing forward, a creative Christianity. Discipleship does not wait to be acted upon, but instead acts upon men and circumstances to make things better. (*Really Are*, p. 100.)

The act of loving one's enemies and submissiveness are the greatest and crowning things in discipleship. It shouldn't surprise us that they don't come early in one's discipleship. Instead they come near the end of the trail, when we are less selfish and less caught up with ego. (*Searching for God in America*, p. 132.)

Keeping our sense of proportion *whatever* we do, keeping our precious perspective *wherever* we are, and keeping the commandments *however* we are tested—these reflect being "settled in our discipleship." (*Prove*, p. 12.)

True discipleship is for volunteers only. Only volunteers will trust the Guide sufficiently to follow Him in the dangerous ascent which only He can lead. (*Not My Will*, p. 89.)

Sustained discipleship includes resisting, and chopping back again and again, the encroaching crabgrass cares of the world. (*Not My Will*, p. 123.)

Taking up the cross daily is an affirmation of the meaning of life, even if we log only a few miles a day in the journey of discipleship. Each increment not only moves us along but also, what is very important, maintains the desired direction. The lack of daily affirmation, on the other hand, such as through service, prayer, and forgiveness, can be a perilous pause. Resuming the journey after any pause is not automatic. Every delay risks the difficulty of resumption. (*Faith*, p. 104.)

We can tell much by what we have already willingly discarded along the pathway of discipleship. It is the only pathway where littering is permissible, even encouraged. In the early stages, the debris left behind includes the grosser sins of commission. Later debris differs; things begin to be discarded which have caused the misuse or underuse of our time and talent. (*Ensign*, November 1995, p. 24.)

DISCOURAGEMENT

Discouragement is not the absence of adequacy but the absence of courage. (*Deposition*, p. 31.)

DISOBEDIENCE

Those few in deliberate noncompliance includ[e] some who cast off on intellectual and behavioral bungee cords in search of new sensations, only to be jerked about by the old heresies and the old sins. (*Ensign*, November 1992, p. 65.)

Those who wrongly and heedlessly do their own thing are really doing Lucifer's thing in an unconscious pattern of sobering servility. (*Not My Will*, p. 8.)

DIVINE NATURE

Because our view of brotherhood is that men are not merely biological brothers—because we know that we are more than stranded passengers on an earthship that is about to blink, quiver, and die—we can accept each other in a more full and complete way. We look for the day when as children of our Father in Heaven, the designations Appalachian, Asian, or American will no longer be significant, nor will using words like Dutch or Nigerian. When that day comes, salutations from our Heavenly Father to us will be "son," "daughter," and among ourselves, "brothers," "sisters." (*Press Forward*, pp. 127–28.)

DOCTRINE

Deeds *do* matter as well as doctrines, but the doctrines can move us to do the deeds, and the Spirit can help us to understand the doctrines as well as prompt us to do the deeds. (*My Family*, p. 87.)

Difficult doctrines [are teachings that are] "hard sayings"—hard not only because they stretch one conceptually, but also because the "guilty taketh the truth to be hard, for it cutteth them to the very center." (1 Nephi 16:2.) . . . Cotton-candy concepts are soothing to the taste, but there is no nourishment in them. (*Deposition*, p. 23.)

False doctrines are carnally convenient! (*Deposition*, p. 90.)

There is contained in the simple LDS hymn "I Am a Child of God" or in the anthem "O My Father" more true doctrine than in the communiques from various synods and councils of centuries past! Discussion is not a substitute for revelation! (*Flood*, p. 40.)

It seems that the more spiritually significant the doctrine, the more quickly it comes under attack from the devil, hence the more quickly it is discarded when apostasy occurs. Furthermore, one false doctrine usually leads to another. By way of example, premortality, the reality of a physical resurrection, and the concept that man can become god-like were early casualties in the attack by false doctrines. (*Flood*, p. 40.)

When weary legs falter and detours and roadside allurements entice, the fundamental doctrines will summon from deep within us fresh determination. Extraordinary truths can move us to extraordinary accomplishments! (*Experience*, p. 4.)

The doctrines are God's, not ours. His power is His to delegate, not ours to manipulate. Those who want to shape and remake things to their own liking have ample opportunities to do so by establishing their own secular organizations. For us, the goal is clearly to make God's work our own—not the other way around. (*Endure*, p. 101.)

While carrying our individual crosses, we can greatly help each other if we "hold fast" to the doctrines as well as to each other. (*Endure*, p. 119.)

DOUBT

The shouts and barbs from those in doubt are sometimes not criticism at all, but frustration at not yet having found the "iron rod"— something solid in a world of too many marshmallow men and too many chameleon causes. (*Choose*, p. 6.)

To host an *if* is like hosting an insect that breeds and multiplies in the sun of circumstance. Soon one is crawling with *ifs* and is thereby overcome. (*As I Am*, p. 74.)

Doubters often pool their doubts by associating with like-minded individuals, each bringing his own favorite "dish" as if to a potluck dinner. (*Believe*, p. 191.)

Scanning, but doing so while doubting, is the flipside of Moroni's methodology [Moroni 10:3–5], and it produces flippant conclusions. (*Not My Will*, p. 26.)

By not being actively involved in the process of faith, doubters simply do not receive reinforcing rewards. They also resent the lack of sympathetic vibrations from the faithful each time doubters themselves oscillate in response to what they suppose is some "new evidence" to the contrary. (*Faith*, p. 89.)

DRUGS

Those determined to escape the present by using alcohol and drugs will ruin the future too. (*Believe*, p. 76.)

DUTY

Our Christian duties are like keys on a piano keyboard: touch them correctly and in concert and renewing music is inevitable; if one chord doesn't lift us, another will! But one must do the touching himself, for we are not dealing with a player piano. (*Notwithstanding*, p. 114.)

The truly converted will not be diverted from their duties to God or to each other. (*Endure*, p. 89.)

EARTH

The adversary regards this telestial turf as his own. ("'All Hell Is Moved,'" p. 175.)

The disciple knows that just as the star that shone over Bethlehem was no random, mutant star but was placed in precise trajectory centuries before Bethlehem, so this is not a random, mutant planet. It is a special place, a planet with a purpose. (*Choose*, p. 50.)

EGO

Ego trips are almost always made on someone else's expense account. (*Endure*, p. 42.)

The dangers flowing from an excess of ego are real and constant. Would that we first placed an ego-filtering screen over all our thoughts, words, and actions *before* they hurt others or embarrassed us. If we are steadily becoming more and more the man or woman of Christ, the filtering mesh in that ego screen will become finer, fewer things will slip through to harm. (*Faith*, p. 48.)

The larger and the more untamed one's ego, the greater the likelihood of his being offended. (*Ensign*, May 1989, p. 62.)

As one ponders attributes like meekness and humility, he cannot help but observe how much of our mortality is spent in rearranging the furniture of our relationships and in interminable organizational shufflings because of ego rather than for genuine improvement. How many new emphases and new thrusts are simply new extrusions of untamed ego? Or represent a drunkenness of conscientiousness? (*As I Am*, p. 61.)

Does not meekness mean at least holding back one's own ego (the only one we can control, after all) from the congested daily collisions of so many other egos in the midst of life's fray? Sensitive and defensive driving protects riders in both cars when a foot is removed from the accelerator of ego. (*Faith*, p. 115.)

If we do not acknowledge God and His ordering principles we will end up walking stubbornly in our own ways, thus producing the worst form of inflation and the hardest to cure: inflated egos. (*Endure*, p. 15.)

There are . . . a few men in the Church who boast about how they hold the priesthood, while they are actually in the grip of their own egos. (*Endure*, p. 99.)

EMPATHY

Empathy during agony is a portion of divinity. (*Ensign*, May 1978, p. 10.)

When, for the moment, we ourselves are not being stretched on our particular cross, we ought to be at the foot of someone else's—full of empathy and proffering spiritual refreshment. (*Ensign*, May 1990, p. 34.)

We are so busy checking our own temperatures, we do not notice the burning fevers of others even when we can offer them some of the needed remedies, such as encouragement, kindness, and commendation. The *hands which hang down and most need to be lifted up* often belong to those too discouraged even to reach out anymore. (*Ensign*, November 1995, p. 23.)

There are different kinds of tears: tears of joy, tears we shed for those who have no hope of a glorious resurrection, tears evoked by the tears of others. The latter tears are tenderness and empathy responding to the tears of others in a mutual sympathy. Jesus was approached with news saying that Lazarus was ill. Would Jesus come? Jesus said that Lazarus would be raised, but did not go right away. When He finally did go to Lazarus' home, He found friends weeping. Though Jesus knew He was about to raise Lazarus from the dead, He, too, wept because of His empathy. Likewise, when He blessed the Nephite children, He wept for joy twice. Thus tears are evoked for a variety of reasons, so we should not be surprised when tenderness responds to tenderness, and empathy evokes tears. (Dictated December 1996.)

How could our personal empathy be genuinely and lastingly established and enlarged without refining experiences in the furnace of affliction? Even so, you and I do not loiter around these furnaces waiting for extra tours in those ovens. (*Endure*, p. 3.)

ENDURING

With gospel perspective, we can know that when we endure *to the very end*, we are actually enduring *to the very beginning*. Thus, rather than viewing this virtue as delivering us expiring in exhaustion to a finish line, we are brought intact and victorious to a starting line! (*Press Forward*, p. 112.)

The trek will be proving and trying. Faith, patience, and obedience are essential (see Mosiah 23:21; Abraham 3:25), but he who completes the journey successfully will be immeasurably added upon (see Abraham 3:26). And he who does not will have subtracted from the sum of his possibilities. (*Ensign*, May 1986, p. 36.)

The very process of daily living makes and breaks followers. Life's stern seasons and storms overturn those not grounded and rooted. (See Ephesians 3:17; Colossians 1:23; 1 Peter 5:10.) However, those who "believe and are sure" (John 6:69) about Jesus' divinity do not panic, for instance, at the arrival of a new volley of fiery darts; they merely hold aloft the quenching shield of faith. (*Ensign*, November 1988, p. 32.)

Enduring is vital, and those who so last will be first spiritually! (*Ensign*, May 1990, p. 33.)

If certain mortal experiences were cut short, it would be like pulling up a flower to see how the roots are doing. Put another way, too many anxious openings of the oven door, and the cake falls instead of rising. (*Ensign*, May 1990, p. 33.)

Old-timers should not speak so much of the good old days but rather labor to bring even better days. (*Notwithstanding*, p. 84.)

Endurance is more than pacing up and down within the cell of our circumstance; it is not only acceptance of the things allotted to us, but to "act for ourselves" by magnifying what is allotted to us. (Alma 29:3, 6.) (*Ensign*, May 1990, p. 33.)

True enduring represents not merely the passage of time, but the passage of the soul—and not merely from A to B, but sometimes all the way from A to Z. To endure in faith and do God's will (see D&C 63:20; 101:35) therefore involves much more than putting up with difficult circumstances. (*Ensign*, May 1990, p. 34.)

Part of enduring well consists of being meek enough amid our suffering to learn from our relevant experiences. Rather than simply passing through these things, they must pass through us—in ways which sanctify all these experiences for our good. Likewise, our empathy is enriched everlastingly as we comfort and assist those in the midst of "all these things" which can give us experiences for our good. (D&C 122:7.) ("Fulness in the Fulness of Times.")

Rather than shoulder-shrugging, true enduring is soul-trembling. Jesus bled not at a few but at "every pore." (D&C 19:18.) (*Ensign*, May 1990, p. 34.)

Patient endurance permits us to cling to our faith in the Lord and our faith in His timing when we are being tossed about by the surf of circumstance. Even when a seeming undertow grasps us, somehow, in the tumbling, we are being carried forward, though battered and bruised. (*Ensign*, May 1990, p. 34.)

Enduring is one of the cardinal attributes; it simply cannot be developed without the laboratory time in this second estate. Even the best lectures about the theory of enduring are not enough. (*Ensign*, May 1990, p. 34.)

Some of us will have to be most courageous, not when we're alone but when we're in a crowd. Whatever the form the test takes, we must be willing to pass it. We must reach breaking points without breaking. We must be willing, if necessary, to give up our lives—

not because we have disdain for life as some do, but even though we love life—because we are the servants of Him who did that in such an infinite way for all of us. ("But for a Small Moment," p. 457.)

To be spiritually successful, Jesus' yoke cannot be removed part way down life's furrow, even after a good showing up to that point; we are to endure well to the end. ("'Meek and Lowly,'" p. 54.)

Merely knowing that some have prevailed is vital in a society filled with "give-up-itis." (*Excellent*, p. 130.)

The temptation to loiter is sometimes greatest at the end of the spiritual feasts following the last hymn, the last handshake, and the last amen. We must move on. We do not read that the Lord lingered after the Last Supper. (*Press Forward*, p. 75.)

But does not God know beforehand if we can endure? Yes, per-fectly. But *we* need to know, firsthand, about our capacity. So much of a life well lived consists of coming to know what God knows already. (*Press Forward*, p. 110.)

Why is non-endurance a denial of the Lord? Because giving up is a denial of the Lord's loving capacity to see us through "all these things"! Giving up suggests that God is less than He really is. It is a denial of His divine attributes—and also, a denial of our own pos-sibilities! (Talk given December 2, 1984.)

There cannot be immunity from all afflictions. Whether the af-flictions are self-induced, as most of them are, or whether they are of the divine-tutorial type, it matters not. Either way, the Lord can help us so that our afflictions, said Alma, can be "swallowed up in the joy of Christ" (Alma 31:38). Thus afflictions are endured and are overcome by joy. The sour notes are lost amid a symphony of salvational sounds. Our afflictions may not be extinguished. Instead, they can be dwarfed and swallowed up in the joy of Christ. This is how we overcome most of the time, not the elimination of afflictions, but the placing of these in that larger context. (Talk given December 2, 1984.)

Endurance is even more than elasticized courage, for it underwrites all the other virtues across the expanse of life. Without endurance, the other virtues would be episodic; faith would be fitful, and virtue transitory. (*Press Forward*, p. 112.)

Even yesterday's righteous experience does not guarantee us against tomorrow's relapse. A few who have had supernal spiritual experiences have later fallen. Hence, enduring well to the end assumes real significance, and we are at risk till the end! (*Prove*, p. 4.)

Learning to "endure well" is being able to lose face without losing heart. It is being able to pass through seeming or real injustice, as did Job, without "charging God foolishly" (Job 1:22). (*Not My Will*, p. 122.)

An experience is thus not only endured but also absorbed and perused, almost unconsciously, for its value. Such a process takes time. Therefore it is we, not God, who need more time. This fact should give us pause in our prayers when we would hasten the day even as, for others, God must hold back the dawn. (*Not My Will*, pp. 124–25.)

Our premortal choices were made earlier. Our consent was given—in the first estate—concerning our second estate. This being so, enduring well becomes not only a prime quality but also a reasonable requirement. It calls for shoulder squaring and not shoulder shrugging. (*Not My Will*, p. 125.)

Enduring well is clearly an essential part of mortality's planned refining process. Refining requires heat. Refining also requires time.
Furthermore, if whatever constitutes "it" is to be endured well, refining also requires of its recipients a genuine and continuing confidence in the Refiner. (*Endure*, p. 3.)

Much refining needs to occur. Unless we endure it well, we will
not have the right reflexes needed for the rest of eternity, reflexes
we ourselves can trust completely and upon which others also can
safely rely forever. (*Endure*, p. 8.)

ENOCH (CITY OF)

A confluence of conditions and characteristics led to the disinte-
gration of Sodom, for Sodom was not just a place but a way of life.
A confluence of sharply different conditions and characteristics
created the sublime city-culture of Enoch. Countless secular and
sectarian utopian schemes have been stillborn or have soon gone
awry, but, significantly, a sustained Christ-centered society did
exist. (*Heart*, p. v.)

There appear to be no new or complex doctrines that would account for the unique outcome in the city of Enoch. One will look
in vain in the scriptures for a single spectacular teaching that accounts for this singular and spectacular event. Clearly, what made
these people unique was their serious and steady application of the
simple teachings of Jesus Christ. (*Heart*, p. vi.)

ENTHUSIASM

Enthusiasm needs to be effective enthusiasm. We must distinguish between the contribution and enthusiasm of the cheerleader and the enthusiasm of the player. While cheerleaders serve an important purpose, the real contest involves players on the field or on the court of life. We must not go through life acting only as enthusiastic cheerleaders available for hire; we must be anxiously and personally engaged. (*Deposition*, p. 95.)

ENVIRONMENT

The instructions to Adam and Eve about the garden earth . . . have not been rescinded. They were, and we are, to dress it—not destroy it. They were to take good care of it instead of abusing it. Our increasing interdependence on this planet makes some forms of individual selfishness the equivalent of a runaway personal bulldozer. If we have no concern for the generations to follow, the means are at hand to tear up the terrain much more than was ever possible anciently. Today's polluter or terrorist, for instance, can claim the lives of so many more than a mad owner of a long-bow could have done centuries ago! (*Believe*, p. 75.)

This restored work not only involves the things of eternity but is also drenched in daily significance. True disciples, for instance, would be consistent environmentalists—caring both about maintaining the spiritual health of a marriage and preserving a rain forest; caring about preserving the nurturing capacity of a family as well as providing a healthy supply of air and water; caring for both the prevention and the treatment of the miseries caused by the diseases of transgression. (*Flood*, p. 103.)

Equality in the Church

The requirements of the gospel are deeply democratic. All are to walk the same straight and narrow path. All are to keep the same commandments and covenants. But what will result is an eventual aristocracy of Saints. It will be the only safe, deserving, and righteous aristocracy in all of history! (Believe, p. 16.)

A Who's Who is not needed in a church which teaches us all our real identity and which features a democracy of dress in the holy temples. (Ensign, November 1980, p. 14.)

Error

When we become too encrusted with error, our spiritual antennae wilt and we slip beyond mortal reach. This can happen to entire civilizations. (Choose, p. 59.)

We should learn from our errors, but then forget them as soon as we can. There may be some value in "instant replay" in order to learn what we can and then move on. But some of us engage in "constant replay," which can be enervative and destructive of our self-confidence. (Experience, p. 87.)

Example 107

Eternal Life

Upon receiving eternal life, whatever the deprivations of the faithful will have been in mortality, fulness will follow. Mortal deprivations will give way to God's celestial benefactions. And He does not give grudgingly. Being a perfect Father, He delights to honor those who serve Him (see D&C 76:5). (*Flood*, p. 58.)

Evil

Evil is not only erotic, it is erratic, since it must entice so many in such a multitude of ways. (*Heart*, p. 25.)

Evil always seeks company, for it cannot be by itself alone. Satan detests solitude, for solitude turns him in upon himself, reminding him of what glories might have been. (*Heart*, p. 50.)

Example

We can be walking witnesses and standing sermons to which objective onlookers can say a quiet amen. (*Ensign*, November 1980, p. 15.)

We worry about sensory deprivation because of noise pollution, about nutritional deprivation because of poverty—and we are right to be so concerned. But emulatory deprivation—being without models and exemplars—may be the greatest deprivation of all. For exemplars not only show us that walking the straight and narrow way is possible, but that it is worth doing! (*Smallest Part*, p. 26.)

If the challenge of society's growing secular church becomes too assertive, let us, as in all other human relationships, be principled but pleasant. Let us be perceptive without being pompous. Let us have integrity and not write checks with our tongues which our conduct cannot cash. ("Meeting the Challenges of Today," p. 151.)

We can't be examples if we're on an ego trip, if we are preoccupied with our needs rather than the needs of those whom we serve. (*Deposition*, p. 94.)

As in all things, the Ultimate Example is Jesus. I never tire of bearing witness of Him—not alone that He lived and lives—but also *how* He lived! Even in what might be described as small episodes, He gave us such large lessons. He was a fully integrated, righteous Individual, perfectly congruent in character. ("Integrity . . . The Evidence Within.")

Not only do we have perfect Jesus as our ultimate Exemplar, but also His servants, the men and women of God, are proximate examples. Though imperfect, these individuals mirror significantly in their lives qualities perfected in the Master. (*Flood*, p. 123.)

When we learn to "shine as lights in the world" (Philippians 2:15) there is no need to seek to be in the spotlight. Such lesser incandescence is of no interest. (*Men and Women*, p. 28.)

Experience

So many spiritual outcomes require saving truths to be mixed with time, forming the elixir of experience, that sovereign remedy for so many things. (*Ensign*, May 1990, p. 34.)

In our approach to life, patience also helps us to realize that while we may be ready to move on, having had enough of a particular learning experience, our continued presence is often needed as a part of the learning environment of others. ("Patience," p. 217.)

[Christ] shares with us His work; does that not suggest the need for our sharing, too, some of the suffering as well as the genuine cheer that He has known? Should not we also learn to distinguish, as did He, between temporary sadness and everlasting sorrow? between joy and mere pleasure? In dark days, therefore, we can make our own contribution to illumination by going about our lives just as He has commanded—"with cheerful hearts and countenances." (*As I Am*, p. 109.)

Faith

Faith is not devoid of intellectual content, nor is it antireason. Spiritual things belong to an encircling and larger realm. This realm has its own culture, its own evidence, its own interior consistency, and, indeed, its own language. Toward this realm, ironically, the "natural man" will not extend even a mild form of diplomatic recognition. (*Precious Things*, p. 60.)

While faith is not a perfect knowledge, it brings a deep trust in God, whose knowledge is perfect! Otherwise, one's small database of personal experience permits so few useful generalizations! But by searching the holy scriptures, we access a vast, divine data bank, a reservoir of remembrance. In this way, the scriptures can, as the Book of Mormon says, enlarge the memory. (See Alma 37:8.) (*Ensign*, May 1991, pp. 89–90.)

Poorly defined, faith not only produces little conviction but also is difficult to nurture and increase. Faith has several specific dimensions. Each facet is important. President Brigham Young illustratively taught that we must have "faith in [Jesus'] name, character, and atonement . . . faith in his Father and in the plan of salvation." Only such faith, said Brigham, will produce steady and enduring "obedience to the requirements of the Gospel." (*Faith*, p. 2.)

Our capacity for personal revelation, personal inspiration, or personal insight come rooted in and depend upon our faith. This is why some among us in the Church do so well quietly and modestly at the process of knowing and discovering certain things, and for others it is such a struggle, probably because of their lack of faith in the plan of salvation, in Jesus' character and atonement. ("'Lord, Increase Our Faith.'")

Just as the capacity to defer gratification is a sign of real maturity, likewise the willingness to wait for deferred explanation is a sign of real faith and of trust spread over time. (*Ensign*, May 1985, p. 71.)

One cannot have adequate faith in a Christ whom he does not adequately know, "who is a stranger . . . far from the thoughts and intents of his heart." (Mosiah 5:13.) (*Ensign*, May 1986, p. 35.)

Sensual individuals crave and live by sensations. Disciples, instead, walk and "overcome by faith" (D&C 76:53), accepting gratefully the evidence of things not seen which are true (see Hebrews 11:1; Alma 32:21) and using quietly God's spiritual gifts. (*Ensign*, November 1988, p. 32.)

Serving, studying, praying, and worshiping are four fundamentals in perfecting "that which is lacking in [our] faith." (1 Thessalonians 3:10.) If we cease nurturing our faith in any of these four specific ways, we are vulnerable. (*Ensign*, May 1991, p. 88.)

Deliberately cultivating our spiritual memories becomes a large part of maintaining daily faith. Clearly it is the case that our past blessings will help us to discount our present anxieties. ("'Lord, Increase Our Faith.'")

It is better to so nourish our faith in what seems to be an ordinary process than to experience extraordinary things only to stumble later over life's ordinary challenges. (*Ensign*, May 1991, p. 89.)

If we lack faith, it shows up in interesting ways. You and I see it expressed as a failure to pay a full tithing, failure to wear the holy temple garments, refusal to work more meekly at making a marriage more successful or a family happier, the resentment of personal trials, trying to serve the Lord without offending the devil (we have quite a few Church members who are trying to do just that!), failing to sustain the Brethren, neglecting prayer, neglecting the holy scriptures, neglecting neighbors, neglecting sacrament meetings, and neglecting temple attendance. ("'Lord, Increase Our Faith.'")

Faith . . . includes faith in God's developmental purposes, for "the Lord seeth fit to chasten his people; yea, he trieth their patience and their faith." (Mosiah 23:21.) Still, some of us have trouble when God's tutoring is applied to us! We plead for exemption more than we do for sanctification. (*Ensign*, May 1991, p. 90.)

Patience permits us to cling to our faith in the Lord when we are tossed about by suffering as if by surf. When the undertow grasps us, we will realize that even as we tumble, we are somehow being carried forward; we are actually being helped even as we cry for help. ("Patience," p. 218.)

The Lord told Moses that the children of Israel needed initially only to look on the brass serpent and they would be healed. (Numbers 21:8.) That is the beginning of salvation. Yet, we should not be surprised if some of our friends do not desire to look through the theological telescope. Like Galileo's friends, they are afraid of what they will see. (*Deposition*, p. 78.)

Previous satisfaction in Church service—isolated by time or inactivity—is not a sufficient basis for faith to meet today's challenges. Without incoming experiences to reinforce us, our faith is often at the mercy of our moods and circumstances. (*Choose*, p. 64.)

Unlike Thomas, some of us ask not only for absolute proof, but also for its perpetual renewal, contradicting the Father's plan by which, essentially, we are to walk by faith and overcome by faith. (*As I Am*, p. 52.)

If we can trust the answers God has already given, why not the answers yet to be given, including patiently awaiting the data from our first estate that will illuminate the imponderables of our second estate? (*As I Am*, p. 53.)

Faith induces the quiet scrubbing of the soul that is part of our being anxiously engaged. (*Men and Women*, p. 27.)

No sooner do we begin to display a little faith . . . than that faith is tried—just as happened in the Sacred Grove. Yet without the trials which come even to early faith, greater things cannot subsequently be revealed to us. Only after our faith is tried can we receive the witness which is subsequently needed to sustain us (see Ether 12:6). (*Faith*, p. 41.)

If one is without the faith that remembers, past benefactions are forgotten because of present deprivations. Thirst for water caused some to forget that they were once rescued from far too much water at the Red Sea. It is ironical that the very repetition of some blessings can routinize these blessings. The ration of the daily miracle of manna was taken for granted, even complained about by some. (*Men and Women*, p. 90.)

Faith in God includes faith in His purposes as well as in His timing. We cannot fully accept Him while rejecting His schedule. We cannot worship Him but insist on our plans. (*Believe*, p. 84.)

Faith in the plan of salvation with its developmental dimensions makes allowance for the fact that so many undesirable things occur "in process of time." Exercising one's faith "in process of time" involves . . . the steady isometrics of pitting the old self against the new self. No wonder patience is also required in this, the most grinding and exhausting form of calisthenics. (*Faith*, p. 35.)

The acceptance of the reality that we are in the Lord's loving hands is only a recognition that we have never really been anywhere else. (*Small Moment*, p. 89.)

We sometimes must do the hard things we have been asked to do *before* we will be blessed. Joshua and his priests, in a little-read replication of the parting and crossing of the Red Sea, crossed the flooded Jordan River in another miracle. But the miracle did not begin for ancient Israel until *after* Joshua and his priests got the soles of their feet wet. (Joshua 3:15–17.) (*Experience*, pp. 44–45.)

Unlike those ancient Israelites, once we are settled in our minds, surely we need not overreact to each new crisis or criticism or each new fiery dart of doubt any more than we who are scientists need to recheck the chemical composition of water to be sure, one more time, that it consists of two parts hydrogen—not three—and one part oxygen. . . . We should not demand of God "perpetual renewal of absolute truth." (We Talk of Christ, p. 7.)

Believing is not a matter of accessing antiquity to obtain its evidence, though we welcome such evidence. Nor is it solely dependent upon accumulating welcome historical evidence. Rather it is a matter of believing in "Jesus' words." Real faith, like real humility, is developed "because of the word," and not because of surrounding circumstances. (Alma 32:13–14.) (Not My Will, p. 31.)

In the life of each of us there is intermittent shade brought by passing cloud cover. It takes operative faith in the Father's plan to survive, whether in the shade or under the scorching, secular sun. Both discouraging shade and the heat of the sun bring out our weaknesses. By relying on faith, we repent and improve in honest recognition of those inadequacies. (Faith, p. 51.)

Whether experiencing a severe wind on Galilee (see Matthew 8:23–27), or a fierce wind on the high seas such as pounded Lehi's vessel (see 1 Nephi 18:15), or the turbulence in our own lives, it is the same. If we know Jesus is our Lord and that He watches over us, we can handle—though we will surely feel them—all the winds of strange doctrines and all the surging commotion (see Matthew 24:23–28). (Faith, p. 93.)

If everything in one's immediate context were constantly clear, God's plan would not work. Hard choices as well as passing through periodic mists of darkness are needed in order to maintain life's basic reality—that we are to overcome by faith. (Faith, p. 110.)

Though we rightly speak of "faith and works," faith by itself . . . is constant work! It is a work to be done and a process best pursued while being not only "anxiously engaged" but also engaged with "fear and trembling." Otherwise we may lose our concentration on Christ. (*Faith*, pp. 111–12.)

Does our faith in Jesus include faith in His timing, whether in His macro-management of the entire universe or in His micro-shepherding of us? (*The Christmas Scene*, p. 8.)

FALSE DOCTRINE

The Lord distinguishes between the "doctrines of devils" and "the commandments of men." (D&C 46:7.) One may be more sinister than the other or more invidious in its motivation, but the consequences of following an incorrect principle are the same, regardless of its source. (*Deposition*, p. 13.)

The injunction given in the Sacred Grove to Joseph Smith at the time of the Restoration is totally consistent with the character and standards of Jesus at the time he was here in his earthly ministry in the Holy Land. The Savior condemned the errors in both behavior and doctrine that had grown up in ancient Judaism; later he did the same regarding supposed Christianity. It shouldn't surprise us if he still condemns doctrinal falsity or casualness today. If Jesus of Nazareth described the way as straight and narrow (with few finding it), could he endorse the broad way with hundreds of competing and disagreeing Christian churches? (*Really Are*, p. 38.)

FALSE PROPHETS

Satan's order of battle is such that if it is necessary to encourage a hundred false prophets in order to obscure the validity of one true prophet, he will gladly do so. (*Experience*, p. 115.)

FAMILY

When the real history of mankind is fully disclosed, will it feature the echoes of gunfire or the shaping sound of lullabies? The great armistices made by military men or the peacemaking of women in homes and in neighborhoods? Will what happened in cradles and kitchens prove to be more controlling than what happened in congresses? When the surf of the centuries has made the great pyramids so much sand, the everlasting family will still be standing, because it is a celestial institution, formed outside telestial time. (*Ensign*, May 1978, pp. 10–11.)

Even with its flaws, the family is basic, and since no other institution can compensate fully for failure in the family, why then, instead of enhancing the family, the desperate search for substitutes? Why not require family impact studies before proceeding with this program or that remedy, since of all environmental concerns the family should be first? Hundreds of governmental departments and programs protect various interests, but which one protects the family? (*Ensign*, May 1993, p. 77.)

The human family—without the gospel or without strong families—is not going to go very far. Unless we can fix families, you can't fix anything else. Most of the problems that are most vexing are things government can't fix. They have to be fixed at a different level. That's the urgency of our message. I'd rather have ten commandments than ten thousand federal regulations. . . . Unless we rebuild marriages and families, then we really are just straightening deck chairs on the Titanic. (*Searching for God in America*, pp. 132–33.)

Society should focus anew on the headwaters—the family—where values can be taught, lived, experienced, and perpetuated. Otherwise . . . we will witness even more widespread flooding downstream, featuring even more corruption and violence (see Genesis 6:11–12; Matthew 24:37). (*Ensign*, May 1994, p. 90.)

Why should it surprise us, by the way, that life's most demanding tests as well as the most significant opportunities for growth in life usually occur within marriage and the family? How can revolving door relationships, by contrast, be as real a test of our capacity to love? Is being courteous, one time, to the stranger on the bus as difficult as being courteous to a family member who is competing for the bathroom morning after morning? Does fleeting disappointment with a fellow office worker compare to the betrayal of a spouse? Does a raise in pay even approach the lift we receive from rich family life? ("'Thanks Be to God.'")

Father Lehi once described himself as a "trembling parent" (2 Nephi 1:14). There are trembling parents and grandparents today! Some of today's families already exist in a worse wilderness than did Father Lehi's. Healthy, traditional families are becoming an endangered species! Perhaps, one day, families may even rank with the threatened spotted owl in effective attention given! (*Ensign*, May 1994, p. 89.)

Nostalgically, many wish for the family life of yesteryear; they regard family decline as regrettable but not reversible. Others, genuinely worried over the spilling social consequences, are busy placing sandbags downstream, even when the frenzied use of sandbags often destroys what little is left of family gardens. A few regard the family as an institution to be drastically redefined or even to be rid of. (*Ensign*, May 1994, p. 89.)

Alas, in some families things do go wretchedly wrong, but these gross failures are no reason to denigrate further the institution of the family. We should make course corrections and fix the leaks, not abandon ship! (*Ensign*, May 1994, p. 89.)

Every year should be the Year of the Family. (*Ensign*, May 1994, p. 89.)

There should be less wringing of hands and more loving arms around our families. (*Ensign*, May 1994, p. 89.)

If the combination of rainmakers prevails, . . . the rains will continue to descend, and the floods will continue to come. Dikes and sandbags downstream will be no match for the coming crests. More and more families, even nations, if built upon secular sand instead of gospel granite, will suffer. (*Ensign*, May 1994, p. 90.)

Sickness of spirit in a family is carried to the office or classroom just as surely as the flu. (*Deposition*, p. 20.)

Someday a real history can be written that will tell us how many misshapen mortals came from homes fatally flawed and who then made the whole human family an enlarged audience before and on which they acted out the drama of that original deficiency. (*Deposition*, p. 26.)

We are emphasizing family life in an age when the modern family appears to be disintegrating, when homes are becoming "hollow hotels," and when relationships with family and kinsmen are seen as burdens to be jettisoned as soon as possible. (*Excellent*, p. 8.)

Those who have known the sweetness of service in the kingdom and who have looked at life through the lens of the gospel will ever be restless with a divine discontent until their families do partake of that precious fruit and thereby witness for themselves. (*My Family*, p. 1.)

Just as certain people must be prepared to do God's work, so, too, families are prepared beforehand to host special individuals. (*My Family*, pp. 2–3.)

Family life is a constant challenge, not a periodic performance we can render on a stage and then run for the privacy of a dressing room to be alone with ourselves. (*My Family*, p. 3.)

Countless families are living in "quiet desperation," held together with the Scotch Tape of sentiment or existing merely on the ice floes of indifference. The good family is the salt of society; if it loses its flavor, what will give savor to a tasteless society—"wherewith shall it be salted"? (See Matthew 5:13.) (*My Family*, p. 3.)

Looking beyond the family to other institutions, programs, or activities—which may be good and helpful in their spheres—can be disastrous. The family is still the most efficient means for producing human happiness and human goodness, as well as for preparing us for the world of immortality that is to follow. (*My Family*, p. 7.)

The health of the family is a better barometer of things to come in our political and economic world than we may care to admit. The malcontents and assassins and militants who will do so much to harm society tomorrow are already aflame in the overheated family furnaces of today. It could be said of our increasing social interdependency that never have so few been able to hurt so many so much. (*My Family*, p. 13.)

Just as a giant solar flare reaching skyward from our sun ends up causing stormy weather on the earth, today's failure—or success—in an obscure family thousands of miles away may touch us later far more than we know. (*My Family*, p. 13.)

Ironically, some individuals who cannot handle the challenge of family life so often veer off in dramatic causes to save mankind—like a drop-out from Little League demanding a place in the batting order in baseball's World Series! (*My Family*, p. 31.)

The flame of family can warm us and at the same time be a perpetual pilot light to rekindle us. (*My Family*, p. 86.)

In a world filled with much laboring and striving in parliaments, congresses, agencies, and corporate offices, God's extraordinary work is most often done by ordinary people in the seeming obscurity of a home and family. (*My Family*, p. 122.)

As with all of the eternal virtues, the family garden is the best place in which to grow and nurture the capacity for long-suffering. Daily family life is filled with opportunities to extend love and mercy. (*Believe*, p. 12.)

Even though he gains the world of music through composing significant songs, a composer who goes rutting about while neglecting his wife and family has broken their tender hearts (see Jacob 2:35) even though putting musical notes together. In the family's next generation, tragic anger or imitation may be acted out. The music which flows from such a composer cannot compensate fully for his folly. In eternal perspective, a soothing symphony does not compensate for jarring cacophony in personal conduct. Besides, better music is ahead (see 1 Corinthians 2:9). (*Flood*, p. 98.)

The prophets teach all of the gospel, but choose to emphasize those truths that are most relevant and most needed in the times in which they live. In an age, for instance, when the institution of the family was quite secure, prophets apparently felt less need to speak about that issue. Family life was a given fact. But in our time, it has been necessary for prophets (particularly in the last part of this last dispensation) to remind all of society, as well as the Saints, about the tremendous importance of the home. (*Really Are*, p. 66.)

In the search for peace, can we ask for God's help in rallying the human family to avoid a nuclear holocaust, if we neglect the nuclear family wherein we can learn, first and best, about love, taking turns, negotiating, and restraining selfishness? (*Prove*, p. 90.)

FATALISM

Those who are surfeited with fatalism, whose diet is the equivalent of a constant clash of cymbals, are not only apt to lose their capacity to feel, but may find themselves losing the very sensitiveness to other humans which the lyrics of much modern music celebrate. (*Choose*, p. 71.)

Surely Paul, who stressed so rigorously the importance of pressing forward and running the race the full distance in our discipleship, did *not* intend a casual Christianity, in which some had won even before the race started. (*Really Are*, p. 23.)

FATHERS

A father who truly loves his children, and who is truly striving, for instance, to become a better man, sends off to his children all kinds of messages, in a variety of ways, that let them know he loves them and that he is a serious disciple of Jesus Christ. Then his children can more easily forgive him the tactical errors, because his basic message is intact: he believes in God and he cares for his family. On the other hand, for the father who is not truly serious in his discipleship, no number of compensatory techniques or humanistic sentiments can ever compensate for the failure of that father to teach the truth by precept and by example. (My Family, p. 108.)

As you become Latter-day Saint mothers and fathers, remember, therefore, not only the shared duties that you have, but that fathers need to be significantly involved in the religious life of their families. Precious, indeed, is the formal training such as family home evenings, family scripture reading, fast and testimony meetings, seminary and institute, and Church classes, but likewise important are the deep but informal moments of sharing religious feelings between parents and their children—the private moments when you talk together, discuss the gospel, pray with your children and bless them. These are profoundly shaping moments much needed to fortify you to survive spiritually in the world in which you live. (Church Educational System Fireside, June 4, 1995.)

Even marvelous mothers cannot fully compensate for malfunctioning fathers. (My Family, p. 16.)

Today . . . we have more functioning gadgets of convenience but fewer functioning fathers! (Endure, p. 24.)

FAULT-FINDING

People who spend their time searching for feet of clay will not only miss seeing the heavens wherein God moves in His majesty and power, but God's majesty as He improves and shapes a soul. (*Ensign*, May 1982, p. 39.)

Unevenness in the spiritual development of people means untidiness in the history of people, and we should not make an individual "an offender for a word," (Isaiah 29:21; 2 Nephi 27:32), as if a single communication could set aside all else an individual may have communicated or stood for! (*Ensign*, November 1984, p. 11.)

In a church established, among other reasons, for the perfecting of the Saints—an ongoing process—it is naive to expect, and certainly unfair to demand, perfection in our peers. A brief self-inventory is wise before we "cast the first stone." Possessing a few rocks in our own heads, it is especially dangerous to have rocks too ready in our hands. (*Not My Will*, p. 74.)

FEAR

The only things we should really fear are those things which can keep us from going where there is no fear. (*Press Forward*, p. 94.)

FELLOWSHIPPING

In the city of Zion, there are constantly new kids on the block! Since priesthood leaders have determined that the newcomers' visas are in order, let us greet them genuinely—not with frowns and skepticism. It will be our job to lift them up—not to size them up. They will have known much rejection; now let them know much acceptance. (*Ensign*, November 1980, p. 14.)

Precious returnees . . . like the prodigal son, have come to their senses (see Luke 15:11–32). Filled with tender resolve, they, too, need a warm welcome. Let us emulate the father of the prodigal son, who ran to greet his son while the son was still a great distance away, rather than waiting passively and then skeptically asking the son if he had merely come home to pick up his things! (*Ensign*, November 1980, p. 14.)

Regrettably we sometimes see an individual get classified, and no matter how well he or she does thereafter, it is difficult to get reclassified. It is sometimes like the chicken whose comb gets bloodied; all the chickens then peck at it, making the situation even worse. These "walking wounded" are all about us, and they need someone else to help them bind up—not add to—their wounds. (*Experience*, p. 76.)

Involve newcomers quickly in the Lord's work. They have been called to his vineyard not just to admire but to perspire—not to "ooh" and "aah" but to "hoe and saw." Let us make of them friends—not celebrities; colleagues—not competitors. Let us use their precious enthusiasm to beckon still others to come within. (*Ensign*, November 1980, p. 15.)

We poorly serve the cause of the Lord, at times, with program-
matic superficiality and by our lack of empathy for those who drift
in despair. (*Ensign*, May 1983, p. 10.)

Truly, we live and walk on "a streetful of splendid strangers,"
whom we are to love and serve even if they are uninterested in us!
(*Ensign*, May 1983, p. 10.)

When [converts] have come from so great a distance to join the
Church, surely we can go a second mile in friendshipping and
fellowshipping them. If with quiet heroism they can cross the border into belief, surely we can cross a crowded foyer to extend the
hand of fellowship. Has it been so long that we have forgotten our
first anxious day at a new school or our timidity in a new town?
(*Notwithstanding*, p. 83.)

So often what people need so much is to be sheltered from the
storms of life in the sanctuary of belonging. Such a service cannot
be rendered by selfish people, however, because the response of the
selfish will always be that there is no room in their inn. Chronic
self-concern means that the "No Vacancy" sign is always posted.
(*Experience*, p. 55.)

Our capacity as Church members to love and to forgive will be
freshly and severely tested as battered and bruised souls come into
the Church in ever-larger numbers. Some come in from the cold
shivering. Others are breathless, having caught what was for them
the last train out of Babylon. Their own continued process of repentance will be much aided if they see, all about them, more regular emphasis in the lives of the rest of us on faith unto repentance. (*Not My Will*, p. 74.)

FIRST VISION

When we say "He lives," we mean all that that glorious truth implies. The theophany at Palmyra, for instance, was a deeply profound statement, not solely an affirmation to that youthful audience of one, *but to all mankind.* (*As I Am*, pp. 8–9.)

Jesus Christ is the Jehovah of the Red Sea and of Sinai, the Resurrected Lord, the spokesman for the Father in the theophany at Palmyra—a Palmyra pageant with a precious audience of one! (*As I Am*, p. 120.)

FOLLOWERSHIP

Serious sinners who regard themselves as free are the most obvious satellites in our human solar system. If one is going to be a satellite, he had better pick his Saturns carefully. Indeed, followership in the kingdom leaves no place for static, satellite relationships, for individual growth based on eternal principles is the criterion. To mix metaphors, Pied Piper situations are not only hard on the followers but are bad for the Pied Pipers too. (*Press Forward*, p. 102.)

FOLLY

If, over the decades, one could have been agelessly situated on a space platform and could have thus watched the recurring human drama from a distance, among the strongest impressions he would have acquired would be the dull repetitiveness of human folly. He would see the almost childish intensity with which each new set of players on this planet pursues the cares of the world. The age-old drama goes on, with each group pursuing the cares of the world as if they were pioneers in the process instead of constituting just another legion of lemmings marching to the secular sea. (*Sermons*, p. 14.)

FOREORDINATION

The combined doctrine of God's foreknowledge and of foreordination is one of the doctrinal roads least traveled by, yet these clearly underline how very long and how perfectly God has loved us and known us with our individual needs and capacities. Isolated from other doctrines or mishandled, though, these truths can stoke the fires of fatalism, impact adversely upon our agency, cause us to focus on status rather than service, and carry us over into predestination. ("Meeting the Challenges of Today," p. 151.)

Just because we were chosen "there and then," surely does not mean we can be indifferent "here and now." Whether foreordination for men, or foredesignation for women, those called and prepared must also prove "chosen and faithful." (See Revelation 17:14; D&C 121:34–36.) (*Ensign*, November 1985, p. 17.)

Foreordination is like any other blessing—it is a conditional bestowal subject to our faithfulness. Prophecies foreshadow events without determining the outcomes, because of a divine foreseeing of outcomes. So foreordination is a conditional bestowal of a role, a responsibility, or a blessing which, likewise, foresees but does not fix the outcome. ("Meeting the Challenges of Today," p. 152.)

God knew beforehand each of our coefficients for coping and contributing and has so ordered our lives. ("Meeting the Challenges of Today," p. 155.)

The doctrine of foreordination . . . is not a doctrine of repose; it is a doctrine for the second-milers; it can draw out of us the last full measure of devotion. It is a doctrine of perspiration, not aspiration. Moreover, it discourages aspiring, lest we covet, like two early disciples, that which has already been given to another (Matthew 20:20–23). Foreordination is a doctrine for the deep believer and will only bring scorn from the skeptic. ("Meeting the Challenges of Today," p. 156.)

When we say God has a plan, he truly has a plan—not simply a grand scale, but for each of us as individuals, allocating some special talent to this dispensation and some to another. (*Deposition*, p. 45.)

It has always been the case—that the Lord has raised up men as His prophets who have just the cluster of talents needed for a particular time. It is no different in the culminating days of the dispensation of the fulness of time. The Lord measured and ordained these men before they came here. Knowing perfectly the conditions that would obtain, He has sent, and will send, men to match the mountains of challenges that are just ahead of us. (*Experience*, p. 122.)

Foreordinations for men and foredesignations for women happened a long, long time ago. Let us be true to those anticipations by striving to journey "home" complete with our families. (*Faith*, p. 51.)

FORGIVENESS

Saints fashion forgiveness where others would revel in resentment! (*Ensign*, May 1983, p. 11.)

We cannot repent for someone else. But we can forgive someone else, refusing to hold hostage those whom the Lord seeks to set free! (*Ensign*, November 1991, p. 32.)

If you have been offended, recall that while you may have been bumped by an ecclesiastical elbow, the chip was on your shoulder long before the elbow appeared. (*Ensign*, November 1974, p. 13.)

In families with spiritual perspective, yesterday need not hold tomorrow hostage. If we sometimes act the fool, loving families know this is not our last act; the curtain is not rung down. (*Ensign*, May 1994, p. 90.)

Disciples are to make for themselves "a new heart" by undergoing a "mighty change" of heart (Ezekiel 18:31; Alma 5:12–14). Yet we cannot make such "a new heart" while nursing old grievances. Just as civil wars lend themselves to the passionate preservation of ancient grievances, so civil wars within the individual soul—between the natural and the potential man—keep alive old slights and perceived injustices, except in the meek. (" 'Meek and Lowly,' " p. 55.)

Since the past is not plastic, the disciple must not moodily contemplate the sores and wounds of life. For us to incessantly pick at the soul scabs of the past, rather than let the healing influence of the Gospel operate fully in our lives, reflects on our capacity for self-forgiveness. (*Choose*, p. 50.)

Divine forgiveness is possible even when men do not forgive us. If we have the justified assurance that God has forgiven us, we can forgive ourselves and outlast any unforgiving attitude of those about us. (*Excellent*, p. 64.)

Some of us let the past lock us in, rigidly refusing to reclassify other people, which can be devastating to the development of anyone. We must permit others to press forward, too. (*Press Forward*, p. 91.)

One important dimension of loving-kindness is forgiveness. Our generosity, forgetfulness, and forgiveness can often be the equivalent of an "emancipation proclamation" for someone who has erred, as "with the breath of kindness," we "blow the chaff away." (*Believe*, p. 22.)

There is no expiation in retaliation; vengeance not only prolongs conflict, but also deepens and widens it. Thus, forgetfulness and forgiveness, by being intertwined, make strong the chords of brotherhood. (*Heart*, p. 34.)

If we are submissive, we will not be as easily offended. Jesus was not offended because of the wrongs done to Him, rather, He was worried over the offender. He could look upon offenses caused by others as reflecting deficiencies or earlier wounds in their lives. If they would yield to Him, Jesus could heal all these (3 Nephi 18:32). Otherwise, healing scabs are sometimes torn off by fresh offenses, bringing needless, repetitive pain. (*Not My Will*, p. 108.)

The tendency to strike back whenever we are offended makes us brusque and rude, as if others were merely functions, not brothers and sisters. (*Ensign*, May 1995, p. 68.)

FREE SPEECH

One wonders if the first amendment could flourish in a climate of serious degeneration in the morality of the people. It may be true that the people of Sodom and Gomorrah had absolute free speech, but it is also probably true that they had nothing worth saying, preoccupied as they were with various sins. Those surfeited in sensualism produce sounds all right, but not necessarily the informed speech John Stuart Mill and our Founding Fathers had in mind. (Fourth of July Celebration, Midway, Utah, July 4, 1991.)

An otherwise permissive society, which tolerates almost everything, usually will not tolerate speech that challenges its iniquity. Evil is always intolerantly preoccupied with its own perpetuation. (*Believe*, pp. 74–75.)

FREEDOM

Ultimately, freedom involves choice between eternal alternatives, *but not the altering of the alternatives.* We can choose wickedness or happiness, but not wickedness with happiness. ("Insights from My Life," p. 199.)

Sensuous souls often love their neighbors as themselves—i.e., not at all! Thus, Sodom was a free-wheeling, but very unfree society. (*Smallest Part*, p. 11.)

FRIENDS

A wise lady once said that what we hope our friends will do is to separate the wheat from the chaff and, with a breath of kindness, blow the chaff away. I am grateful now, as I have been over the years, for friends who have had strong lungs. ("Insights from My Life," p. 188.)

Friends who would hold us back spiritually are not true friends at all. (*Ensign*, November 1992, p. 66.)

Sometimes, in the mutual climb along the straight and narrow path . . . we need friends to shout warnings to us or to give us instructions, but we also need those moments when warm whispers can help us to keep putting one foot in front of the other. ("Insights from My Life," p. 191.)

The finest of friends must sometimes be stern sentinels, who will insist that we become what we have the power to become. The "no" of such stern sentinels is more to be prized than a "yes" of others. ("Insights from My Life," p. 199.)

Friendships formed in the context of floating values are apt to be floating friendships—devoid of real acceptance, depth, and continuity, the very things that friendship is intended to supply in the first place. (*My Family*, p. 90.)

One of the reasons we love each other in the Kingdom is that our friendships are not friendships of initiation at all, but are, instead, friendships of resumption. ("'Brim with Joy,'" p. 1.)

FUNERALS

Though otherwise "lively," hope stands quietly with us at funerals. Our tears are just as wet, but not because of despair. Rather, they are tears of appreciation evoked by poignant separation. They will change, ere long, to tears of glorious anticipation. Yet the emptiness is so real and so restless it initiates a retroactive inventory of what is now so painfully missing, doing so, however, while forecasting fulness and resplendent reunion! (*Ensign*, November 1994, p. 36.)

GANGS

In their search for identity and belonging, too many supposedly savvy teens are now confined to the solitude of a lonely gang. What is the lasting advantage of becoming streetwise if one is on a street to nowhere? Gangs mark the failure of both families and communities as well as symbolizing the pervasive revolt against authority. (*Ensign*, May 1993, pp. 76–77.)

GOALS

Progress is measured by milestones. What many good people lack are markers that might tell them how they are actually doing. Goals can become a ritual or a fetish, but in the right measure they can give us some much needed reference points. (*Deposition*, p. 32.)

God

God's ultimate power is safe, precisely because He possesses ultimate love, justice, mercy, and knowledge. We cannot share in His power without sharing in His attributes. (*Ensign*, November 1986, p. 54.)

He is not a passive God who merely watches lights on a cosmic computer and presses buttons to implement previously laid plans; He is a personal God who is just, merciful, and kind. His great desire is not to count His creations like so many coins, but to bind up the broken hearts of the inhabitants of each world: sanctification, not quantification, is His work. (*As I Am*, p. 30.)

What is past is truly prologue; hence an unvarying, all-seeing God desiring to save mercurial and myopic man, is not interested in our retroactive adulation, but in preventing our prospective ruination. (*Ensign*, November 1986, p. 54.)

A universal God is actually involved with our small, individual universes of experience! In the midst of His vast dominions, yet He numbers us, knows us, and loves us perfectly (see Moses 1:35; John 10:14). (*Ensign*, November 1987, p. 30.)

Along with knowing that God is there, it is equally vital to know what He is like, including His perfected attributes of justice and mercy. More mortals die in ignorance of God's true character than die in actual defiance of Him. (*Ensign*, November 1987, p. 30.)

We need not be atop high mountains or in sacred groves for God to be there. God is also there even in the mildest expressions of His presence. (*Ensign*, November 1987, p. 32.)

God never can justify us "in committing a little sin." (2 Nephi 28:8.) He is the God of the universe, not some night-court judge with whom we can haggle and plea bargain! (*Ensign*, November 1988, p. 33.)

One of the dimensions of worshipping a living God is to know that he is alive and living in the sense of seeing and acting. He is not a retired God whose best years are past, to whom we should pay a retroactive obeisance, worshipping him for what he has already done. He is the living God who is, at once, in all the dimensions of time—the past and present and future—while we labor constrained by the limitations of time itself. ("Meeting the Challenges of Today," p. 155.)

The cosmos cries out convincingly that God lives, for those with eyes to see and ears to hear. (*Deposition*, p. 18.)

God cares little for cosmetic public relations and *everything* for human relations! (*Choose*, p. 23.)

God is a loving Father who wants us to have the happiness that results from proven righteousness, not from mere innocence. At times, he will not deflect life's harsh learning experiences that may come to each of us, even though he will help us cope with them. God is neither a silent, indifferent monarch in the sky, nor is he an indulgent grandfather figure who will give his children the incomplete therapy of partial truth. (*Choose*, p. 47.)

His governance of galaxies does not prevent His giving us collective and individual attention, just as He watched over nomadic, ancient Israel by day and gave them light by night. (*As I Am*, p. 30.)

In searching the scriptures that describe God the Father and His Son, Jesus Christ, both as to their *actuality* and their *personality*, one finds that all mortal adjectives, however laudatory, are too anemic. Superlatives are overtaken by ordinariness when applied to them. (*As I Am*, p. 114.)

It is one of the ironies of religious history that many mortals err in their understanding of the nature of God and end up rejecting not the real God but their own erroneous and stereotypical image of God. (*Sermons*, p. 17.)

The living God never leaves us alone even when we seek to move away from him. When the living God called Jonah to go to Nineveh, the prophet, out of fear of men, strove to go to Tarshish instead. The living God was not busy elsewhere or slumbering; he delivered Jonah unceremoniously to Nineveh! That is the sort of thing the living God does. A passive life force or an indulgent grandfather God wouldn't worry about that sort of detail—as long as we are being basically good boys and girls who might find some good to do in Tarshish. But we have a precise and loving Father in heaven who knows what we need and who loves us enough to get us to Nineveh instead of settling for the chores of Tarshish. (*Really Are*, p. 36.)

The living God not only stays with his plan, but also with his standards. (*Really Are*, p. 38.)

Decrease the belief in God . . . and behold the large increase in the numbers of those who wish to play at being God. Such societal supervisors may deny the existence of divine ways but they are very serious about imposing their own ways. (*Endure*, p. 17.)

GOD'S LOVE

God's is a loving and redeeming hand which we are to acknowledge, for "eye hath not seen nor ear heard." Even His children in the telestial kingdom receive ". . . the glory of the telestial, which surpasses all understanding" (D&C 76:89); He is an exceedingly generous God! . . . One later day, Jesus' *hand* will not give the faithful merely a quick, approving pat on the shoulder. Instead, both Nephi and Mormon tell of the special reunion and welcome at the entrance to His kingdom. There, we are assured, He is "the keeper of the gate . . . and He employeth no servant there." (2 Nephi 9:41.) Those who reject Him will miss out on a special personal moment, because, as He laments, He has "stood with *open arms* to receive you." (Mormon 6:17.) The unfaithful—along with the faithful—might have been "clasped in the arms of Jesus" (Mormon 5:11). The imagery of the holy temples and holy scriptures thus blend so beautifully, including things pertaining to sacred moments. This is the grand moment toward which we point and from which we should not be deflected. Hence, those who pass through their fiery trials and still acknowledge but trust His hand now will feel the clasp of His arms later! (Talk given October 14, 1996.)

Sometimes the discussions we have in the Church over the nature of God's love end up mostly as reactions to the positions of others in the Church. Those, for instance, who feel God's love is unconditional see themselves moving to the "starboard side" in order to balance those who feel God's love is conditional, and vice-versa. I find it helpful to understand that God loves all His spirit children. How could it be otherwise, since He is a perfect Father? In that sense, His love is universal and everlasting for all of His children; but He does not and cannot love our wickedness: "For I the Lord cannot look upon sin with the least degree of allowance." (D&C 1:31.) He does not say and cannot approve of that which we do which is wrong, nor will He say on judgment day, "Well done thou good and faithful servant" to those who have been wicked or to those who have been poor performers. His perfect integrity and His perfected attributes of truth and justice would not permit it. Nor can our Heavenly Father reward us evenly because our deeds and our degrees of righteousness are so uneven. Of necessity, therefore, we are told there are "many mansions" in His house and only of the comparative few can it be said, "all that my Father hath shall be given." (D&C 84:38.) It is because He loves us that He seeks with such vigor to separate us from our sins, which He hates. We cannot go where He is, unless He fully approves of us. . . . Likewise, it is because He loves us that His redemptive arm is lengthened out all the day long. (2 Nephi 28:32.) Yet, even after all of His outreaching and loving long-suffering, there will follow the judgment and justice of God. Thus His long-suffering is not indulgence masquerading as mercy. God will never stop loving all of His spirit children, including those who go to the telestial kingdom, a kingdom of glory which, in God's generosity, "surpasses all understanding" (D&C 76:89). Even so, where God the Father and Jesus Christ are, telestial beings cannot come. (D&C 76:112.) Thus the hard, cold fact is that how we use our moral agency does not result in a withdrawal of God's love, but does determine the ways and the degrees to which a loving God can express His love of us. Only the most righteous will receive His praise, His approval, and enjoy His presence. . . . If we are unrighteous, "the spirit of the Lord is grieved." (D&C 121:37.) He is "grieved," precisely because He loves us so deeply, but do we love Him enough to set things right? This is the continuing test. (Neal A. Maxwell letter to a Church member, August 9, 1995.)

GOODNESS

It isn't that random goodness lacks heroism. Rather, in isolation it lacks effectiveness. Sharpshooters can irritate and delay an advancing enemy, but they cannot mount a counteroffensive. Random goodness leads to Dunkirks, not to D-Days. (*Deposition*, p. 35.)

General goodness is no excuse for failing to work on those things which we yet lack. (*Ensign*, May 1995, p. 68.)

GOSPEL

There is . . . no other "plan of happiness" (see Alma 42:8), only multiple-choice misery. (*Ensign*, November 1980, p. 15.)

The gospel is not merely a gospel for one age, for one people, or for one place—it is a gospel for the galaxies! (*Ensign*, May 1975, p. 101.)

What precious perspective we obtain from the gospel of Jesus Christ concerning things that really matter—against which we measure the disappointments of the day! (*Ensign*, November 1982, p. 66.)

Every doctrine of the gospel is a door to delight that, when opened, exposes us to a vista of things we have not yet fully comprehended. ("'Brim with Joy,'" p. 147.)

Enclosed in this mortal cocoon, or classroom, we would be totally provincial in outlook except for faith in, and knowledge of, the "great plan of the Eternal God." (*Ensign*, May 1984, p. 22.)

His [Jesus'] doctrines are like glistening diamonds with many dimensions, displaying their verity and beauty, facet by facet, depending on the faith and preparation of the beholder. (*Ensign*, November 1988, p. 33.)

The fulness of the gospel of Jesus Christ is greater than any of its parts and larger than any of its programs or principles. (*Ensign*, May 1993, p. 79.)

The gospel of Jesus Christ is specific because God cares specifically for each of us and, caring for us, will mark the way carefully lest we fall out of happiness. ("But for a Small Moment," p. 456.)

When one sees life and people through the lens of His gospel, then one can see forever. (*Ensign*, May 1974, p. 112.)

So far as its view of truth is concerned, the gospel is galactic whereas secularism is so insular! Little wonder the prophets have been so concerned with theological truancy—for it reduces human happiness. (*Smallest Part*, p. 15.)

The gospel does provide structure in life-style—a scaffolding for shaping the soul especially in the formative years. So shaped, later in life the individual can stand resolutely in holy places and on holy issues and not be moved. (*Deposition*, pp. 16–17.)

The gospel is not a religion of repose nor does it let us reside in an Eden of ease. (*Deposition*, p. 31.)

Far from suppressing individuality, the Gospel opens new doors to individual development, doors we can open in no other way. How much more interesting was the Peter of Pentecost than the Simon who stood on the shores of Galilee a few years earlier. (*Choose*, p. 11.)

Seeing the landscape of life illuminated briefly by lightning can be helpful, but we walk through a mortal minefield which requires the full steady light of the Gospel in order to survive. (*Choose*, p. 11.)

Being in the world but not of it can be a special challenge. We see the world and the people in it differently because the Gospel is like the lens of a cosmic kaleidoscope which enables us to see pattern, design, beauty, and purpose in our lives. It is this particularized vision which can give us a special sense of proportion about the things in life which matter most. (*Choose*, p. 22.)

In a sense, the world has the slogans; the Gospel has the solutions, which, if applied, will carry us to "a state of happiness which hath no end." (*Choose*, p. 80.)

It is not just mercy and justice which are to be balanced. In the ecology of God, all His truths and commandments are principles in perpetual partnership. Together, they can produce human happiness here and salvation and exaltation in the world to come. (*Sermons*, p. 5.)

Those who have lived in the midst of the famine foreseen by Amos, one of not hearing the full word of God (Amos 8:11–12), have never known the taste and nourishment of the whole-grain gospel. Instead, some have subsisted on the fast foods of philosophy. (*Men and Women*, p. 39.)

In living together as Saints, we surely feel and see each other's faults, but when we look at each other through the lens of the gospel and by the light of heaven, we also see in others attributes and qualities that we little imagined were there. The gospel does not ask us to close our eyes to any reality; rather it helps us to open our eyes both more widely and more appreciatively. (*Press Forward*, p. 87.)

GOSPEL LIVING

The men and women of Christ are constant, being the same in private as in public. We cannot keep two sets of books while Heaven has but one. (*Ensign*, November 1990, p. 16.)

There is an inseparable connection between the keeping of the commandments and the well-being of society. (*Ensign*, November 1974, p. 12.)

God asks us now to give up only those things which, if clung to, will destroy us! (*Ensign*, November 1974, p. 13.)

Do not look too deeply into the eyes of the pleasure-seekers about you, for if you do, you will see a certain sadness in sensuality, and you will hear artificiality in the laughter of licentiousness. (*Ensign*, November 1974, p. 12.)

Reflect on the practicality of gospel standards such as abstaining from alcohol; for if you do, a surf of statistics will wash over you, confirming that abstinence is ultimately the only cure for alcoholism that is both preventive and redemptive. (*Ensign*, November 1974, p. 12.)

Young people, too, must come to see that the Gospel is something we do, not simply something we talk about. (*Choose*, p. 8.)

And when we tear ourselves free from the entanglements of the world, are we promised a religion of repose or an Eden of ease? No! We are promised tears and trials and toil! But we are also promised final triumph, the mere contemplation of which tingles one's soul. (*Ensign*, November 1974, p. 13.)

May we be different in order to make a difference in the world. (*Ensign*, November 1974, p. 13.)

The "man of Christ" does not divorce the Sermon on the Mount from the sermon at Capernaum with its hard teachings which caused many to walk "no more with" Jesus. (John 6:66.) (*Ensign*, May 1975, p. 101.)

We cannot reenter His [God's] house until our behavior would let us feel at home. (*Ensign*, November 1986, p. 54.)

There are so many little, focusing moments in which the reflexes of faith are either in place or they are not. Defining moments are preceded by preparatory moments. If previously we have behaved properly, though tempted, or if we have been gentle, though irritated, and if we have reached out to help others, though beset with personal problems, as we meet the defining moments these reflexes will steady us. Reflexes do not introduce new and sudden surges. Rather, they represent the harvest of what has passed. How good, for instance, are we at receiving bad news? If we have buckled in the past, that is one thing; but if we have absorbed bad news and moved on, we are likely to be able to gird up our loins again. If we have hedged instead of trusted in the Lord, then we are likely to hedge again. Equivocation followed by equivocation can become its own destination. (*Faith*, pp. 108–9.)

GOSPEL SCHOLARSHIP

The need for greater individual study of the gospel—more scholarship on the part of individual members who do not demand of the

Church that it supply them with intellectual handouts—is also something which can start to be met in the home. We can be much more effective as leaders and followers if we engage in individual gospel scholarship. (*Excellent*, p. 126.)

GOSSIP

False accusations can linger like a bad odor. The victim may even be vindicated without being re-established. He may be exonerated but remain excluded. (*Believe*, p. 8.)

GOVERNMENT

The living of one protective principle of the gospel is better than a thousand compensatory governmental programs—which programs are, so often, like "straightening deck chairs on the *Titanic*." (*Ensign*, November 1974, p. 12.)

It is no accident that the lessening, or loss, of belief in certain absolute truths, such as the existence of God and the reality of immortality, has occurred at the same time there has been a sharp gain in the size and power of governments. Once we remove belief in God from the center of our lives, as the source of truth and as a determiner of justice, a tremendous vacuum is created into which selfishness surges, a condition that governments delight in managing. (*Notwithstanding*, p. 34.)

In our members' diverse and sometimes stressful situations the world over, can we not follow the twelfth article of faith, rendering appropriately unto God and Caesar? After all, Jesus' immediate audience was a repressed people living under a military protectorate supporting corrupt civil authority. (*Ensign*, November 1988, p. 31.)

Misguided governments mean to live, even if they live beyond their means, thereby mortgaging future generations. (*Ensign*, November 1990, p. 15.)

I fear that, as conditions worsen, many will react to the failures of too much government by calling for even more government. Then there will be more and more lifeboats launched because fewer and fewer citizens know how to swim. Unlike some pendulums, political pendulums do not swing back automatically; they must be pushed. History is full of instances when people have waited in vain for pendulums to swing back. ("Insights from My Life," p. 196.)

If citizen appetites, once aroused, merely look to a new agency to do what a disestablished agency once did, it won't be enough. Addicts can always find new pushers. ("Insights from My Life," p. 196.)

Had Noah lived in our highly regulated day, he probably would have been refused a building permit! (*Believe*, p. 100.)

One of the disciple's major challenges will be to render to Caesar that which is Caesar's—but to know what to do when a swollen Caesar asks too much. (*Really Are*, p. 17.)

Mounting concerns do not necessarily mean "back to the catacombs" for Christians, or that secular Caesars will soon reopen the Colosseum. But, already, there are would-be Caesars who will refuse to settle for citizens who render to Caesar only that which is his—and unto God all that is His. (See Matthew 22:21.) (*Ensign,* May 1983, p. 10.)

For the person involved in government or politics, the constant striving for preeminence or the challenge over turf can get in the way of giving service to others. Some civil servants are barely civil. For some politicians, "getting even" is, somehow, seen as succeeding. Nor are "protective dog-in-the-manger" types likely to give place and priority to Him who was placed in a manger after His birth! (*Sermons,* p. 11.)

GRANDPARENTS

Grandparents are often the strategic reserve who can overlook dirty clothes and untied shoelaces and sibling rivalries—not because they fail to see such, but rather, because their unconditional love for their grandchildren is so irrepressible. (*My Family,* p. 101.)

Grandparents have usually experienced enough peaks and valleys with offspring so that they do not overreact and also so that they don't get overinvolved. (*My Family,* p. 101.)

GRATITUDE

Comparatively, we are so much quicker to return favors and to pay our debts to mortals—and we should be responsive and grateful. But what of Him who gave us mortal life itself, who will ere long give us all immortality, and who proffers to the faithful the greatest gift of all, eternal life? We are poor bookkeepers, indeed! (*Ensign*, November 1988, p. 31.)

There will be times when we applaud and no one notices our pair of happy hands, and no one even hears our added decibels—except us and the Lord. (*Experience*, p. 63.)

Mortal mathematics . . . is forever mistaking who and what counts. Even so, we should be more quick to express genuine appreciation to others. The arithmetic of appreciation is far less practiced and known than the multiplication tables. (*Believe*, p. 55.)

To receive God's blessings without acknowledging their Source is to be unrealistic as well as ungrateful. (*Ensign*, November 1988, p. 31.)

[God] experiences a deep, divine disappointment in us when we are ungrateful and when we are unwilling to confess God's hand in all things. (D&C 59:21.) But it is because of what our sustained ingratitude does to us, not to Him. Failure to see His hand in human affairs in bringing to pass His eternal purposes and plans in the world (at the same time leaving us to exercise our agency) is a fatal misreading of life. It also represents a profound spur to selfishness and self-centeredness. It is these faults which lead to the celebration of the appetites rather than of spiritual things. And God knows perfectly what the end results of such trends are so far as human misery is concerned. It is our true happiness which He desires for us, His children, and "wickedness never was happiness" (Alma 41:10). (*Sermons*, p. 85.)

We can't dwell upon another's ingratitude without using up our time and talents unprofitably. (*Really Are*, p. 56.)

Greatness

Greatness is not measured by coverage in column inches, either in newspapers or in the scriptures. (*Ensign*, May 1978, p. 10.)

The laboratory of life only appears to be a quiet and uneventful place. Even so, some let the seeming ordinariness dampen their spirits. Though actually coping and growing, some lack the quiet, inner-soul satisfaction that can steady them. Instead, some experience a lingering sense that there is something more important they should be doing and that their chores are somehow not quite what was expected—as if, for instance, what is quietly achieved in righteous, individual living or in parenthood is not sufficiently spectacular. (*Prove*, p. 13.)

Gripes

Sometimes, in expressing our gripes, you and I are merely leaving dirty laundry at someone else's feet for them to worry about—and without even turning the socks inside out! When we really care, we will try to transform our complaints into recommendations and our observations into solutions. (*Believe*, p. 91.)

GROWTH

The enlarging of the soul requires not only some remodeling, but some excavating. (*Ensign*, May 1990, p. 34.)

The harrowing of the soul can be like the harrowing of the soil to increase the yield with things being turned upside down. (*Ensign*, May 1990, p. 34.)

While the Master repeatedly said that we are to follow in His footsteps, it is not as if we were headed toward some *geographical* destination but, rather, toward a *developmental* destination. (*As I Am*, p. 66.)

God is more concerned with growth than with geography. Thus, those who marched in Zion's Camp were not exploring the Missouri countryside but their own possibilities. (*Ensign*, November 1976, p. 14.)

I don't think God [is] too interested in real estate. He owns it all anyway. He does seem to be incredibly interested in what happens to us individually and will place us in those circumstances where we have the most opportune chances to grow and to carry out our purposes. ("But for a Small Moment," p. 451.)

Along with believing in the gospel, we need to believe in our own possibilities—not as to status, but as to power to do good. God could surprise—yes, even stun—each of us here today if we could manage such divine disclosures. Such must usually be kept from us (or can only be hinted at) for now. But specific and special opportunities are pending for every person here today, if we can trust God and do each day's duties and bear our present pain. ("Insights from My Life," p. 190.)

We must not expect personal improvement without pain or some "remodeling." (*Deposition*, p. 34.)

As the object of the shaping, we can scarcely be expected to understand everything in the sculpturing of our souls. In our imperceptivity, we may, for instance, believe we are already quite symmetrical in certain portions of our personality, only to encounter an experience in which God suddenly and publicly shears off a whole encrustation. We had not even noticed the need, but we feel the pain; perhaps we were too pleased with our lives. In acknowledging that we cannot comprehend all that God comprehends, this attitude should not apply alone to the galaxies, but also to the constellation of characteristics that make up our present personalities. (*As I Am*, p. 59.)

Could it be that Father has customized chores for us to do in the eternities and therefore chooses to give us now a growth experience we do not seem to need—but that he knows we need? (*Really Are*, pp. 36–37.)

If our soul is to be stretched, how can that happen without growing pains? (*Prove*, p. 14.)

He who has arranged this planet for us with adequate natural resources ("enough and to spare") has also supplied a surplus of opportunities for the stretching of our souls, if we but desire to do so. (*Press Forward*, p. 34.)

Jesus' brief stumbling while carrying the cross is a reminder as to how close to the very edge of our strength God stretches us at times. (*Really Are*, p. xii.)

Change and improvement are . . . blocked by an inordinate fear of the unknown and the risks of change. This kind of fear can immobilize us; it can block us from accepting challenges that might permit us to grow. Significantly, the pioneers did not constantly look over their shoulders out of nostalgia for Nauvoo; they moved into the unknown—but guided by God. (*Excellent*, p. 48.)

Inwardly and anxiously we may worry, too, that an omniscient and loving God sees more stretch in us than we feel we have. Hence when God is actually lifting us up, we may feel He is letting us down. (*Faith*, p. 3.)

We may murmur a little now over the calisthenics of being stretched, and we may complain over enduring the exhausting isometrics of individual development in the moral gymnasium. But if we were deprived of all these experiences in mortality, how would we feel later, as immortals, upon discovering that our smallness of stature was due to that earlier deprivation? (*Endure*, p. 119.)

GRUMPINESS

The gravel of grumpiness . . . keeps us off balance and annoyingly turns ankles. Even though we do not fully fall or stumble, we progress more slowly, painfully, and fitfully. (*Meek*, p. 57.)

One wonders, even in good people, if peevishness is not one of the last tendencies to be conquered. Littleness in big people is always disappointing. Perhaps such littleness is like litter on an otherwise lovely lawn; we must not be judgmental, of course, but we cannot help noticing. Even so, we'd best look first to our own lawns. (*Notwithstanding*, p. 51.)

HABITS

We must remember that tomorrow always exists prenatally in today; the fetus of tomorrow is being formed now, and this is true of nations and individuals. (*Choose*, p. 14.)

HANDBOOKS

There can be no all-purpose handbook to cover all human situations with a page for every problem; each of us must develop his own responses to such dilemmas, and those responses must be given to us by the Holy Ghost, who is the unerring guide in telling us "all things" we need to do. (*Press Forward*, p. 38.)

HAPPINESS

Only by aligning our wills with God's is full happiness to be found. Anything less results in a lesser portion (see Alma 12:10–11). (*Ensign*, November 1995, p. 23.)

Too much anxious opening of the oven door and the cake falls instead of rising. So it is with us. If we are always selfishly taking our temperatures to see if we are happy, we will not be. ("Patience," p. 216.)

There can be no true felicity without true identity. (*Ensign*, November 1986, p. 53.)

Man's search for . . . bedrock purpose and for core values will be a search in vain if it searches for new answers, or if it moves in the direction of false religion or merely in the direction of political ideology. These will prove to be only conceptual *cul-de-sacs*, not the solitary path to happiness. (*My Family*, p. 96.)

Those who prevent human happiness include those who traffic in drugs, narcotics, and child pornography. Because God loves His children and He is our friend, He is angry at our enemies and those foolish and misery-producing acts inculcated by our enemies. (*Sermons*, p. 86.)

HARDNESS OF HEART

Perhaps the worst curse that finally falls upon those who are hard of heart and who fight against God is the curse of being consigned to be with each other. (*Heart*, p. 50.)

Hardness of heart in many will produce other manifestations of hardness and coarseness. Civility will be one casualty of these conditions, and a lowered capacity to achieve reconciliation, whether in a marriage or between interest groups, will be another. (*Notwithstanding*, p. 18.)

HEAVEN

Like Alma, we will "long to be there" (Alma 36:22), in the "royal courts on high." It is the only destination that really matters. Resplendent reunion awaits us! What is more reasonable and more wonderful than children going home? Especially to a home where the past, the present, and the future form an everlasting and eternal now! (*Men and Women*, p. 51.)

HEDONISM

Regarding certain destructive things, abstinence is so much easier than moderation! Meanwhile, you will see those about you who are surfing life's pleasures indulgently. They will eventually crash against the reefs of reality. ("'Brim with Joy,'" p. 4.)

Humdrum hedonism camouflages much critical data. By diminishing our capacity to feel, it also diminishes our capacity to serve others. (*Sermons*, p. 62.)

Of all today's malevolent "isms," hedonism takes the greatest toll. It is naive to say that hedonists merely march to the beat of a different drummer. So did the Gadarene swine! (*Ensign*, May 1995, p. 67.)

HEROES

We must be careful as parents not to canonize all predecessors—not to dry all the human sweat off them, not to put ceaseless smiles on their faces, when they really struggled and experienced agony. Real people who believe and prevail are ultimately more faith-promoting and impressive than saccharine saints with tinsel traits. (*Excellent*, p. 130.)

So it is that the real but unheralded heroes and heroines of our time are the men and women of the earth who uncommonly resist the world's common temptations, who surmount the common tribulations of the world and continue to the very end in righteousness, arriving home battered slightly, yet much bettered. Such individuals may get little mortal applause or recognition, but there is real rejoicing elsewhere by those who really know what a good performance is! (*Prove*, p. 45.)

HISTORY

Seen through the eye of faith, the sweep of history is not evidence of a purposeless world. Instead, we see successive waves of humans, as the cast on this mortal stage changes, again and again. And, however articulate some of those despairing actors are in this human drama, without the gospel light they view only a tiny portion of one scene, not even a whole act. And certainly not the whole play. Such are invited to understand the purposes and instructions of the Author of this drama. But when He finally "comes on the stage, the play is over!" (*Ensign*, May 1983, p. 10.)

The boneyard of history is full of the debris of those who thought they could handle a little power, a little liquor, and a little adultery—of those who thought their particular adultery was somehow noble—of those who loved mankind but not their neighbor. (*Choose*, pp. 27–28.)

Secular history is usually silent concerning spiritual things. (*Ensign*, November 1984, p. 9.)

One day, the historical record will be complete; but, meanwhile, the scriptures will be our guide concerning those transcending spiritual events in human history which are saturated with significance. (*Ensign*, November 1984, p. 9.)

Men must sometimes ponder the past prayerfully, if they desire to fashion a future fit to live in. (*Look Back*, p. 25.)

Some treat the pieces of information which comprise history as if they were the fragments in a kaleidoscope—with the facts rearranging themselves at the mere shake of the next viewer. Hence, we get revisions of revisions of revisions. (*Sermons*, p. 52.)

Deafness to secular history is dangerous with its muted memories of past errors. Deafness to scriptural history is fatal. (*Press Forward*, p. 6.)

HOLY GHOST

Life is no labyrinth; mortality is no maze if a man possesses the gift of the Holy Ghost to guide him. (*Heart*, p. 47.)

In a "wheat and tares" world, how unusually blessed faithful members are to have the precious and constant gift of the Holy Ghost with reminders of what is right and of the covenants we have made. "For behold, . . . the Holy Ghost . . . will show unto you all things what ye should do." (2 Nephi 32:5.) Whatever the decibels of decadence, these need not overwhelm the still, small voice! Some of the best sermons we will ever hear will be those prompted from the pulpit of memory—to an audience of one! (*Ensign*, May 1993, p. 77.)

Repentance takes care of the past, faith the future, and the Holy Ghost helps us with today. (*Heart*, p. 30.)

Tongue cannot always transmit the truths of the gospel. Its truths are too powerful for us to manage on occasion. . . . That is why we are so in need of the Spirit—so that knowledge can arc like electricity from point to point, aided and impelled by the Spirit—aid without which we are simply not articulate enough to speak of all the things which we know. ("But for a Small Moment," p. 451.)

The Holy Ghost never waits to leave until he is formally asked to leave, for his influence has already departed even as we, by our thoughts, slide toward sin. (*My Family*, p. 86.)

Jesus' influence on the tutored [does not] depend upon His personal proximity. The Comforter will teach us and strengthen us. (*As I Am*, p. 64.)

One of the greatest sources of hope is the Comforter, for He can keep us at our lonely posts when it appears that our comrades have been routed or have deserted. (*Press Forward*, p. 61.)

My humble praise today flows not only to God the Father for his loving plan of salvation and to Jesus, the Lord of the universe, for His marvelous and remarkable Atonement, but also to the Holy Ghost, about whom we speak less. Among His many roles I express my particular and personal gratitude for the recent ways in which He has been the precious Comforter, including in the mid-night moments! (*Ensign*, May 1997, p. 12.)

HOME

The act of deserting home in order to shape society is like thoughtlessly removing crucial fingers from an imperiled dike in order to teach people to swim. (*Ensign*, May 1978, p. 11.)

Sometimes, unintentionally, even certain extracurricular Church activities, insensitively administered, can hamper family life. Instructively, after the resurrected Jesus taught the Nephites, He said, "Go ye unto your homes, and ponder upon the things which I have said," and pray and prepare "for the morrow" (3 Nephi 17:3). Jesus did not say go to your civic clubs, town meetings, or even stake centers! (*Ensign*, May 1994, p. 89.)

Failure in the home clearly calls for compensatory institutions, but the home lies at the headwaters of the stream of civilization, and we must keep it happy and pure. When the home fails or is polluted, we must, of course, support "treatment" efforts downstream. But we must not become so fascinated with the filtering operation that we ignore prevention and desert our post at the headwaters. (*Choose*, p. 85.)

When our homes help us to be compassionate and selfless . . . then we have a school on whose graduates all of society depends. (*My Family*, p. 29.)

The home is usually the place where most of our faith is established and increased, for there we witness the examples of righteous parents as we work out our salvation in a setting that requires love, forgiveness, patience, and all the other virtues. How sad, therefore, that some homes are merely a pit stop, when they should be a prep school for the celestial kingdom. (*Faith*, p. 117.)

HONORS OF MEN

Playing to the gallery in all its forms involves a wearying regimen. We cannot finally be concerned about pleasing Him if we are too concerned about pleasing *them*. Besides, playing to the roar of the crowd, be it a few peers or an imagined multitude, ends as an empty exercise. One realizes finally that he is in the wrong theater. (*Prove*, p. 104.)

Time makes of the praise and honors of men so much cotton candy—it is sweet, but melts in one's mouth quickly. Yet how many have paid such a terrible price for that transitory taste. The problem with approaching life on the basis of "now" is that "now" is over, even as one says the very word. (*Really Are*, p. 7.)

While recognition is a basic human need and is important in the
public service, there are those who do too many things to be seen
of men. ("Insights from My Life," p. 194.)

They err who, instead of concentrating on commandment keeping
and personal spiritual progress, desire sweeping significance and
high visibility in the second estate. Is it really numbers of people
touched at the moment which measure the impact of an individual?
Did tens of thousands hear the Sermon on the Mount? Did it make
the six o'clock news? ("Grounded, Rooted, Established, and Settled,"
p. 17.)

Those who "shine as lights in the world" have no need to seek the
spotlight! (See Philippians 2:15.) The world's spotlights are not
only fleeting, but they employ inferior light! ("'In Him All Things
Hold Together,'" p. 105.)

Aside from the consideration of proper balance in our lives, those
who make commendable contributions may in one sense have already received their recognition and reward—here and now (see
Matthew 6:2, 5, 16). This may be just as well, for some honors—
justifiable enough here—would be embarrassing to receive later in
a celestial setting. (*Flood*, p. 104.)

Both premortally and after the astonishing atonement, Jesus said
"Glory be to the Father" (see Moses 4:2; D&C 19:19). What a
contrast to those of us unprofitable servants who, after doing a few
good deeds, insist on keeping score! We worry over whether or not
our little deed is noticed. We notice the size of the letters on the
mortal marquees over the tiny little theaters where our "own little
plot is always being played." (*Men and Women*, p. 127.)

How could we have any greater recognition anyway than that of
being a spirit son or daughter of God? or of finally deserving to be

known as a man or woman of Christ? How could we possibly ever be given more than "all that my Father hath"? There isn't any more! (*Men and Women*, p. 128.)

For those too concerned with credit, the mortal books, however well kept and well intended, are incomplete anyway. They could not stand a real "outside audit." The real and complete Book of Life is kept elsewhere! One day it will be opened and we will all be judged out of it (see Revelation 20:12). There will be no challenge then to the justice or mercy of God (see Mosiah 27:31; Alma 12:15). (*Believe*, p. 55.)

I have become more and more persuaded that our transparent drives for recognition are somehow subtly bound up with our seeming need to verify that we matter. We wish neither to be taken for granted nor to be regarded as a mere cipher. Attention becomes a form of validation. (*Believe*, p. 55.)

Mortal monuments, however pretentious, and the passing praise of the world, however lavish, do not really and finally matter. (*Believe*, p. 135.)

When the secular applause has died down and the bands have stopped playing—when the mortal measuring of those compensatory successes has concluded—such individuals are often left with a tragic emptiness (insofar as eternal things are concerned), "for they have their reward." (*My Family*, p. 75.)

Speaking of being surprised, what, one wonders, were the feelings of the architect for the Tower of Babel? He probably would have been named "architect of the year." But his plans went a floor too far! (*Believe*, p. 172.)

If we condition our "metabolism" of interpersonal relations to require large doses of recognition or constant response from others, we will be disappointed—as much as deserved praise and response are helpful and appreciated when they do come our way. Our need for response can become narcotic, and we may find that we do good things for the wrong reasons simply to elicit attention. (*Power*, p. 27.)

Each of us seeks deserved and legitimate recognition, but a wrong approach can produce an awful addiction, for the passion for preeminence is a dangerous passion. (*Prove*, p. 25.)

To seek place above others is one of our greatest temptations; it is the most fatiguing form of climbing. (*Prove*, p. 105.)

Sometimes the less heralded but highly developed individuals are "no less serviceable" (Alma 48:19) in the cause of God than those who may be much more in the spotlight. (*Faith*, p. 50.)

HOPE

Real hope is much more than wishful musing. It stiffens, not slackens, the spiritual spine. It is composed, not giddy, eager, without being naive, and pleasantly steady without being smug. Hope is realistic anticipation taking the form of determination—a determination not merely to survive but to "endure . . . well" to the end (D&C 121:8). (*Ensign*, November 1994, p. 35.)

When individuals are without hope regarding life to come, death becomes terribly controlling so far as this life is concerned. The second estate is lived out as if it were a final and concluding *excla-mation point* rather than another *comma* in the continuum of man's existence. (*Deposition*, p. 14.)

When we speak of hope as a Christian virtue . . . it is necessary to disengage ourselves from the world's notions of hope. The latter are, at best, rather vague and are often tied to ephemeral enthusi-asm, such as Richard Cobden's 1846 speech in England celebrating the "most important event in history" since the coming of Christ—"the repeal of the corn laws." Human hyperbole is an un-reliable source of perspective. (*Notwithstanding*, p. 40.)

Gospel hope is a very focused and particularized hope that is based upon justified expectations. (*Notwithstanding*, p. 41.)

Relying on defective hope . . . is like using a parachute that works most of the time. Hopes not grounded in the gospel are too much at the mercy of men and circumstance. (*Press Forward*, p. 72.)

Having ultimate hope does not mean we will always be rescued from proximate problems, but we will be rescued from everlasting death! (*Ensign*, November 1994, p. 35.)

In the geometry of restored theology, hope has a greater circumfer-ence than faith. If faith increases, the perimeter of hope stretches correspondingly. (*Ensign*, November 1994, p. 35.)

Souls can be roused and rallied by hope's "reveille" as by no other music. Even if comrades slumber or desert, "lively hope" performs like a reconnoitering scout out in advance of God's columns; "there is hope smiling brightly before us" (see 1 Peter 1:3; *Hymns*, 1985, no. 19). (*Ensign*, November 1994, p. 35.)

Ultimate hope and daily grumpiness are not reconcilable. It is ungraceful, unjustified, and unbecoming of us as committed Church members to be constantly grumpy or of woeful countenance. Do we have some moments of misery or some down days? Yes! But the promise is that Christ will "lift thee up" (Moroni 9:25.) The disciple can note the depressing signs of the times without being depressed. He can be disappointed in people without being offended at life. Thus it is that ultimate hope, if it does not finally dissolve our daily disappointments, at least puts them in perspective. (Local Thanksgiving speech [untitled], November 26, 1980.)

Those with true hope often see their personal circumstances shaken, like kaleidoscopes, again and again. Yet with the "eye of faith," they still see divine pattern and purpose (Alma 5:15). (*Ensign*, November 1994, p. 36.)

HOPELESSNESS

Behavioral permissiveness flourishes amid a sense of hopelessness. If human appetites are mistakenly viewed as the only authentic reality, and "now" as the only moment that matters, why should one checkrein any impulse or defer any gratification? Hence individual accountability and belief in individual immortality are intertwined. (*Small Moment*, p. 72.)

If one is devoid of hope and thanksgiving, he cannot for long remain sinless, for he will in despair have slackened his resolve. (Moroni 10:22.) Feelings of futility foster vulnerability. Self-pity is such a busy stagehand, rearranging the scenery to help sin make its entrance. No wonder the prophets say that without faith in the Lord, "there is no hope." (D&C 10:21.) (Local Thanksgiving speech [untitled], November 26, 1980.)

One can certainly be entrapped by the adversary in dramatic ways, but the economy of temptation apparently does not require drama, if minor moods serve the same purpose. Major sin can destroy an individual quickly, but a sustained feeling of hopelessness can cause slow spiritual suicide with the same ultimate result. (*Excellent*, p. 65.)

HUMILITY

The gospel requires us to yield our minds as well as bend our knees. Minds are often more arthritic than knees. (*Believe*, p. 101.)

Isn't it marvelous how Jesus deflected credit from himself? Even after his excruciating atonement, he meekly said, "Glory be to the Father"! ("Out of the Best Faculty," p. 48.)

The enthusiasm of "I'll baptize a thousand on my mission!" is best tempered by "I'll go where you want me to go, dear Lord . . . I'll do what you want me to do," letting "God give the increase" (*Hymns*, no. 270; 1 Corinthians 3:6). (*Men and Women*, p. 25.)

Humility is not the disavowal of our worth; rather, it is the sober realization of how much we are valued by God. Nor does true humility call for the denigration of what truth we already know; rather, it is the catching of one's breath, as he realizes how very little that which we mortals presently know really is! (*Experience*, p. 127.)

We have no evidence of Jesus' ever reflecting upon or discoursing immodestly upon His masterful performances, such as in the miracle of the loaves and fishes, in the raising of Lazarus, or in the healing of the ten lepers. He let his deeds speak for themselves, and He always attributed His power to the Father. Dare we do less as regards the much less we have achieved? (*Not My Will*, pp. 93–94.)

[Jesus] rejoices in our genuine goodness and achievement, but any assessment of where we stand in relation to Him tells us that we do not stand at all! We kneel! (*Ensign*, November 1981, p. 8.)

HUMOR

The true believer is serious about the living of his life, but he is of good cheer. His humor is the humor of hope and his mirth is the mirth of modesty—not the hollow laughter or the cutting cleverness of despair. Unlike those of a celebrated "devil-may-care" lifestyle, his is the quiet "heaven-does-care" attitude. ("'True Believers in Christ,'" p. 139.)

How wonderful it is to see those whose sense of humor includes the capacity to see themselves and their frailities laughingly—not in the chronic, self-deprecating, biting way. Those who can see themselves and their incongruities with smiles (not sarcasm) suggest to the rest of us that they have an inner security, and this encourages the rest of us to take heart in a world in which too many of us are much too serious about ourselves and in which too much of the laughter is nervous laughter. (*Power*, p. 25.)

Humor as a reflection of the incongruities of life can be helpful. The living prophets I have known have all had such a sense of humor. (*Deposition*, p. 52.)

Indeed, the Brethren are happy while they cope with serious and somber problems. Someone said it is too bad we don't preserve the small talk of great men; so, too, the humor of holy men who serve as special witnesses. (*Deposition*, p. 19.)

IDEALISM

We must nurture and keep youthful idealism alive to serve as an infusion of adrenaline throughout the Church—something which is very much needed in our time—without making the tragic error of being taken in by irrelevant "relevancies." (*Choose*, p. 7.)

IDENTITY

Having faith in the plan of salvation includes steadfastly refusing to be diverted from our true identities and responsibilities. In the brief season of our existence on earth we may serve as plumber, professor, farmer, physician, mechanic, bookkeeper, or teacher. These are useful activities and honorable designations; but a temporary vocation is not reflective of our true identities. Matthew was a tax collector, Luke a physician, and Peter a fisherman. In a salvational sense, "so what!" (*Faith*, p. 47.)

IDLENESS

Idleness brings about idolatry and increase in iniquity. There is something holy about work; even in times of plenty, it is a necessity. While work is not all of life, it nevertheless can keep us mindful of our blessings. (*Look Back*, p. 10.)

IMMORALITY

Take away regard for the seventh commandment, and behold the current celebration of sex, the secular religion with its own liturgy of lust and supporting music. Its theology focuses on "self." Its hereafter is "now." Its chief ritual is "sensation"—though, ironically, it finally desensitizes its obsessed adherents, who become "past feeling." (Ephesians 4:19; Moroni 9:20.) (*Ensign*, November 1990, pp. 15–16.)

There is a last irony—but only for those who need it: The great apostle of love, John, reminded us that this world will pass away "and the lust thereof." (See 1 John 2:17.) This means, quite frankly, that not only can lust ruin this life, but it is also a pandering to an appetite that will have *no* existence at all in the next world! (*Notwithstanding*, p. 100.)

We must not be intimidated or lose our composure even though the once morally unacceptable is becoming acceptable, as if frequency somehow conferred respectability! One of the most subtle forms of intimidation is the gradual normalization of aberration! (*Ensign*, May 1993, p. 76.)

When one seeks to be prescriptive with regard to [the seventh commandment], society is not interested. They react as if we are offering them unlimited access to root canals. Remedy would require significant cessation of fornication and adultery with all the resultant illegitimacy, divorce, and failed families. ("'Build Up My Church,' 'Establish the [Lord's] Righteousness.'")

The notion that private immorality is somehow acceptable rests on the notion that certain behavior is "safe" because it is confined. Just as there can be no private smallpox or cholera, at least one other individual is usually affected by our sin, and usually more, whether immediately or eventually. (*Sermons*, p. 62.)

Strip-mining scars the landscape, causes floods, and leaves an economic emptiness which haunts the coming generations. Similarly, unchastity leaves terrible scars, brings floods of tears and anguish, and leaves a moral emptiness. Significantly, both strip-mining and unchastity rest on a life-style which partakes of an "eat, drink, and be merry" philosophy—gouge and grab now without regard to the consequences! Both strip-mining and unchastity violate the spirit of stewardship over our planet and our person. (*Power*, p. 2.)

IMPERFECTIONS

Imperfections in predecessors should be expected, but their faults should be seen as an opportunity for improvement—not as damaging evidence. (*Choose*, p. 24.)

Satanic "salesmen" must try to make up in cleverness what they lack in content, while righteousness often has advocates who are, unintentionally, halting, even clumsy in their advocacy of that which is right. This points up our need to fall in love with the Gospel itself and to make allowance for each other—the faulty human conduits through whom the message comes. (*Choose*, pp. 30–31.)

INDIVIDUAL

The kingdom begins with the individual and lets reform radiate outward from him to society and its institutions. The world strives to do it the other way. (*Deposition*, p. 99.)

The Gospel places heavy stress on the individual and his ultimate challenge to govern himself according to righteous principles. It rests on changing the inner man, not the outward circumstances. That is a slow, unglamorous way to lift the quality of life on this planet, especially since the world usually seeks its goals by imposing new laws or outer controls on man. (*Choose*, p. 27.)

INSPIRATION

Someone afflicted with physical deafness could sit amid a symphony of sound but hear nothing, while those about him would enjoy the thrill of great music. His would be an involuntary deprivation, of course. One who is deaf to spiritual sounds also sits unnoticing amid a different kind of symphony. Yet the reality is likewise there, since others, attuned, partake. (*We Talk of Christ*, pp. 57–58.)

Reflection and pause are even more necessary than we had supposed in order to wipe clean the busy chalkboard of our lives; fresh impressions need a place to be recorded. (*Press Forward*, p. 122.)

The prompting that goes unresponded to may not be repeated. Writing down what we have been prompted with is vital. A special thought can also be lost later in the day in the rough and tumble of life. God should not, and may not, choose to repeat the prompting if we assign what was given such a low priority as to put it aside. (*Press Forward*, p. 122.)

IRONY

Irony is the hard crust on the bread of adversity. Irony can try both our faith and our patience. Irony can be a particularly bitter form of such chastening because it involves disturbing incongruity. It involves outcomes in violation of our expectations. We see the best laid plans laid waste. (*Ensign*, May 1989, p. 62.)

Our planning itself often assumes that our destiny is largely in our own hands. Then come intruding events, first elbowing aside, then evicting what was anticipated and even earned. Hence, we can be offended by events as well as by people. Irony may involve not only unexpected suffering but also undeserved suffering. We feel we deserved better, and yet we fared worse. We had other plans, even commendable plans. Did they not count? A physician, laboriously trained to help the sick, now because of his own illness, cannot do so. For a period, a diligent prophet of the Lord was an "idle witness." (Mormon 3:16.) Frustrating conditions keep more than a few of us from making our appointed rounds. Customized challenges are thus added to that affliction and temptation which

Paul described as "common to man." (1 Corinthians 10:13.) (*Ensign*, May 1989, p. 63.)

We need to make allowance for the role of irony in our individual lives and as a people. For instance, those chosen for service by the Lord would appear to be improbable selections. The same God who had his Only Begotten Son born in a manger and reared in despised Nazareth as the least appreciated but most beneficial individual in human history, also improbably chose Moses, who was not eloquent but "slow of speech, and of a slow tongue," to lead one of the greatest migrations in history. God also chose shepherds and fishermen, sent a mere boy to face Goliath, chose Paul (a persecutor of Christians) as an apostle, and selected an obscure boy to receive the remarkable divine manifestations at Palmyra. (*Choose*, pp. 43–44.)

In coping with irony, as in all things, we have an Exemplary Teacher in Jesus. Dramatic irony assaulted Jesus' divinity almost constantly. For Jesus, in fact, irony began at His birth. Truly, He suffered the will of the Father "in all things from the beginning." (3 Nephi 11:11.) This whole earth became Jesus' footstool (see Acts 7:49), but at Bethlehem there was "no room . . . in the inn" (Luke 2:7) and "no crib for his bed." (*Hymns*, 1985, no. 206.) At the end, meek and lowly Jesus partook of the most bitter cup without becoming the least bitter. (See 3 Nephi 11:11; D&C 19:18–19.) The Most Innocent suffered the most. Yet the King of Kings did not break, even when some of His subjects did unto Him "as they listed." (D&C 49:6.) Christ's capacity to endure such irony was truly remarkable. (*Ensign*, May 1989, p. 63.)

If we had all the data which is available to God, we could see that what looks like irony is simply the smooth flow of events and decisions that are part of a much larger plan. (*Choose*, p. 45.)

IRRITATIONS

Big people are simply less irritated by little things. (*My Family*, p. 45.)

JEALOUSY

For us to jettison our jealousies is to stop yet another form of waste, for we cannot go where He is if we worry rather than rejoice over who else will be there. Jousting for position among peers and friends is to waste what could better be used in the battle against the enemy of evil. (*Press Forward*, p. 94.)

JESUS CHRIST

If you sense that one day every knee shall bow and every tongue shall confess that Jesus Christ is the Lord, why not do so now? For in the coming of that collective confession, it will mean much less to kneel down when it is no longer possible to stand up! (*Ensign*, November 1974, p. 13.)

Some crusaders without a cross have actually removed the divinity of Jesus Christ from the center of their doctrines—only to see all the other doctrinal dominoes tumble too. (*Ensign*, May 1976, p. 26.)

The Atonement not only rescues us but also exemplifies Jesus' character. His character can guide us, beacon-like, in the midst of our own afflictions, since these constitute the necessary crucible for the further refining and confirmation of our own character. (*Faith*, p. 17.)

[The prophet] Jacob said that we will see "things as they really are, and as they really will be." That is how we should view Jesus, and because of His character He makes that possible. The more you and I come to understand God and Jesus, the more we want to be like Them and to be with Them. That yearning takes on a strength and an intensity that dims other things in comparison. Their character is so marvelous. No wonder the Prophet said, "If men do not comprehend the character of God, they do not comprehend themselves." How can we know who we are if we don't know who He is? How can we understand what our character should be like if we do not understand His? Christ's character is without flaw, and He is perfect in His love and empathy so you and I can trust Him completely. If He were not, imagine where we would be. ("'Lord, Increase Our Faith.'")

The more we know about the character of God and Jesus, which ensures their desire to help us, and also about their capacity to help us, the more we will have faith that the Lord's "grace is sufficient" to see us through our personal trials and troubles (see Ether 12:26–27.) (*Faith*, p. 19.)

I thank Jesus for foregoing fashionableness and for enduring not only the absence of appreciation but also for speaking the truth, knowing beforehand that misunderstanding and misrepresentation would follow. I thank him for his marvelous management of time, for never misusing a moment, including the moments of meditation. Even his seconds showed his stewardship. (*Ensign*, May 1976, p. 27.)

How dare some treat His ministry as if it were all beatitudes and no declaratives! How myopic it is to view His ministry as all crucifixion and no resurrection! How provincial to perceive it as all Calvary and no Palmyra! All rejection at a village called Capernaum and no acceptance in the City of Enoch! All relapse and regression in ancient Israel and no Bountiful with its ensuing decades of righteousness. (*Ensign*, November 1981, p. 8.)

We can wait, as we must, to learn later whether . . . Matthew's or Luke's account of Jesus' Davidic descent is correct. (See Matthew 1; Luke 3.) Meanwhile, the Father has, on several occasions, given us Jesus' crucial genealogy: "This is My *Beloved Son*, in whom I am well pleased. Hear Him!" (See Matthew 3:17; 17:5; 3 Nephi 11:7; Joseph Smith—History 1:17; italics added.) (*Ensign*, November 1984, p. 11.)

Though crucified briefly between two thieves, Jesus now sits eternally on the right hand of God! (See Luke 22:69; 1 Peter 3:22.) He is the Lord of the constructed universe, yet He was known merely as "the carpenter's son." (Matthew 13:55.) (*Ensign*, November 1988, p. 33.)

Christ never brushed aside those in need because He had bigger things to do! (*Ensign*, November 1990, p. 16.)

Each of us is an innkeeper who decides if there is room for Jesus! (*Ensign*, November 1992, p. 66.)

As Jesus begins to have a real place in our lives, we are much less concerned with losing our places in the world. When our minds really catch hold of the significance of Jesus' atonement, the world's hold on us loosens. (See Alma 36:18.) (*Ensign*, November 1992, p. 67.)

Consider, what if Jesus' Mortal Messiahship had consisted only of remarkable sermons? Or was further enhanced with healings and other miracles—but without Gethsemane's and Calvary's awful but consecrated hours of the Atonement? How then would we regard Jesus' ministry? Where would mankind be? (*Ensign*, November 1992, p. 67.)

Christ on the cross gave out the cry "My God, my God, why hast thou forsaken me?" That cry on the cross is an indication that the very best of our Father's children found the trials so real, the tests so exquisite and so severe, that he cried out—not in doubt of his Father's reality, but wondering "why" at that moment of supreme agony—for Jesus felt so alone. ("But for a Small Moment," p. 445.)

We may turn from Him, but He is still there. We may feel that He is hidden from us because of the cloud cover of our concerns, but He is still close to us. We—not He—let something come between us, but no lasting eclipse need ensue. Our provincialism cannot withstand His universalism. Our disregard of Him is no match for His love of us. Yes, Jesus of Nazareth lived! He lives now! He guides His Church! ("'All Hell Is Moved,'" p. 181.)

Unlike servitude to sin, by wearing his yoke we truly learn of the Yoke Master in what is an education for eternity as well as for mortality. ("'Meek and Lowly,'" p. 53.)

Though he was actually the Creator of this world, the earth being his footstool, Jesus' willingness to become from birth a person of "no reputation" provides one of the great lessons in human history. He, the leader-servant, who remained of "no reputation" mortally, will one day be he before whom every knee will bow and whose name every tongue will confess (see Philippians 2:10–11). ("'Meek and Lowly,'" p. 55.)

It does not surprise me that Satan would thus try to influence the painting of pictures of a Jesus Satan *never saw*. Satan encountered no effeminate Lord on the Mount of Temptation. Satan did not go up against a frail Lord in the preexistence, nor was he dispatched out of the presence of a fragile Lord. Indeed, the Lord whom Satan often has had represented in religious art is just the opposite of that Being of whom he is so fearfully jealous. There is no truth in Lucifer's art. (*Deposition*, pp. 59–60.)

Jesus is the only perfect leader to grace this globe, and he was the only individual who was perfect in his love. (*Excellent*, p. 4.)

The only real *veneration* of Jesus is *emulation* of Him. Indeed, striving to become like Him is a special way of bearing and sharing our testimony of Him. (*As I Am*, p. 2.)

Who but merciful and discerning Jesus could be betrayed, arrested, and forsaken, and yet extend to a one-time persecutor, Saul, the great apostolic calling? Later on, the same Creator of this and other worlds stood by a jailed and persecuted Paul in the night. [Acts 9:5; 23:11.] (*As I Am*, p. 30.)

Only when what and who *He is* begin to dawn more fully upon us—and to fill us with awe instead of respect—will we really follow Him. (*As I Am*, p. 36.)

Jesus refused to be one of "woeful countenance." Not only did He refuse to let the establishment of the time tell Him with whom he might dine; He also refused to insist that people look mournful when they were fasting. Though He was called "man of sorrows," that description refers to His bearing of *our* sorrows—not His; it does not describe His day-to-day bearing! (*As I Am*, p. 103.)

His duties have long been galactic, yet He noticed the widow casting in her mite. I am stunned at His perfect, unconditional love of all. Indeed, "I stand all amazed at the love Jesus offers me." I thank Him for His discerning way of loving us without controlling us, for never letting the needs of now crowd out the considerations of eternity. I thank Him, in every situation, for maintaining His grip on Himself, which was also mankind's hold on the eternal future. (*As I Am*, p. 115.)

Did not this good and true Shepherd forgo repose after the glorious but awful Atonement in order to establish His work among the lost sheep who were disobedient in the days of Noah? Did He not then visit still other lost sheep in the Americas? Then still other lost sheep? What can we tell Him about conscientiousness? (*As I Am*, p. 119.)

Jesus lifts us up in a world which so often puts people down. (*Flood*, p. 115.)

Jesus could not have done the things He did if He had been like some of us—fretting over dominion, fearing the criticism of the world, and seeking glory and praise. In contrast there was Lucifer, whose ascendancy was more important to him than our agency (see Moses 4:1, 3). (*Flood*, p. 119.)

In the great premortal council, when Jesus meekly volunteered, saying, "Here am I, send me" (Abraham 3:27), it was a most significant moment: a few words were preferred to many, for the meek do not multiply words. Never has one individual offered to do so much for so many with so few words as did Jesus when, having created this and other worlds, He then meekly proffered Himself as ransom for all of us on this planet, billions and billions of us! (*Meek*, p. 8.)

Christ's remaining possession, a cloak, was gambled for even as He died. (John 19:23–24.) Yet the very earth was the footstool of Him who was meek and lowly! Jesus gave mankind living water so that we shall never thirst again. In return, on the cross He was given vinegar. (*Meek*, p. 11.)

Jesus did not find pleasure in hanging on the cross; joy came after duty and agony. He went to Gethsemane and Golgotha out of a sense of supreme service, not because it would meet his needs. He fulfilled *all* things by giving *all* in that remarkable and special act of service. He descended below all—taking more than all of us put together have taken—before being lifted up. (*Experience*, p. 60.)

When Jesus said, "Come, follow me," it was an invitation, not a taunt. Moreover, His firm footprints are especially recognizable. They reflect no hesitancy, and no turning aside; they lie in a straight path. The prints are also sunk inerasably deep into the soil of the second estate because of the heavy burdens He bore. A portion of that depth is attributable to us, individually, because we added to the heaviness of His pressing yoke. (*Not My Will*, p. 13.)

Each of the Savior's names implies so much! The name *Jesus* denotes "God's help" and "Savior." The name *Christ* means "Anointed One," "Messiah." We are to have faith in those names and in their implications for all mankind and for us personally. These names are profound, especially when compared to the understandable but understated appellations "the carpenter's son" or "Jesus of Nazareth." Designations by vocation or location are far too provincial when describing the Lord of the universe. (*Faith*, p. 9.)

If we do not regard Him highly enough to pay heed to His words about *who* He is, we will pay less heed to *what* He says and requires of us. The resulting diminution of regard and comprehension will result in little faith. What "think [we] of Christ" inevitably determines His operative relevance for our lives. (*Faith*, p. 9.)

Ever observant, in both the first and second estates, consecrated Jesus always knew in which direction He faced: He consistently emulated His Father. (*Ensign*, November 1995, p. 23.)

JOSEPH SMITH

Those who revile Joseph Smith will not change Joseph's status with the Lord (see 2 Nephi 3:8)—merely their own! (*Ensign*, November 1983, p. 56.)

His prayer [in the Sacred Grove] was for personal and tactical guidance. The response, however, was of global and eternal significance. (*Ensign*, May 1992, p. 37.)

Yes, Joseph received remarkable manifestations, along with constant vexations. True, for instance, there were periodic arrivals of heavenly messengers, but these were punctuated by the periodic arrivals of earthly mobs. (*Ensign*, May 1992, p. 38.)

While Joseph was befriended by heavenly notables, he was also betrayed by some of his earthly friends. Receiving keys and gifts was real, but so was the painful loss of six of the eleven children born to him and Emma. Granted, Joseph had revealed to him glimpses of far horizons—the first and third estates. But these periodic glories occurred amid Joseph's arduous daily life in the second estate. (*Ensign*, May 1992, p. 38.)

Whenever we speak of the Prophet Joseph Smith . . . it should be in reverent appreciation of the Lord who called him and whom Joseph served so well. ("'A Choice Seer,'" p. 113.)

What came *through* Joseph Smith was *beyond* Joseph Smith, and it *stretched* him! In fact, the doctrines that came through that "choice seer" (2 Nephi 3:6–7) by translation or revelation are often so light-intensive that, like radioactive materials, they must be handled with great care! ("'A Choice Seer,'" p. 114.)

The Everest of ecclesiastical truth built from the translations and revelations of the Prophet Joseph Smith speaks for itself as it towers above the foothills of philosophy. . . . Revelations came to us through an inspired prophet, Joseph Smith. His spelling left something to be desired, but how he provided us with the essential grammar of the gospel! ("'A Choice Seer,'" p. 115.)

Yet another way of testing and appreciating the significance of the ministry of the Prophet Joseph Smith is to ask oneself: (1) "What would we know about the holy temples and about the sealing power *without* the Prophet Joseph Smith?"; (2) "What would we know about the plan of salvation with its different estates *without* the Prophet Joseph Smith?"; (3) "What would we know about the precious and plain doctrine of premortality of mankind *without* the Prophet Joseph Smith?" The answer to each question is the same: "Very, very little; certainly not enough." ("'A Choice Seer.'")

Joseph Smith reflected some of the anxieties and activities of his time and period. Yet a torrent of truth came through that brilliant, good, but imperfect conduit, almost more than Joseph could communicate. (*Sermons*, p. 5.)

There was another factor at work in the soul stretching of the Prophet in the [Liberty,] Missouri dungeon. Earlier, Joseph had Oliver Cowdery and Sidney Rigdon to be not only his *aides-de-camp* but also in a measure as his spokesmen. After the Liberty Jail experience, however, Joseph was clearly his own spokesman. From that time forward, we begin to receive Joseph's stretching sermons, involving some of the gospel's most powerful doctrines. (*Small Moment*, p. 17.)

The prophecy given by the angel Moroni was that Joseph's name "should be had for good and evil among all nations" [Joseph Smith—History 1:33]. The adversary will be doing his relentless part with regard to the negative portion of that prophecy. (See D&C 122:1.) By word and deed, faithful Church members must see to it that the positive portion is fulfilled. (*Small Moment*, p. 133.)

Let us examine an important verse in the third chapter of Second Nephi in which ancient Joseph spoke of the latter-day seer and said, "And he shall be like unto me." (2 Nephi 3:15.) The comparisons between the two Josephs, of course, reflect varying degrees of exactitude, but they are, nevertheless, quite striking. Some similarities are situational, others dispositional. First, both Josephs had inauspicious beginnings. Initially, they were unlikely candidates to have had the impact they did on Egyptian history and American history, respectively; indeed, upon world history. Next, both were falsely accused. Further, both were jailed. Both, in their extremities, helped others who later forgot them. In the case of ancient Joseph, it was the chief butler. (Genesis 40:20–23.) Joseph Smith had many fair-weather friends, including Sidney Rigdon, who, finally, did not merit Joseph's full confidence. Both Josephs were torn from their families, although ancient Joseph for a much, much longer time. Very significantly, both were "like unto" each other in being amazingly resilient in the midst of adversity. It is a truly striking quality. Indeed, good but lesser men could not have borne what the "Josephs" bore; the Lord knew His prophets—from back of the beyond. Both Josephs were generous to those who betrayed them. Ancient Joseph was generous to his once-betraying brothers whom he later saved from starvation. Joseph Smith, in but one example, was generous to W. W. Phelps whose brief betrayal, ironically, helped put Joseph Smith in Liberty Jail. Both were understandably anxious about their loved ones and friends. Ancient Joseph, when his true identity became known, inquired tenderly of his brothers, "Doth my father yet live?" (Genesis 45:3.) From Liberty Jail, the Prophet Joseph Smith, doubtless with comparative awareness, wrote, "Doth my friends yet live, and if they do, do they remember me?" (*Writings*, p. 409.) (" 'A Choice Seer.' ")

Mine is an apostolic witness of Jesus, the great Redeemer of mankind. It was He who called the Prophet Joseph Smith, tutored him, and nurtured him through his adversities, which were to be "but a small moment" (D&C 121:7). Once the Prophet Joseph hoped aloud that he might so live amid his own suffering that one day he could take his place among Abraham and the "ancients," hoping to "hold an even w[e]ight in the balances with them" (*The Personal Writings of Joseph Smith*, ed. Dean C. Jessee [1984], 395). I testify that Joseph so triumphed, which is why we rightly sing of his being "crowned in the midst of the prophets of old." (*Hymns*, no. 27). (*Ensign*, January 1997, p. 41.)

JOY

Joy is nondeductible; it is an addition to one that does not require subtraction from someone else. (*Deposition*, p. 28.)

Joy is obviously of a higher order than mere pleasure. Pleasure is perishable. It has a short shelf life. Mere pleasure is not lasting, because it is constantly feeding on itself. Thus, the appetites of the natural man, though frequently fed, are never filled. ("'Brim with Joy,'" p. 144.)

Exclaiming "Joy to the world!" provides a much-needed antidote to those who say, "Eat, drink, and be merry, for tomorrow we die" (2 Nephi 28:7). Truly, "men are, that they might have joy" (2 Nephi 2:25)—unless they choose questionable, perishable pleasure instead! (*The Christmas Scene*, p. 3.)

Joy not only helps us do our gospel duties but it also increases our individuality. It is sinners who reflect such a stale sameness.

Righteousness lends itself to individuality. Think, in contrast, of poor Lemuel, who "hearkened unto the words of Laman." (1 Nephi 3:28.) He was Laman's satellite. One wonders if poor Lemuel ever had any thoughts of his own. ("'Brim with Joy,'" p. 147.)

When we reach a point of consecration, our afflictions will be swallowed up in the joy of Christ. It does not mean we won't have afflictions, but they will be put in a perspective that permits us to deal with them. With our steady pursuit of joy and with each increasing measure of righteousness, we will experience one more drop of delight—one drop after another—until, in the words of a prophet, "our hearts are brim with joy." At last, the soul's cup finally runs over! ("'Brim with Joy,'" p. 13.)

JUDGMENT

The Man of Galilee will finally judge each of us on the basis of a rigorous celestial theology, instead of the popular "no-fault theology" of this telestial world. (*Ensign*, May 1975, p. 101.)

When we are finally judged in terms of our performance in this second estate, we will see that God, indeed, is perfect in his justice and mercy. We will also see that when we fail here it will not have been because we were truly tempted above that which we were able to bear. There was always an escape hatch had we looked for it! We will also see that our lives have been fully and fairly measured. In retrospect, we will even see that our most trying years here will often have been our best years, producing large tree rings on our soul, Gethsemanes of growth! Mortality is moistened by much opportunity if our roots of resolve can but take it in. ("Taking Up the Cross," p. 253.)

JUSTICE

Moses, in that moment on Mount Pisgah overlooking the Holy Land, must have been sobered by the realization that even sterling past performance, when tarnish is present, cannot rob justice of its polishing part. (*As I Am*, p. 45.)

God's love balances justice and mercy in divine due process—beside which our mortal due process is, comparatively, either a kangaroo court or an orgy of unredeeming indulgence. (*As I Am*, p. 46.)

We must not automatically assume that time wounds all heels, for the bad are not always exposed—but eternity *will* bring a fulness of justice. (*Press Forward*, p. 32.)

The gospel guarantees ultimate, not proximate, justice. (*Press Forward*, p. 116.)

KNOWLEDGE

All knowledge is not of equal significance. There is no democracy of facts! They are not of equal importance. Something might be factual but unimportant. . . . Some truths are salvationally significant, and others are not. ("The Inexhaustible Gospel," p. 141.)

Knowledge rises with us in the resurrection, and the limitations on our luggage then will not be limitations of volume but of kind. ("Taking Up the Cross," p. 252.)

Knowledge is intended to travel in a convoy of other Christian virtues. It does not have final meaning by itself. ("The Inexhaustible Gospel," p. 141.)

The mere accumulation of knowledge without purpose and of information without wisdom constitutes ever learning but never coming to a knowledge of the truth. (See 2 Timothy 3:7.) (*Ensign*, May 1983, p. 10.)

Without divine guidance, our cerebral calisthenics, though often fascinating to engage in, can be empty exercises. (*Smallest Part*, p. 9.)

Knowledge, if possessed for its own sake and unapplied, leaves one's life unadorned. A Church member, for instance, might describe the Lord's doctrines but not qualify to enter the Lord's house. One could produce much brilliant commentary without being exemplary. One might be intellectually brilliant but Bohemian in behavior. ("The Inexhaustible Gospel," p. 141.)

Being saturated with data even brings to mind a prophecy about those who are "ever learning, and never able to come to the knowledge of the truth" (2 Timothy 3:7). Megabytes, however large and helpful, are no substitute for partaking of the bread of life. (*Endure*, p. 93.)

LAST DAYS

So as the shutters of human history begin to close as if before a gathering storm, and as events scurry across the human scene like so many leaves before a wild wind—those who stand before the warm glow of the gospel fire can be permitted a shiver of the soul. Yet in our circle of certitude, we know, even in the midst of all these things, that there will be no final frustration of God's purposes. God has known "all things from the beginning, wherefore, he prepareth a way to accomplish all his works among the children of men." (1 Nephi 9:6.) (*Ensign*, November 1981, p. 10.)

The true believer knows that in the awful winding-up scenes human deterioration will be finally and decisively and mercifully met by divine intervention. He understands, therefore, that in such conditions the sooner he renounces the world, the sooner he can help to save some souls in it. ("'True Believers in Christ,'" p. 139.)

Yes, there will be wrenching polarization on this planet, but also the remarkable reunion with our colleagues in Christ from the City of Enoch. Yes, nation after nation will become a house divided, but more and more unifying Houses of the Lord will grace this planet. Yes, Armageddon lies ahead. But so does Adam-ondi-Ahman! (*Ensign*, November 1981, p. 10.)

We are living in a time in which we shall see things both wonderful and awful. There is no way that we can be a part of the last days and have it otherwise. Even so, we are instructed by our Lord and Exemplar, Jesus Christ, to "be of good cheer." (D&C 61:36; 78:18.) (*Ensign*, November 1982, p. 66.)

We must not underestimate . . . the difficulty of the last days. Joel and Zephaniah both speak of the last days as being "a day of . . . gloominess." (Joel 2:2; Zephaniah 1:15.) The coming decades will be times of despair. Why? Because, as Moroni said, despair comes of iniquity. (See Moroni 10:22.) The more iniquity, the more despair. And unless there is widespread repentance, despair will both deepen and spread—except among those who have gospel gladness. (*Ensign*, November 1982, p. 67.)

In case you hadn't noticed it, in the last days discipleship is to be lived in *crescendo*. Our adversities and extremities will merely bring out the strong simplicities and the reassuring realities of the gospel. Likewise, brisk challenges to basic beliefs, and some afflictions, will aid in the development of even greater convictions concerning these basic beliefs. Though it will be the key doctrines which are assailed, after the dust of this dispensation has settled it will be the key doctrines which will have prevailed. (*Ensign*, November 1985, p. 15.)

What we mortals encounter as the unforeseen, God has already seen, such as how the oil deposits of this earth would shape the latter-day conflicts among nations. . . . He has anticipated the impact of continental drifts on the frequency and intensity of latter-day earthquakes. He . . . also knows where and when, in latter days, the seas' tidal waves will heave themselves savagely "beyond their bounds." (D&C 88:90.) (*Ensign*, November 1987, p. 31.)

Today, the assembled agonies of the world pass in reminding review on the nightly news. (*Ensign*, May 1988, p. 8.)

The last days will be rampant with the cardinal sins, just "as in the days of Noah." Society in the days of Noah, scriptures advise, was "corrupt before God" and "filled with violence." (Genesis 6:11–12; Moses 8:28.) Corruption and violence—sound familiar? Both of these awful conditions crest because of surging individual selfishness. When thus engulfed, no wonder men's hearts in our day will fail them because of fear. (See Luke 21:26; D&C 45:26.) Even the faithful can expect a few fibrillations. (*Ensign*, November 1990, p. 14.)

The challenge is surviving spiritually in a deteriorating "wheat and tares" world. [D&C 86:7.] Granted, occasionally a few defectors or dissidents may try to vex us as they hyperventilate over their particular concerns, but it is the engulfing effects of that deteriorating world on Church members which is the "clear and present danger." "Evils and designs" really do operate through "conspiring [individuals] in the last days." (D&C 89:4.) The Lord has even announced, "Behold, the enemy is combined." (D&C 38:12.) (*Ensign*, May 1993, p. 76.)

Even during these difficult times, members "armed with righteousness" can do so many things. (1 Nephi 14:14.) We can have love at home, even though the love of many waxes cold in the world. (See Matthew 24:12.) We can have inner peace even though peace has been taken from the earth. (See D&C 1:35.) . . . We can stand fast "in holy places," even though in the world "all things shall be in commotion." (D&C 45:32; 88:91.) (*Ensign*, May 1993, p. 79.)

In the days ahead, "all things shall be in commotion" (D&C 88:91). We may even have nostalgia for past days of obscurity (see D&C 1:30). Amid a drumroll of developments, complex and converging world conditions will bring both trials and opportunities. Faithful Church members, however, will sense the crescendo in it all, even while being carried forward on the crest of breathtaking circumstances. (*Ensign*, November 1993, p. 20.)

There is the increasing presence of choice and talent-laden spirits sent [to earth] now because of what each can add to the symphony of salvation. (*Deposition*, p. 63.)

An avalanche of apocalyptic advice from secular prophets swirls about young and old alike; there is an abundance of earnest Paul Reveres who warn us about what is coming, or is already here. (*Choose*, p. 2.)

We need not be naive about the impending realities in the prophecies, but let us not run to the foothills too soon. (*Choose*, p. 10.)

Surely those of us who live in the last days cannot expect to be immune from the sufferings and feelings that war produces. We hope, however, that we can resist the coarsening effects of war and its tendency to rob us of any progress made in developing mercy, meekness, justice, and so forth. (As I Am, p. 106.)

When we pause to think of nuclear denouement, we find it almost instantly unthinkable. Yet we know that it is avoidable if mankind will keep God's commandments. If we do not, then again, as God told us (long before man so worried about incinerating the world), the earth can be destroyed by fire. The outcome turns on whether mankind chooses to respond as in Nineveh or as in Sodom, for those are now the choices; Eden is long since behind us! (As I Am, p. 106.)

Today's world trembles because of ancient grievances and hatreds, now nourished anew amid growing nuclear capacity. (Precious Things, p. 73.)

It is clear to all thoughtful souls that life on this planet is precariously perched as never before—except for the days of Noah and the deluge. (Sermons, p. 27.)

The "whole earth shall be in commotion" [D&C 45:26], contributing undoubtedly to a condition in which "men's hearts shall fail them" and in which fear "shall come upon all people" [D&C 88:91]. Some of that fear will exist because of "those things which are coming" [Luke 21:26]. Much of this "commotion" may be geophysical, with earthquakes, seas heaving themselves beyond their bounds, and other cataclysmic events. . . . But the basic unsettlement of "all things" may reflect the seismology of a sensual, secular society. The sense of being unanchored will be pervasive. (Sermons, pp. 28–29.)

To ponder signs without becoming paranoid, to be aware without frantically matching current events with expectations, using energy that should be spent in other ways—these are our tasks. (*Power*, p. 20.)

Latter-day Saints need to remember that we who live now are being called upon to work out our salvation in a special time of intense and immense challenges—the last portion of the dispensation of the fulness of times during which great tribulation and temptation will occur, the elect will almost be deceived, and unrighteous people will be living much as they were in the days of Noah. . . . Therefore, though we have rightly applauded our ancestors for their spiritual achievements (and do not and must not discount them now), those of us who prevail today will have done no small thing. The special spirits who have been reserved to live in this time of challenges and who overcome will one day be praised for their stamina by those who pulled handcarts. (*Notwithstanding*, pp. 18–19.)

The gigantic, global collapse that is yet to come will not be that of a failing stock market, but the fall of hardened mindsets and collective pride when it all finally tumbles. (*Meek*, p. 53.)

In the topsy-turvy last days, it is important to realize that as "the eternal purposes of the Lord shall roll on," His disciples will surely know what it is to be tumbled. (Mormon 8:22.) It will be no time to be proud, especially when the tumblings may not at the moment seem purposeful. Yet the Lord's work will roll on; His meek disciples will understand. (*Meek*, p. 56.)

We do not worship a God who simply forecasts a generally greater frequency of earthquakes in the last days before the second coming of His Son. He knows precisely when and where all these will occur. God has even prophesied that the Mount of Olives will cleave in twain at a precise latter-day time as Israel is besieged. (Zechariah 14:4.) (*Experience*, p. 7.)

The young will live to see a certain madness in some majorities in the world in a way heretofore thought impossible. Pilate yielded Barabbas instead of Jesus to just such a crowd. Someone has recently coined what is called the Gadarene Swine Law, which is, simply put, that just because a group is in formation does not mean that it is going in the right direction. (*Experience*, pp. 63–64.)

These are the winding-up times when there will be a dramatic convergence of the growth of the Church and an intensification of evil in the world—all of which will make for some real wrenching. (*Experience*, p. 101.)

Staying close to the prophets will be vital since, in some ways, the last days in this last dispensation may come to resemble the first days in this dispensation. The middle period through which the Church has recently passed has been essentially a pleasant period—full of growth, understanding, and even some acclaim from the world. But the last days, although they will be characterized by much growth, will also be characterized by much tribulation and difficulty. There will be both wonderful and awful things. (*Experience*, p. 121.)

LAWS

The rules of the spiritual universe are as demanding as those of the physical universe. The immutable laws which must be obeyed for happiness on this spaceship Earth are just as fixed as the physical laws which we also violate at our own peril. (*Choose*, p. 45.)

The Gospel is the counsel of a Super Intelligence as to how we can progress in a cold universe which responds only to law. Man did not get to the moon with random trajectories and with each astronaut "doing his own thing." The price for reaching the moon was obedience to universal law. (*Choose*, p. 22.)

LEADERSHIP

Since the plan of salvation is aimed at our individual spiritual development, it is well for us to take account of life's high-risk situations. One tremendous risk is possessing power, though this is a circumstance for which many crave (see D&C 121:34–46). There is currently much fascination with empowerment but very little interest in the everlasting significance of the attribute of meekness, which was so perfectly embodied in the character of Jesus, our great Exemplar. (*Faith*, p. 45.)

As the Lord's undershepherds, let us take preventive care to set a prudent pace for Church activities and extra financial contributions. The Lord wants dedication, not prostration! (*Ensign*, May 1982, p. 38.)

Imperfect people are, in fact, called by our perfect Lord to assist in his work. (*Ensign*, May 1982, p. 38.)

Prophets need tutoring, as do we all. However, this is something the Lord seems quite able to manage without requiring a host of helpers. The Lord provides discreet but needed feedback, as He did to Peter by the shattering sound of a rooster crowing (see Luke 22:54–62), or to an undelegating Moses through a caring, observing, and wise father-in-law—without Jethro's placing an ad in the *Sinai Sentinel* (see Exodus 18:13–16). (*Ensign*, May 1982, p. 39.)

Sometimes, brothers and sisters, we do too much comparing and too little following. Sometimes also a few resent God's having chosen someone else; perceiving themselves as passed over, they then go under spiritually. (*Ensign*, November 1988, p. 32.)

Often, those who quest for a share in decision-making really do not want power, but merely proximity to the process. A wise leader can often provide this without risking his "sense of command." (*Smallest Part*, p. 56.)

No leader can be fully effective without love, and those who try to serve without it will not be properly motivated and may even feel resentment and a sense of slavery. (*Excellent*, p. 9.)

Personality and *eternity* are irretrievably enmeshed with each other, and leadership is the critical catalyst that can aid the development of the former in order to give greater meaning to the latter. (*Excellent*, p. 1.)

Trying to describe leadership is like having several viewers trying to compare what they see in a kaleidoscope when the mere act of passing the kaleidoscope shakes up its design. (*Excellent*, p. 15.)

Good leaders and followers need to store up "gladness" from previous experiences in order to weather out the tests and the buffetings of today and tomorrow in their relationships. (*Excellent*, p. 51.)

Most followers ultimately like a leader who makes reasonable demands of them, who expects performance and who praises and reproves accordingly. Of course, all of this must be done in the spirit of real love. (*Excellent*, p. 92.)

We ought to listen as carefully to those we supervise as to those who supervise us. You and I are usually pretty good at paying attention upward, but we are not nearly as good at heeding that which comes from other directions. Likewise, while parents are to teach their children, my, how we can learn from them at times! Some of us are humble up but not humble down. (*Experience*, pp. 77–78.)

LIFE

Individual development sometimes requires the march of a Zion's camp, or an arduous Hole in the Rock trek, or special classrooms like the settlements in northern Mexico, wherein special individuals were fashioned. Those episodes, however, had nothing to do with real estate but everything to do with our second estate! (*Ensign*, May 1984, p. 22.)

This life is the second estate over the prospects of which we once shouted for joy (Job 38:7), even though there may be brief moments when we might wonder what all that shouting was about. (*Not My Will*, p. 113.)

In some ways, our second estate, in relationship to our first estate, is like agreeing in advance to surgery. Then the anesthetic of forgetfulness settles in upon us. Just as doctors do not de-anesthetize a patient in the midst of authorized surgery to ask him again if the surgery should be continued, so, after divine tutoring, we once agreed to come here and to submit ourselves to certain experiences and have no occasion to revoke that decision. ("Meeting the Challenges of Today," pp. 151–52.)

It is an incredible irony . . . that some complainingly attempt to use the very tutoring process of the Lord against Him. Or resent the reality that we are to walk by faith during this mortal experience. (*Ensign*, May 1984, p. 22.)

A superficial view of this life . . . will not do, lest we mistakenly speak of this mortal experience only as coming here to get a body, as if we were merely picking up a suit at the cleaners. Or, lest we casually recite how we have come here to be proved, as if a few brisk push-ups and deep knee bends would do. (*Ensign*, May 1985, p. 71.)

One's life . . . is brevity compared to eternity—like being dropped off by a parent for a day at school. But what a day! (*Ensign*, November 1985, p. 17.)

I believe with all my heart that because God loves us there are some particularized challenges that he will deliver to each of us. He will customize the curriculum for each of us in order to teach us the things we most need to know. He will set before us in life what we need; not always what we like. And this will require us to accept with all our hearts the truth that there is divine design in each of our lives and that we have rendezvous to keep, individually and collectively. ("But for a Small Moment," p. 444.)

God gives to us the lessons we need most, not always the ones we think we need. ("Insights from My Life," p. 191.)

In fact, is not managing life's *little* challenges so often the *big* challenge? Those who wait for a single, spectacular, final exam are apt to flunk the daily quizzes. ("'Thanks Be to God,'" p. 10.)

Our second estate can be a first-class experience only if you and I develop a patient faith in God and in His unfolding purposes. ("Patience," p. 215.)

The seeming flat periods of life give us a blessed chance to reflect upon what is past as well as to be readied for some rather stirring climbs ahead. Instead of grumbling and murmuring, we should be consolidating and reflecting, which would not be possible if life were an uninterrupted sequence of fantastic scenery, confrontive events, and exhilarating conversation. . . . We should savor even the seemingly ordinary times, for life cannot be made up all of kettledrums and crashing cymbals. There must be some flutes and violins. Living cannot be all crescendo; there must be some dynamic contrast. ("Patience," p. 217.)

Let the kaleidoscope of life's circumstances be shaken, again and again, and the "true believer of Christ" will still see "with the eye of faith" divine design and purpose in his life. ("'True Believers in Christ,'" p. 139.)

Life is conditioning. It is not a neutral experience. Life is not a limpid pool on which we just float motionless; it is an often-stormy sea with crosscurrents and riptides. (*Deposition*, p. 21.)

Life is neither a pleasure palace through whose narrow portals we pass briefly, laughingly, and heedlessly before extinction, nor is it a cruel, terminal predicament in an immense and sad wasteland. It is the middle (but briefest) estate of the three estates in man's carefully constructed continuum of experience. (*Deposition*, p. 80.)

Life isn't a sandpile to which we go to each day to start from scratch—we inherit yesterday. (*Choose*, p. 13.)

Life in the world is too compromising, too corrosive for most; marching to a celestial cadence requires the meekness of Moses and the simple trust in God that David had when he went forth "in the name of the Lord of hosts" with a sling and five smooth stones. (*Choose,* p. 44.)

We live amid divine design in the enveloping empire of Elohim! (*Flood,* p. 26.)

Once persuaded that life is a continuum, and likewise that one will never cease to exist, and further that the wrongs we do must be painfully undone and any missteps retraced—once so persuaded, how careful we then are concerning what we do and what we think and what we become! This macro and spiritual view is, of course, in stark contrast to those who urge, "Eat, drink, and be merry," because "you only live once!" The gospel response to that assertion is: "Yes, we only live once, but that once is forever!" (*Sermons,* pp. 63–64.)

Our first estate featured learning of a cognitive type, and it was surely a much longer span than that of our second estate, and the tutoring so much better and more direct. The second estate, however, is one that emphasizes *experiential learning* through *applying,* *proving,* and *testing.* We learn cognitively here too, just as a good university examination also teaches even as it tests us. In any event, the books of the first estate are now closed to us, and the present test is, therefore, very real. We have moved, as it were, from first-estate *theory* to second-estate *laboratory.* It is here that our Christlike characteristics are further shaped and our spiritual skills are thus strengthened. (*Experience,* pp. 19–20.)

Life is a school in which we enrolled not only voluntarily but rejoicingly; and if the school's Headmaster employs a curriculum— proven, again and again on other planets, to bring happiness to participants—and if we agreed that once we were enrolled there would be no withdrawals, and also to undergo examinations that would truly test our ability and perceptivity, what would an experienced Headmaster do if, later on, there were complaints? Especially if, in His seeming absence, many of the school children tore up their guiding notebooks and demanded that He stop the examinations since these produced some pain? (*Experience*, p. 27.)

Just as no two snowflakes are precisely alike in design, so the configurations of life's challenges differ also. (*Experience*, p. 48.)

When life is seen as good, a bad day can easily be absorbed. (*Experience*, p. 84.)

Our misuse and abuse of [moral] agency tells us awful things about ourselves! Unsurprisingly, this mortal school, constructed to help us overcome our frailties, creates a history replete with mistakes. But we should not blame the school! Nor the curriculum! Least of all, the Schoolmaster! Besides, finishing schools have a way of knocking off the rough edges. So the debris of our deficiencies, the morass of our mistakes, is of our own making, like tailings around a mine or litter in a nursery. (*We Talk of Christ*, pp. 81–82.)

Clearly, whatever degree of spiritual progress we achieved in the first estate, certain experiences are unique with the second estate. Some of the curriculum carries over, but certain "courses" are offered for the first time here in mortality. Such experiences are largely those associated with learning to subject a mortal body to the things of the Spirit, such as in connection with the law of chastity. (*Prove*, p. 47.)

Life is not intended to be lived in an idyllic Eden. Spiritual submissiveness includes our acceptance of the ups and downs of life. (*Not My Will*, p. 8.)

We should see life . . . as being comprised of clusters of soul-stretching experiences, even when these are overlain by seeming ordinariness or are plainly wrapped in routine. Thus some who are chronologically very young can be Methuselahs as to their maturity in spiritual things. (*Not My Will*, p. 118.)

LIGHT

You and I in our own little circles have been placed here to light up the landscape of life for others, frail and flickering as our own flames seem at times. (*Press Forward*, p. 26.)

Any man may blink as the rays of morning first touch his eyes, but some blink and then turn with irritation away from all light. So it is also when some men encounter an individual illuminated by the light of truth. (*Look Back*, p. 13.)

When the light of the gospel was bent by processing it through a pharisaic prism, it lost its fulness as Jesus so often noted during his ministry. When the light of the gospel was processed through the labyrinth of legalism, it was not only less illuminating, it was distorted. In the case of the Pharisees, scribes, and lawyers, the lessened illumination and the distortion in perspective resulted in a tragic inversion of values. (*Smallest Part*, p. 25.)

Who better than the Light of the world can decide the degree of divine disclosure—whether it is to be flashlights or floodlights? (*As I Am*, p. 120.)

It is not surprising that we should squint and even shield our eyes momentarily—being in some degree in darkness—when we are first struck by the light of the gospel. The danger is that our defensive reflexes will cause us, in effect, to pull down the shade or to tell someone resentfully to put out the light. (*My Family*, p. 26.)

This matter . . . of being a light is even more important in dark times. Our impact, for better or worse, on others is inevitable, but it is intended that we be a light and not just another shadow. (*My Family*, p. 86.)

The same God that placed that star in a precise orbit millennia before it appeared over Bethlehem in celebration of the birth of the Babe has given at least equal attention to placement of each of us in precise human orbits so that we may, if we will, illuminate the landscape of our individual lives, so that our light may not only lead others but warm them as well. (*My Family*, p. 86.)

The light at the end of the tunnel of time is the light of Christ. Happily, while in the darkness of that same tunnel of time each of us is given, at the start of the journey, a portion of the light of Christ. (*Press Forward*, p. 19.)

Sometimes in the deepest darkness there is no external light—only an inner light to guide and to reassure. (*Ensign*, November 1994, p. 35.)

LONELINESS

Widows and widowers whose deprivation stretches into years when the caress of dimmed memories is insufficient, sometimes sob to see purpose in it all. However, they will later know moments when the Lord shall "wipe away tears from off all faces" (Isaiah 25:8). Meanwhile, they can truly testify, "Yet thou art there!" (*Ensign*, November 1987, p. 32.)

LONG-SUFFERING

Our merciful and long-suffering Lord is ever ready to help. His "arm is lengthened out all the day long" (2 Nephi 28:32), and even if His arm goes ungrasped, it was unarguably there! In the same redemptive reaching out, our desiring to improve our human relationships usually requires some long-suffering. Sometimes reaching out is like trying to pat a porcupine. Even so, the accumulated quill marks are evidence that our hands of fellowship have been stretched out, too. (*Ensign*, November 1996, p. 22.)

In the spiritual scheme of things, the lubricant of long-suffering is vital. We depend constantly upon the Lord's long-suffering, but must develop that same virtue ourselves. (*Believe*, p. 12.)

Of all the Father's and Jesus' perfected virtues, the two most to be celebrated in connection with the plan of salvation and the Atonement are their *loving-kindness* and their *long-suffering*, qualities which equipped Jesus to accomplish the Atonement (see 1 Nephi 19:9). These virtues in Him will evoke our everlasting praise. In fact, we will gladly praise His loving-kindness and long-suffering "for ever and ever" (D&C 133:52.) (*Faith*, p. 30.)

LOOKING BEYOND THE MARK

Jacob censured the "stiffnecked" Jews for "looking beyond the mark" (Jacob 4:14). We are looking beyond the mark today, for example, if we are more interested in the physical dimensions of the cross than in what Jesus achieved thereon; or when we neglect Alma's words on faith because we are too fascinated by the light-shielding hat reportedly used by Joseph Smith during some of the translating of the Book of Mormon. To neglect substance while focusing on process is another form of unsubmissively looking beyond the mark. (*Not My Will,* p. 26.)

LOSING ONESELF

Losing oneself means losing concern over getting credit; by knowing our true identity we need not be concerned about seeming anonymity. It likewise means losing our desire to be in the driver's seat; putting our shoulder to the wheel is enough. It means that eagles meekly serve under sparrows—without worrying over comparative wingspans or plumage. (*Flood,* p. 99.)

Losing oneself means yielding the substance of one's own agendum if it does not match the agendum of the Lord. It means losing those elements of our leadership style which are not consistent with His. (*Flood,* p. 99.)

LOVE

The relevancy of "love thy neighbor," if practiced successfully "here and now," one day will demonstrate how it will be applied in the coming "there and then"—in a neighborhood as wide as the universe! (*Endure*, p. 98.)

The lubricant of love must be used in generous proportions. (*Choose*, p. 4.)

Celestial customs will invariably refuse admission to a disciple devoid of love. (*Choose*, p. 16.)

Charity initiates and sustains all the other spiritual qualities in much the same way that courage sustains these qualities at the testing point. ("'Brim with Joy,'" p. 147.)

Has not the Lord with equal truth and relevance told us concerning the resources of this planet, "For the earth is full, and there is enough and to spare"? [D&C 104:17.] Should not this reality sober us in terms of what might be achieved as regards poverty? Clearly, it is the attribute of love, not other resources, that is in short supply—a scarcity that inevitably means misery. (*As I Am*, p. 25.)

Too often we behave as if we were in massive competition with others for God's love. But we have His love; it is our love of Him that remains to be proven, such as through service to others. (*As I Am*, p. 63.)

The adversary, who displays no true love, has sought (with renewed efforts in recent times) to cripple the family, the natural locus of so much love. The adversary, interestingly enough, has even tried to ruin the word *love* itself, making it seem to be a one-dimensional thing, a base act instead of a grand thing. If the adversary could have his way, loving would mean only copulating—and even that in violation of the seventh commandment. Such a narrowing is nonsense, for it is like saying that freedom is merely voting or that literature is simply words in print. (*Experience*, p. 53.)

Love is never wasted, for its value does not rest upon reciprocity. (*Press Forward*, p. 37.)

MANKIND

The perceptions necessary for the ultimate diagnosis of human ills are, in my judgment, contained in the Gospel of Jesus Christ. Some secular prescriptions, ironically, would amount to giving mankind an aspirin when surgery is required. (*Choose*, p. 15.)

We are living on a small planet that is part of a very modest solar system, which, in turn, is located at the outer edge of the awesome Milky Way galaxy. If we were sufficiently distant from the Milky Way, it would be but another bright dot among countless other bright dots in space, all of which could cause us to conclude comparatively, "that man is nothing." (Moses 1:10.) Yet we are rescued by reassuring realities such as that God knows and loves each of us, personally and perfectly. Hence, there is incredible intimacy in the vastness of it all. Are not the very hairs of one's head numbered? Is not the fall of each sparrow noticed? (Matthew 10:29–30.) Has Jesus not borne, and therefore knows, our individual sins, sicknesses, and infirmities? (Alma 7:11–12.) (*Prove*, pp. 1–2.)

MARRIAGE

Why should it surprise us that life's most demanding tests as well as life's most significant opportunities for growth in life usually occur within marriage and the family? How can revolving door relationships, by contrast, be a real test of our capacity to love? (*Prove*, p. 9.)

Brethren, marry someone who is your better in some respects; and, sisters, do likewise, so that your eternal partnership is one of compensating competencies. ("Taking Up the Cross," p. 251.)

Mormon marriages ought not to be marriages in which men are the theologians and women are the Christians; we must press forward together, for men cannot finally go anywhere that matters without women. (*Press Forward*, p. 127.)

MEEKNESS

We admire boldness and dash, but boldness and dash can so easily slip into pomp and panache. By contrast, the meek are able with regularity to peel off the encrustations of ego that form on one's soul like barnacles on a ship. (*Precious Things*, p. 54.)

The meek . . . make stepping-stones of stumbling blocks. (*Meek*, p. 57.)

If meek, we will place all we have on the altar of the Lord and will not ask for a receipt! ("'Meek and Lowly.'")

Occasionally, as we all know, backing off is really going forward. (*Ensign*, May 1989, p. 62.)

Can we remain silent when silence is eloquence—but may be used against us? (*Ensign*, May 1989, p. 64.)

Meekness ranks so low on the mortal scale of things, yet so high on God's: "For none is acceptable before God, save the meek and lowly in heart" (Moroni 7:44). ("'Meek and Lowly,'" p. 53.)

In one of the rarer moments in holy writ, we hear the voice of the Father: "And I heard a voice from the Father saying: Yea, the words of my Beloved are true and faithful." (2 Nephi 31:15.) The meekness of the Father was such that He testified to the truthfulness of what His Son taught. Think, too, about the appearances of the Father with the Son. Never does the Father upstage His Son. There is a kind of *majestic mutual meekness with the Father and the Son.* Jesus is ever deferential to the Father. ("The Book of Mormon: A Marvelous Work and a Wonder," Seminar.)

If sufficient meekness is in us, it will not only help us to jettison unneeded burdens, but will also keep us from becoming mired in the ooze of self-pity. Furthermore, true meekness has a metabolism that actually requires very little praise or recognition—of which there is usually such a shortage anyway. ("'Meek and Lowly,'" p. 55.)

Meekness is thus so much more than a passive attribute that merely deflects discourtesy. Instead, it involves spiritual and intellectual activism. ("'Meek and Lowly,'" p. 57.)

Meekness also protects us from the fatigue of being easily offended. There are so many just waiting to be offended. They are so alerted to the possibility that they will not be treated fairly, they almost invite the verification of their expectations! The meek, not posted on such a fatiguing alert, find rest from this form of fatigue. ("'Meek and Lowly,'" p. 57.)

One day [the Lord] will share all he has with the meek. For everyone else, whatever their temporary possessions, the Creator's reversion clause will take effect. ("'Meek and Lowly,'" p. 60.)

Meekness constitutes a continuing invitation to continuing education. No wonder the Lord reveals His secrets to the meek, for they are "easy to be entreated." (Alma 7:23.) (Precious Things, pp. 54–55.)

Lest we worry overmuch that our meekness might be an open invitation for others to abuse us, it is well to note some of its less-understood features. For example, meekness may not always "win," especially in worldly matters or in the short run; but in the long run the meek will inherit the earth. (Men and Women, p. 59.)

Genius is safest when accompanied by meekness. Competency is most useful when accompanied by humility. The qualities of love, mercy, patience, meekness, and spiritual submissiveness are portable. These—to the degree developed—will go with us through the veil of death; they will also rise with us in the resurrection. (On Becoming a Disciple-Scholar, pp. 19–20.)

Human suffering does not automatically produce sweetness and character unless meekness is present. Meekness is the mulch that must go in the soil of adversity in order for empathy to grow and in order for character to grow. Jesus could not have become the most empathetic person had he not been the most meek person. ("'Build Up My Church,' 'Establish the [Lord's] Righteousness.'")

In Jesus' spiritual submissiveness there was the shining but subdued elegance of marvelous meekness. On our small scale initial meekness may consist of being willing simply to give place to develop that which is lacking in our faith. We are not far into the process of giving place before we encounter our well-developed selfishness. Our schedule is too full to visit the sick. Other papers must be attended to before scriptures can be searched. Private prayers are put off till weariness limits both the quality and the quantity of our pleadings and appreciations. The cares of the world crowd out inward and reflective worship at a sacrament meeting. (Men and Women, p. 104.)

Meekness enables us, after a tumble [from the peak of pride], to pick ourselves up but without putting others down blamefully. (Meek, p. 58.)

When the Lord declared, "My sheep hear my voice, . . . and they follow me" (John 10:27), it was not only an indication that a profound process of recognition and familiarity would be at work; it also bespoke the role of operational meekness—listening long and humbly enough for the recognition to occur. (Meek, p. 67.)

Meekness not only dampens our cravings for ascendancy but also helps us avoid needless pique over the ascendancy of others. (Meek, p. 94.)

A true community of Saints will . . . have a high ratio of those who are meek, being low demanders and high performers. (Endure, p. 98.)

MEMORIES

Memories can become the vigilant sentries needed to challenge our marauding moods, moods which otherwise would carry the day and especially the night! Those sentries can both prod us and point us to the strait and narrow path. (*Flood*, p. 59.)

Caution is called for as to what we choose each day to put in our storehouses of memory. It is a blessed condition if we can be nourished later therefrom rather than remembering with regret. (*Endure*, p. 64.)

MERCY

Let us be merciful with each other. We certainly do not criticize hospital patients amid intensive care for looking pale and preoccupied. Why then those recovering from surgery on their souls? No need for us to stare; those stitches will finally come out. And in this hospital, too, it is important for everyone to remember that the hospital chart is not the patient. (*Ensign*, May 1991, pp. 90–91.)

Life's comparatively few ironies are much more than offset by heaven's many mercies! We cannot count all our blessings every day, but we can carry over the reassuring bottom line from the last counting. (*Ensign*, May 1989, p. 64.)

One important point that must be made about the quality of the eternal attributes: In acknowledging His patience or mercy, even when we do it worshipfully, we are only acknowledging mercy and

patience as we now know them. His perfection of these two attributes places His mercy and patience (and this is true also with all
the other virtues) almost beyond our reach or understanding. The
most clear-cut and laudatory act of mercy we have known or the
most superlative display of patience within our experience does
not even approach His mercy and patience. At best, our degree of
development is only "a type and shadow of things which are to
come." (As I Am, p. 35.)

MILLENNIUM

That millenarian moment will not spring out of senates, will not
be propelled by mortal proclamations, and will not be traceable to
treaties. Rather, the King, Jesus Christ, will have first established
His kingdom and His people, physically and spiritually, and He
will then come and judge all societies according to His standards,
not secular standards. (Press Forward, p. 5.)

MIRACLES

Having daily access to the Spirit . . . is better than periodic miracles. (Faith, p. 113.)

Seeing a prodigal return . . . is a marvelous thing. To see someone,
in the words of scripture, who comes to himself and resolves that "I
will go to my Father" is a marvelous journey for someone to make.
The joy comes in seeing someone who has been crusty and difficult
to deal with become more meek, or to see a family really come to

love and appreciate each other. Those are the real miracles. The multitude were fed five thousand loaves and fishes, yet they were hungry again the next day. But Jesus is the Bread of Life, and if we partake thereof then we will never be hungry again. The most lasting miracles are the miracles of transformation in people's lives. These give one much joy, and while we can't cause these to happen, the Lord lets us, at times, be instruments in that process. This brings us great joy. (*Searching for God in America*, p. 143.)

MIRTH

There is a special gladness that goes with the gospel, and appropriate merriment. Yes, there is a mirth that can be heard among mortals who are estranged from the living God and from things as they really are. But it is a melancholy mirth. (*Really Are*, p. xiv.)

MISSIONARY WORK AND RETENTION

It is important in our relationships with our fellowmen that we approach them as neighbors and as brothers and sisters rather than coming at them flinging theological thunderbolts. (*Press Forward*, p. 127.)

How vital it is that the sheaves (the bundles of converts) are gathered safely into the granary or the garner of the Church. Otherwise, the winds and storms will scatter, destroy, and waste the sheaves. ("Coordination of Full-time and Stake Missionary Work.")

When the Lord directs us to "bring many souls unto me," this means bringing them all the way into the garner of the Church—not simply dropping them off just outside the door. . . . Clearly, when we baptize, our eyes should gaze beyond the baptismal font to the Holy Temple. The great garner into which the "sheaves" should be finally gathered is the Holy Temple! (Satellite, Missionary Training.)

Sometimes even the most articulate and inspiring words fail to bring the desired change because of the hearer's refusal to listen, but we need to be ready even if he is not. Ready not only with content, but with conviction. A casual, uncaring testimony may not be an effective witness at all. (*Choose*, p. 74.)

MISTAKES

We should, of course, learn from our mistakes, but without forever studying the instant replays as if these were the game of life itself. (*Ensign*, November 1976, p. 14.)

We do notice each other's weaknesses. But we should not celebrate them. Let us be grateful for the small strides that we and others make, rather than rejoice in the shortfalls. And when mistakes occur, let them become instructive, not destructive. (*Ensign*, May 1982, p. 39.)

Big mistakes are made over such little things! Little sparks can start such big bonfires. It is well that the sturdy shield of faith can be used not only to quench fiery darts (see Ephesians 6:16) but also to extinguish the small sparks struck by the flint of frustration. In daily life the shield of faith must be ever ready as well as ever sturdy. (*Faith*, p. 91.)

MODERATION

We are rediscovering "moderation" and seeing afresh the importance of "quiet," of "smallness," and of "green." Sound at shock levels, dazzling strobe lights which titillate the senses, if not overwhelm them, are a poor preparation for those who want to see a sunset or watch the grass grow. (*Choose*, pp. 70–71.)

MOODS

Sometimes we make unrealistic demands of life. We seem to expect an unbroken string of green lights and a parking space just in front of every destination—with some time left on the parking meter—or else we have had a bad day. Thus, when little things don't go right, our moods darken with regard to the truly big things when there is no real justification for such. (*Deposition*, pp. 34–35.)

Our faith must ride out our moods, or our discipleship will be too much at the mercy of mood, men, and circumstances. (*Press Forward*, p. 35.)

Our moods do change, so we need to distinguish between a mood and a basic belief. The Book of Mormon doesn't become untrue because we have had a bad day! (*Press Forward*, p. 62.)

Despair about life and about self is a different thing from the transitory moods that may pass over us. The doctrines of the Church can help us to deal with despair, but moodiness seems best dealt with by service and by prayer. Turning inward is a form of looking back, whereas looking out for others requires just that—looking outward. (*Press Forward*, p. 64.)

Do not let your moods maul your faith. Do not allow the absence of social life and dates to color your attitude toward your rendezvous with the resurrection. Do not let a bad day cause you to think that life is bad. ("'All Hell Is Moved,'" p. 179.)

It is so easy for one person's bad day to become another person's bad day. A spreading electrical power outage ends up affecting everybody, because early on, the discipline required was abandoned in favor of passing the problem along. Emotional electricity is much like the real thing. (*Press Forward*, p. 63.)

MORALITY

Only a schizoid society could sanction the delusion that there is a private morality apart from public morality. There are not "indoor" and "outdoor" sets of Ten Commandments! (*Deposition*, p. 21.)

Those committed to the keeping of the stern but sweet seventh commandment in a time of increasing immorality will need to be special. Average won't do now, anymore than average was adequate in the days of Sodom and Gomorrah. (*Ensign*, February 1986, p. 19.)

Diminished moral cleanliness means diminished service to mankind, because uncleanliness dulls the tastebuds of the soul and renders us less sensitive to others, to the beauties of life, and to the promptings of the Spirit. (*Ensign*, February 1986, p. 19.)

Sexual immorality is not only wrong itself, but, as few things do, it nurtures the deadly virus of selfishness. (*Ensign*, February 1986, p. 19.)

If Jesus were only a man, albeit a very good man, His counsel is merely that of a meridian moralist. It is quite another thing, however, for the Creator of multiple worlds, whose central concern is our individual happiness, to command, "Thou shalt not commit adultery." Our task, therefore, is to "reconcile [ourselves] to the will of God, and not to the will of . . . the flesh" (2 Nephi 10:24). (*Ensign*, May 1987, p. 70.)

Our commerce must be the commerce of Christ, for the morals of the marketplace matter and do find their way into families. (*Heart*, p. 20.)

The old mountains of individual morality have been worn down. This erosion has left mankind in a sand-dune society, in a desert of disbelief, where there are no landmarks, no north, no east, no west, and no south. There is only the windblown dust of despair! (*Deposition*, p. 80.)

We spend billions for the rightful rehabilitation of victims of plagues, but only comparative pennies to preach prevention. Jeers even greet those who advocate healthy abstention from various self-destructive acts. (*Believe*, p. 76.)

Moral uncertainty always leads to behavioral absurdity, and prescriptions that are value-free always prove finally to be so costly. Yet absurdity about immorality is achieving a certain momentum today. (*Notwithstanding*, p. 91.)

MORTALITY

Our eventual place in eternity turns on whether our knees bend or shake and what we think and do in daily life. (*Faith*, p. 100.)

Mortality involves teeth to be brushed, beds to be made, cars to be repaired, diapers to be changed, groceries to be bought—such an endless array of mundane matters. In the midst of these, however, is the real business of living—a friendship to be formed, a marriage to be mended, a child to be encouraged, a truth to be driven home, an apology to be made, a Christian attribute to be further developed. (*Not My Will*, p. 125.)

The general proving process of mortality is really the stunning sum of its billions of individual subsets, all of which are overseen by an all-knowing and all-loving Father and Son. But, though overseen by Them, we must, through the mists of the moment, keep our eyes on Them; there is actually nowhere else to look. (*As I Am*, pp. 60–61.)

Someday, when we look back on mortality, we will see that so many of the things that seemed to matter so much at the moment will be seen not to have mattered at all. (*As I Am*, p. 104.)

Mortality, this precious micro-dot on the canvas of eternity, is such a brief moment. While in it, we are to prepare ourselves for the time when there will be no time. (*Not My Will*, p. 11.)

Without our individual refining . . . life would become merely a pass-through, audited course—not a course for credit. . . . Mortality therefore is not a convenient, suburban drive-around beltway with a view. Instead it passes slowly through life's inner city. Daily it involves real perspiration, real perplexity, real choosing, real suffering—and real refining! (*Endure*, p. 8.)

Some of us approach our experience in this mortal school as if it were to be mostly relaxing recesses with only the occasional irritant of summoning bells. In fact, any recesses are merely for renewal and for catching one's breath; and these are not to become a prolonged sigh of relief that introduces protracted leisure or languor. (*Endure*, p. 123.)

MOTHERS

We salute you, sisters, for the joy that is yours as you rejoice in a baby's first smile and as you listen with eager ear to a child's first day at school which bespeaks a special selflessness. Women, more quickly than others, will understand the possible dangers when the word *self* is militantly placed before other words like *fulfillment*. You rock a sobbing child without wondering if today's world is passing you by, because you know you hold tomorrow tightly in your arms. (*Ensign*, May 1978, p. 10.)

The devoted wife and mother who is a quiet but effective neighbor but whose obituary is noticed by a comparative few may well have laid up precious little here in the current coin-of-the-realm, recognition, yet rising with her in the resurrection will be relevant attributes and skills honed and refined in family and neighborhood life. ("Grounded, Rooted, Established, and Settled," p. 18.)

Priesthood and motherhood are the perfect partnership! (*Deposition*, p. 82.)

God trusts women so much that He lets them bear and care for His spirit children. (*Ensign*, May 1978, p. 10.)

Some mothers in today's world feel "cumbered" by home duties and are thus attracted by other more "romantic" challenges. Such women could make the same error of perspective that Martha made. The woman, for instance, who deserts the cradle in order to help defend civilization against the barbarians may well later meet, among the barbarians, her own neglected child. (*Press Forward*, p. 101.)

MURMURING

Those of deep faith do not murmur. They are generously disposed, and they are reluctant to murmur, even while in deep difficulties. (*Ensign*, November 1989, p. 84.)

Strange, isn't it, brothers and sisters, how those with the shortest memories have the longest lists of demands! (*Ensign*, November 1989, p. 83.)

Perhaps when we murmur we are unconsciously complaining over not being able to cut a special deal with the Lord. We want full blessings but without full obedience to the laws upon which those blessings are predicated. (*Ensign*, November 1989, p. 83.)

Damage to ourselves is sufficient reason to resist murmuring, but another obvious danger is its contagiousness. . . . Instead of murmuring, therefore, being of good cheer is what is needed, and being of good cheer is equally contagious. (*Ensign*, November 1989, p. 84.)

Murmuring can also be noisy enough that it drowns out the various spiritual signals to us, signals which tell us in some cases to quit soaking ourselves indulgently in the hot tubs of self-pity! Murmuring over the weight of our crosses not only takes energy otherwise needed to carry them but might cause another to put down his cross altogether. (*Ensign*, November 1989, p. 85.)

One of the great risks of murmuring is that we can get too good at it, too clever. We can even acquire too large an audience. Furthermore, what for the murmurer may only be transitory grumbles may become a cause for a hearer that may carry him or her clear out of the Church. ("'Meek and Lowly,'" p. 58.)

Muttering and murmuring are often the expressions of our conscience gone grumpy; it is precisely because we know we need to respond affirmatively (and have some inkling about what's coming) that we let off steam—we start puffing *in advance* of the climb. (*Deposition*, p. 31.)

Murmurers make good conversational cloakholders (see Acts 7:58). Though picking up no stones themselves, they provoke others to do so. (*Flood*, p. 64.)

Brigham Young called for us to be faithful even if circumstances are "darker than 10,000 midnights" [*JD* 3:207]. Some of us murmur even when only the dusk of difficulty appears. (*Believe*, p. 3.)

Murmurers (and each of us has no doubt taken a turn at it) have sharp tongues and dull memories! Perhaps, too, if the journeying Nephite women can be cited [see 1 Nephi 17:1–2], we need the equivalent of basic rations in our diet and less French pastry before we can settle in for the long journey. We, too, must learn to depend upon the Lord for our manna and our daily bread, and to be of good cheer as He leads us along. (*Notwithstanding*, p. 52.)

There is a difference [of repetition] . . . between the importuning widow and the strident murmurings of ancient Israel in the Sinai. (*Notwithstanding*, p. 53.)

Murmuring (and it is usually against the prophets) can be a mere gripe and complaint or it may reflect a deep difference. But whatever the degree of dissent, it ought to be clear that though a particular leader is the ostensible object of the murmuring, as Moses told his complaining people, "your murmurings are not against us, but against the Lord." (Exodus 16:8.) However, rocks can reach prophets, for they are proximate. But few are seen hurling stones skyward; they may have a grievance with God, but they also have had some experience with gravity. (*Experience*, p. 107.)

MUSIC

The symphonic strains of scriptural music can give our lives lilt and tone, a way of tuning our lives by reference to a celestial scale. The melodies are the marching music for the traveler on the strait and narrow way! (*Choose*, p. 72.)

High-quality music is so desperately needed to counteract secular sounds. (*Not My Will*, p. 76.)

MYSTERIES

Perhaps the need to develop faith about the basics is one of the reasons why we are warned about the mysteries, what might be called the radioactive doctrines. We are ready to experiment, as Alma urged, with basic gospel principles, but we are ill equipped to handle the radioactive doctrines in the tiny laboratories of our minds; they can become a dangerous diversion from what our highest priority really is—to become like Jesus! (Matthew 5:48; 3 Nephi 27:27.) (*We Talk of Christ*, p. 70.)

Heavenly Father and Jesus Christ are actually giving away the secrets of the universe. If only you and I will not become offended by Their generosity, if only we will not be indifferent to the significance of the things revealed to us in holy temples and in holy scriptures. (Talk given January 8, 1995.)

Mysteries consist of truth-laden ordinances, but they are not fully efficacious if received barren of appropriate prerequisite behavior. Instead these ordinances and truths require that the would-be recipient "repenteth and exerciseth faith, and bringeth forth good works, and prayeth continually without ceasing—unto such it is given to know the mysteries of God" (Alma 26:22). Doing brings knowing (John 7:16). (*Not My Will*, p. 132.)

NATURAL MAN

Only to the extent that we are willing to put off the natural man do we have any real hope at all of becoming saints. It is the putting off of the putting off that is our real problem, however. (*Notwithstanding*, p. 73.)

The natural man listens with such a thirsty ear for the approving roar of the crowd. He needs no encouragement to be "of the world," because he is already so much "in the world." Unless the natural man is "put off" (Mosiah 3:19) he will finally put us down. Only when he is put off do we "come off conqueror" (D&C 10:5). (*Faith*, p. 6.)

So much of our fatigue . . . comes from carrying that needless load [of the selfish natural man]. This heaviness of the natural man prevents us from doing our Christian calisthenics; so we end up too swollen with selfishness to pass through the narrow needle's eye. (*Ensign*, November 1990, p. 15.)

The world in its wisdom constantly seeks to accommodate the natural man while gospel wisdom constantly urges us to put off the natural man (Mosiah 3:19). ("The Inexhaustible Gospel," p. 145.)

It should not surprise us that . . . coarse, spiritually unrefined individuals cannot receive the things of the Spirit but are shut out from the very light that could show them, if they were willing, how to put off the natural man. The seeming shutters are but the natural scales on our own eyes. (*Notwithstanding*, p. 73.)

The "natural man" is not free. For instance, in his limiting myopia it is not natural for him to be sensitive to the needs of those who are *behind* or *below* him. By way of simple example, our striving to get ahead in vehicular traffic is usually done without worrying about the person behind us. (*Faith*, pp. 88–89.)

Organizational charts often encourage us to be humble "up" but less humble toward those who are "down." The natural man simply faces in the wrong direction, and in every way his appetites of the flesh take him farther and farther away from God. (*Faith*, p. 89.)

Facing up to gospel truths is not easy for the natural man, since he prefers playing in his local sandpile rather than contemplating the cosmos and thereby seeing God "moving in his majesty and power" (D&C 88:47). (*Faith*, p. 97.)

Mauled by his moods and intimidated by his fears, the natural man overreacts to, while hope overrides, the disappointments of the day. (*Ensign*, November 1994, p. 36.)

Giving up on God and on oneself constitutes simultaneous surrender to the natural man. (*Ensign*, November 1994, p. 36.)

The natural man (see Mosiah 3:19) is often fed but never filled. Even if his appetites are surfeited, his satisfactions are short-lived. The sense of emptiness relentlessly reappears. Even as gluttony digests its latest glob, it begins anticipating its next meal. The same pattern is there when it comes to the praise of men, or lust, or greed. Strange as it seems, the appetites of the natural man carry within themselves a capacity for the quick cancellation of any temporary satisfaction. (*Endure*, pp. 77–78.)

Our spiritual mobility is determined by how much we can jettison, including by putting off the sumo-sized natural man. (*Faith*, p. 29.)

NEEDY

There are many who thirst not only for water or hunger not only for bread but also for the word of the Lord and for friendship. The needy include both the poor in substance and those who are poor as to needed support systems. Losing oneself brings more noticing of others. The more preoccupied we are, the more who will pass by us unnoticed (see Mormon 8:39). (*Flood*, p. 99.)

We must be slow to judge, [King Benjamin] said, why individuals find themselves in poverty. It is not appropriate for us to reason casually or indifferently that "the man has brought upon himself his misery," since we are all, finally, beggars in terms of our dependence upon God. (Mosiah 4:17–23.) Benjamin would not have wanted the poor to covet either, but neither should the rest of us be insensitive to them. Benjamin even went so far as to say that giving to the poor is essential if we intend to retain our remission of sins and to walk guiltless before God (see Mosiah 4:26). We cannot even expect our own petitions to be heard if we neglect others "who stand in need" (Alma 34:28.) (*Heroes from the Book of Mormon*, p. 66.)

The vices of humanity are far more interactive than many people realize. In the societies of Sodom and Gomorrah there was rampant sexual immorality; there was also inordinate pride, idleness, and a neglect of the poor and the needy. (Ezekiel 16:48–50.) A haughty attitude towards God (who had given strict counsel on the need to care for the poor) led to the neglect of the poor and needy. This is something those who would focus all of their attention on poverty, without any concern for adultery and homosexuality—and vice versa—would do well to ponder upon. (*Sermons*, p. 37.)

NEIGHBORS

A man who is too busy to notice a neighbor also has no time to smell the flowers. Smallness of soul keeps us from contemplating both bird and brother, when God would have us exult over all his creations. (*Heart*, p. 32.)

Alas, it is regrettable that those who live in neighborhoods are not necessarily neighbors. (*Endure*, p. 91.)

NEWS

There were no newspapers, as we know them, at the time of Jesus' ministry. Had there been, one can guess that the news coverage would have missed the significance of what was transpiring at, and after, Calvary, while perhaps reporting the return of Pilate to Cae-sarea after a trying weekend in Jerusalem, or while noting the arrival or departure of new trade caravans. The atonement, the central fact of human history, would have been ignored or subordinated to the other busy and important things of the time—unless the publisher had perspective about "things as they were." (*Smallest Part*, p. 44.)

Victory at the polls, winning at a hearing, and dominating the news, even though only over some passing concern, can easily seem to constitute the whole of life. Moreover, reinforcements by the media (with their fascination with sensation and preference for information instead of wisdom) only intensifies the illusion. (*Sermons*, pp. 11–12.)

NOBILITY

The faithful but perhaps plump woman whose nails are worn but who is a giving mother, wife, and neighbor has a queenly beauty and a regal way, if we would but see her as she really is; her beauty will *not* be taken from her by the passing years. The paraplegic in the wheelchair who refuses to indulge himself in self-pity—his giving and achieving has genuine glamour. One day he will stand very tall and straight; he should do so already in our eyes. (*Experience*, pp. 61–62.)

NONBELIEVERS

The barbed questions of the faithless do not deserve answers any more than the taunts which Christ himself suffered while on the cross. The inquiring probes of some nonbelievers are not really questions at all, but simply a reconnaissance aimed at discovering any breeches in the defenses of the believer who holds the fortress of faith. The nonbeliever often does not really care to know. He seeks to have his sport, to work up a semantical sweat, grasping what pleasures he can from a life otherwise filled with forlornness. (*Choose*, p. 32.)

For those who think they can keep the second great commandment without keeping the first, it may be enough for now to say that we cannot really love others unless we know *who* others really are. How can we know their deepest needs without knowing their true identity? Yes, the glass of water given by a disbeliever to the thirsty individual is just as refreshing and the crust of bread just as filling. But irreverence for, or an unwillingness to acknowledge, the Ultimate Source of both the water and the bread keeps that moment of giving and receiving from its completeness. As the Savior said, water from the well is useful, but we will thirst, again and again, unless we drink of the living waters. (John 4:13–14.) Disbelievers do good, but it is a good that is not good enough. (*Experience*, pp. 67–68.)

Fortunately, God neither stops existing nor loving because a mere mortal rejects Him. So far as nonbelievers are concerned, we must not reject them because they reject our message. (*Press Forward*, p. 108.)

NOSTALGIA

Some nostalgia on our part for days past is pardonable—but not much, because nostalgia can be narcotic in the demands it makes on us to fix our faces on the past. (*Excellent*, p. 10.)

OBEDIENCE

Obedience is the outer expression of our inner gospel gyroscope. (*Press Forward*, p. 43.)

It is important to understand that obedience is not simply a requirement of a capricious God who wants us to jump hurdles for the entertainment of a royal court. It is really the pleading of a loving Father for you and me to discover, as quickly as we can, that there are key concepts and principles that will bring happiness in a planned but otherwise cold universe. (*Choose*, pp. 13–14.)

Personal spiritual symmetry emerges only from the shaping of prolonged obedience. Twigs are bent, not snapped into shape. (*Ensign*, May 1990, p. 34.)

We do not always know why our obedience in the *here and now* is so steadily crucial, but it is no doubt bound up in our *usefulness* and *happiness* in the *there and then*! ("'Thanks Be to God,'" p. 11.)

The principle of obedience . . . has fallen on hard times; obedience is low on the world's scale of values. There are causes for this, of course. Some have done terribly wrong things in obedience to unjust leaders. Some have engaged in senseless subordination to bad causes, becoming mere satellites in mindless orbits. Satan always pretzelizes principles in order to increase human misery. But obedience is so essential for the gospel journey; it must be rescued from the careless conclusions reached by sloppy intellects. The tests of obedience are always "to whom?" and "to what?" Obedience is not blind faith but following the glimpses we get when seeing with the eye of faith. ("All Hell Is Moved," p. 179.)

With every ounce of . . . obedience comes a bushel of blessings. (*Deposition*, p. 29.)

Significantly, Abraham did not see the substitute ram on Mount Moriah until *after* the moment that mattered, when he obediently "stretched forth his hand, and took the knife. . . . " (Genesis 22:10.) Sometimes the cross must be taken up just that decisively. There is no time for an agonizing appraisal. (*Deposition*, p. 76.)

Ahead in eternity there may be "narrow passages" yet to be navigated, passages which are unknown to us now. Strict obedience will still be essential. Otherwise we would not really be equipped to live in such a universe, which, for all we know, will require not only our obedience but also spiritual daring in order for us to come safely through. (*Believe*, p. 13.)

Obedience [is not] a mindless shifting of our personal responsibility. Instead, it is tying ourselves to a living God who will introduce us—as soon as we are ready—to new and heavier responsibilities involving situations of high adventure. Obedience, therefore, is not evasion; it is an invasion—one that takes us deep into the realm of our possibilities. (*Experience*, p. 127.)

Those who make demands of the Lord Himself (or His mortal leaders) to perform according to their criteria actually want a God who will serve them, not vice versa! (*Not My Will*, p. 92.)

God's blessings, including those associated with consecration, come by unforced obedience to the laws upon which they are predicated (see D&C 130:20–21). Thus our deepest desires determine our degree of "obedience to the unenforceable." (*Ensign*, November 1995, p. 24.)

OBSCENITY

Grossness in conduct is usually preceded or accompanied by grossness in language. Instead of employing beauty and variety, obscenity exhibits poverty of expression. What jars is not only the mounting crudeness but also the increasing sameness—like the indistinguishable grunts of a herd in a hurry to worship afresh at the shrine of sensualism. (*Believe*, p. 75.)

OFFENSES

Some of us endure life's major afflictions better than we endure small slights. How do we feel, for example, when we are unfairly unmentioned in a public litany of appreciation? Though we may appear outwardly unoffended, do we brood inwardly? Was the oversight deliberate or merely forgetful? For the meek, however, any regret is minimal and concern is reserved for the one who did the overlooking, lest he be embarrassed. (*Believe*, p. 55.)

Our planning usually assumes that our destiny is largely in our own hands. Then come intruding events, first elbowing aside, then evicting, what we had anticipated and even earned. Hence we can be offended by events as well as by people. (*Men and Women*, p. 63.)

OMISSIONS

Most omissions occur because we fail to get outside ourselves. We are so busy checking on our own temperatures, we do not notice the burning fevers of others. (*Ensign*, November 1995, p. 23.)

Many of us thus have sufficient faith to avoid the major sins of commission, but not enough faith to sacrifice our distracting obsessions or to focus on our omissions. (*Ensign*, November 1995, p. 23.)

OMNIPOTENCE

It is one of the hallmarks of human vanity that we assume, because we cannot do something, that God cannot do it either. Is it not marvelous that the Father and the Son blend perfect love and perfect power? (*As I Am*, p. 27.)

Furthermore, because the centerpiece of the Atonement is already in place, we know that everything else in God's plan will likewise finally succeed. God is surely able to do His own work (see 2 Nephi 27:20–21). In His plans for the human family, long ago God made ample provision for all mortal mistakes. His purposes will all triumph, and will do so without abrogating man's moral agency. Moreover, all His purposes will come to pass in their time. (See D&C 64:32; see also *Teachings of the Prophet Joseph Smith*, p. 220.) (*Men and Women*, p. 12.)

Whether in a micro or a macro mode, God is "able to do [His] own work." Parting the Red Sea for ancient Israel was easy for Him who, centuries before, had brought to pass the parting or dividing of the earth's oceans and continents (see Genesis 10:25; 1 Chronicles 1:19; D&C 133:24). (*Flood*, p. 122.)

Impotence cannot dictate terms to Omnipotence. (*Choose*, p. 18.)

Having genuine faith in God clearly requires not only believing that He is there but also that He is cosmically competent—that He can really bring to pass His purposes (2 Nephi 27:20, 21). (*The Christmas Scene*, p. 7.)

OMNISCIENCE

God's omniscience permits Him to take all things into account. He is perfectly aware, perfectly loving, perfectly empathic. But He is also deeply committed to our moral agency and to our spiritual development. His interventions are His decisions, and they will always reflect His divine attributes at the center of which is His loving-kindness. (*Believe*, p. 34.)

The Lord, who was able to say to his disciples, "Cast the net on the right side of the ship," knew beforehand there was a multitude of fishes there (John 21:6). If he knew beforehand the movements and whereabouts of fishes in the little Sea of Tiberias, should it offend us that he knows beforehand which mortals will come into the gospel net? ("Meeting the Challenges of Today," p. 153.)

When we are unduly impatient with circumstances, we may be suggesting that we know what is best—better than does God. Or, at least, we are asserting that our timetable is better than His. Either way, we are questioning the reality of God's omniscience as if, as some seem to believe, God were on some sort of post-doctoral fellowship, trying to complete His understanding and, therefore, needing to use us as consultants. (*Notwithstanding*, pp. 59–60.)

When the Lord asks us to confess His hand in all things, He is not seeking our ritualistic incantation concerning His powers. Again, He is after realism in us, including our acknowledgment that His omniscience has made allowance even for human errors of which He does not approve, but which are not allowed to frustrate His overall plan. We can count on His plans—even when He cannot count on us! (*As I Am*, p. 57.)

God, who knows the end from the beginning, knows, therefore, all that is in between. He could not safely see us through our individual allotments of "all these things" that shall give us experience if He did not first know "all things." (*Experience*, p. 7.)

There are no qualifiers, only flat and absolute assertions of the omniscience of God. (*Experience*, p. 7.)

God can see into the hearts of the malcontents even before they form a mob, just as He saw where civil rebellion in America was to begin. (D&C 87:1; 130:12.) (*Experience*, p. 13.)

By foreseeing, God can plan and His purposes can be fulfilled, but He does this in a way that does not in the least compromise our individual agency, any more than an able meteorologist causes the weather rather than forecasts it. (*Experience*, p. 19.)

It is crucial . . . to remember that while we often fail our opportunities, God is neither pleased nor surprised that we do not rise to those opportunities. But we cannot say to him later on that we could have achieved had we only been given the chance. This is all part of the justice of God. (*Really Are*, p. 28.)

God does not live in the dimension of time as do we. We are not only hampered by our finiteness (experiential and intellectual), but also by being in the dimension of time. Moreover, God, since "all things are present" with him, is not simply predicting based solely on the past. In ways that are not clear to us, he *sees* rather than *foresees* the future, because all things are at once present before him. (*Really Are*, p. 29.)

While a person is thinking his way through his particular hesitations or reservations about faith, he might ask, "Does God really know what I am passing through?" The answer is "Yes!" He knows! He also *knew*—through His foreknowledge. (*Faith*, p. 39.)

The new star [of Bethlehem] would have had to be placed in its precise orbit long, long before it shone so precisely! By reflecting such careful divine design, it underscored what the Lord has said: "All things must come to pass in their time" (D&C 64:32). His planning and precision pertain not only to astrophysical orbits but to human orbits as well. (*The Christmas Scene*, pp. 2–3.)

OPPOSITION

Even though it is true that there must be an "opposition in all things" [2 Nephi 2:11], none of us has the personal obligation to provide that opposition. (*Experience*, p. 108.)

ORDINANCES

Ordinances thus blend faith and works. They are not, however, rituals which save all by themselves, that is, if unaided by the righteous life. Covenants must be kept before blessings flow. On the other hand, random goodness, unaccompanied by divine ordinances, is not of full salvational effect either: "Wherefore he that prayeth, whose spirit is contrite, the same is accepted of me if he obey mine ordinances" (D&C 52:15). (*Faith*, pp. 76–77.)

Ordinances are necessary milestones in this mortal march, marking and showing the way, signifying those things which are both endings and beginnings, such as baptism, which signifies both a burial and a resurrection. (*Heart*, p. 48.)

We can and should have faith in [the] saving ordinances, just as we do in Him whose prescribed ordinances they are. The ordinances are not merely quaint and reminding rituals. They are essential, both for the "here and now" and to qualify us for the "there and then." (*Faith*, p. 73.)

Developing . . . saintly qualities is every bit as essential as receiving the ordinances of the gospel. . . . Thus developing charity is clearly just as essential for admission to the upper realms of the celestial kingdom as is baptism! (*Endure*, p. 33.)

ORTHODOXY

Orthodoxy in thought and behavior brings safety and felicity as the storms come, including "every wind of doctrine." (See Ephesians 4:14.) Happily, amid such winds the Holy Ghost not only helps us to recognize plain truth but also plain nonsense! (*Ensign*, May 1993, p. 78.)

True orthodoxy consists of keeping the doctrines, ordinances, covenants, and programs of the Church and Christian service in proper balance. In this daily balancing process, we are not excused from exercising good judgment—after all that manuals and handbooks can do. (*Ensign*, November 1988, p. 31.)

Great care must be exercised . . . so that . . . we do not pass off our personal preferences as the Lord's program; we must not confuse our personal religious hobbies with His orthodoxy. Nor must we ever pass off a personal obsession as a spiritual impression. ("'True Believers in Christ,'" p. 136.)

In orthodoxy lies real safety and real felicity! Flowing from orthodoxy is not only correctness but happiness. Orthodoxy is especially vital in a time of raging relativism and belching sensualism. The world's morality is constantly being improvised. Some views are politically correct one day, but not another. ("The Inexhaustible Gospel," p. 146.)

The orthodox Latter-day Saint scholar should remember that his citizenship is in the Kingdom and that his professional passport takes him abroad into his specialty. It is not the other way around. That fact is true not only for the professor but also for the plumber in his relationships with his union. (*Deposition*, p. 15.)

Preserving orthodoxy is a delicate challenge. It is also one of the missions of the Church, because human happiness will be greater with orthodoxy than it will be following satellite belief systems whose outcome is always less than the sum required for full happiness. (*Choose*, p. 12.)

PACIFISM

The contagious pacifism of which we read in the scriptures describes those who would not make war, even in self-defense, but instead trusted in the blessings of God (see Alma 24:17–27). Can we recommend unconditional pacifism or unilateral disarmament for any people who are not otherwise righteous and therefore are unable to rely on the Lord to bless them? Would the citizens of

Sodom have been spared if they had been pacifists but otherwise unrighteous? Or does unilateral disarmament constitute undue reliance upon the arm of flesh and natural man? (*Sermons*, p. 33.)

Parents

As parenting declines, the need for policing increases. There will always be a shortage of police if there is a shortage of effective parents! Likewise, there will not be enough prisons if there are not enough good homes. (*Ensign*, May 1994, p. 89.)

Just as the leaning Tower of Pisa is a persistent rebuke to architectural pessimism, so parental hope—by refusing to topple merely because of the gravity of the current family situation—is a repudiation of despair. Giving parents never give up hope! (*Ensign*, November 1994, p. 36.)

When we return to our real home, it will be with the "mutual approbation" of those who reign in the "royal courts on high." There we will find beauty such as mortal "eye hath not seen"; we will hear sounds of surpassing music which mortal "ear hath not heard." Could such a regal homecoming be possible without the anticipatory arrangements of a Heavenly Mother? (*Ensign*, May 1978, p. 11.)

What in you is merely casualness about Christianity may, in your children, become hostility; for what you have not defended your children may reject angrily. (*Ensign*, November 1974, p. 12.)

We see our near-perfect parents, Adam and Eve, coping with challenges in the first family, for their children too, came trailing traits from their formative first estate. (*Ensign*, November 1976, p. 13.)

We [should] allow for the agency of others (including our children) *before* we assess our adequacy. Often our deliberate best is less effectual because of someone else's worst. (*Ensign,* November 1976, p. 14.)

Parents, striving to reach and to rescue the truculent teenager, experiencing disappointment after disappointment and wondering when it all will end, can be assured, "Yet thou [God] art there!" (*Ensign,* November 1987, p. 32.)

"Glory be to the Father" for allowing His special Son to suffer and to be sacrificed for all of us. On Judgment Day, brothers and sisters, will any of us want to rush forward to tell our Father how we, as parents, suffered when we watched our children suffer? (*Ensign,* May 1989, p. 64.)

When some choose slackness, they are choosing not only for themselves, but for the next generation and the next. Small equivocations in parents can produce large deviations in their children! Earlier generations in a family may have reflected dedication, while some in the current generation evidence equivocation. Sadly, in the next, some may choose dissension, as erosion takes its toll. (*Ensign,* November 1992, p. 66.)

The fifth commandment's laudable emphasis upon honoring parents, unless checked by the first commandment, could result in unconditional loyalty to errant parents rather than to God. (*Ensign,* May 1993, p. 78.)

Malfunctioning fathers are a much more common phenomenon in the Church than are malfunctioning mothers. Often the success-oriented male leaves untended some of his responsibilities to his wife and family. Even so, having one "sentry" who has gone AWOL joined by another "sentry," the wife and mother, is no help. (*Deposition,* p. 84.)

When parents fail to transmit testimony and theology along with decency, those families are only one generation from serious spiritual decline, having lost their savor. The law of the harvest is nowhere more in evidence and nowhere more relentless than in family gardens! (*Ensign*, May 1994, p. 90.)

Sincere parents are anxious to make their house a home and not merely a hotel—where mother is maid and chef and father is a desk clerk and a bell captain with the car keys. (*My Family*, p. 2.)

Without the guides of the gospel and of living prophets, we can all be caught up into various fads and fashions having to do with child rearing. In such a situation, we can very easily slide into permissiveness. (*My Family*, p. 15.)

Parents who crave the approval of their children at the expense of principle will find that they worship a jealous and capricious god. (*My Family*, pp. 75–76.)

Sometimes as parents . . . when we sound "general quarters," it isn't because the enemy has been sighted, but rather because we have a need to demonstrate to the "crew" that the "captain" is on the bridge. (*My Family*, p. 98.)

We, as parents, would . . . do well to hold one partner and/or some of ourselves in reserve so that we are not entirely spent on tactical matters. Strategic reserves are intended to be just that: something held in reserve for the moments that are decisive. If both parents commit themselves simultaneously to the field of action on every issue, as a pair, they will miss those opportunities when it is wise to have one parent held in reserve so that if the other parent, in a sense, has spent himself, or herself, there is still someone left to shape the final outcome; sometimes parents need to pass the baton, so to speak, so that one of them is fresh for the next lap. (*My Family*, p. 99.)

It is in the very nature of parenting that parents need to be authoritative, yet without being authoritarian. (*Believe*, p. 16.)

Parents and teachers . . . are planting little intellectual time bombs that will helpfully be set off by certain pressures of circumstances and human chemistry. This perspective ought to give teachers and parents reason to reflect on the nature of their teaching investment. The parental portfolio needs balance between teaching on current matters and the teaching whose dividends will be deferred till a time when they will be much needed—in four years or in a decade. (*Power*, pp. 24–25.)

There are wise limits in daily life. For instance, how many of the various "lessons" for their children can young parents sustain, financially as well as transportationally? How much such "good" can their children actually stand? We sometimes do so much *for* our children that we can do nothing *with* them! (*Faith*, p. 117.)

PATIENCE

Patience is . . . clearly not fatalistic, shoulder-shrugging resignation. It is the acceptance of a divine rhythm to life; it is obedience prolonged. Patience stoutly resists pulling up the daisies to see how the roots are doing. ("Patience," p. 218.)

Patience is a willingness, in a sense, to watch the unfolding purposes of God with a sense of wonder and awe, rather than pacing up and down within the cell of our circumstances. ("Patience," p. 216.)

The patient person can better understand how there are circumstances when, if our hearts are set too much upon the things of this world, they must be broken—but for our sakes, and not merely as a demonstration of divine power. ("Patience," p. 217.)

Patience is not indifference. Actually, it means caring very much but being willing, nevertheless, to submit to the Lord and to what the scriptures call the "process of time." ("Patience," p. 215.)

A patient willingness to defer dividends is a hallmark of individual maturity. ("Patience," p. 216.)

Clearly, without patience, we will learn less in life. We will see less. We will feel less. We will hear less. Ironically, "rush" and "more" usually mean "less." The pressures of "now," time and time again, go against the grain of the gospel with its eternalism. ("Patience and the Law of the Harvest.")

Sometimes that which we are doing is correct enough but simply needs to be persisted in patiently, not for a minute or a moment but sometimes for years. Paul speaks of the marathon of life and of how we must "run with patience the race that is set before us" (Hebrews 12:1). Paul did not select the hundred-meter dash for his analogy! ("Patience," p. 216.)

Very importantly, it is patience, when combined with love, which permits us "in process of time" to detoxify our disappointments. Patience and love take the radioactivity out of our resentments. These are neither small nor occasional needs in most of our lives. ("Patience," p. 217.)

God's timing, which calls for our patience, is often His way of preserving our agency. We halt at a busy intersection when we hear sirens; we pull over for fire trucks. Spiritual emergencies are no different, except that, alas, there are no loud sirens to be heard! (*Flood*, p. 68.)

In our approach to life, patience also helps us to realize that, while we may be ready to move on, having had enough of a particular learning experience, our continuing presence is a needed part of the learning environment for others. Patience is thus closely connected with other central attributes of Christianity—love and humility. ("Patience and the Law of the Harvest.")

Patience is not only a companion of faith but is also a friend to moral agency. Inside our impatience there is sometimes an ugly reality: we are plainly irritated and inconvenienced by the need to make allowances for the agency of others. In our impatience we would override others, even though it is obvious that our individual differences and preferences are so irretrievably enmeshed with each other, that the only resolution which preserves agency is for us to be patient and long-suffering with each other. ("Patience and the Law of the Harvest.")

Patience permits us to cling to our faith in the Lord when we are tossed about by suffering as if by surf. When the undertow grasps us, we will realize that we are somehow being carried forward even as we tumble; we are actually being helped even as we cry for help. (*Notwithstanding*, p. 67.)

PERFECTION

Our perfect Father does not expect us to be perfect children yet. He had only one such Child. Meanwhile, therefore, sometimes with smudges on our cheeks, dirt on our hands, and shoes untied, stammeringly but smilingly we present God with a dandelion—as if it were an orchid or a rose! If for now the dandelion is the best we have to offer, He receives it, knowing what we may later place on the altar. It is good to remember how young we are spiritually. (*Believe*, p. 100.)

Striving to become like the Father and the Son is more than an optional objective. Focusing on the personality of Jesus is an intellectual and behavioral as well as theological imperative. (*As I Am*, p. 13.)

In a Kingdom where perfection is an eventual expectation, each other's needs for improvement have a way of being noticed. (*Ensign*, November 1976, p. 12.)

The Church is for the perfecting of the Saints, hence new arrivals are entitled to expect instant community but not instant sainthood—either in themselves or in others. (*Ensign*, November 1980, p. 15.)

Jesus called upon us to be "perfect even as your Father which is in heaven is perfect." (Matthew 5:48.) Would a Lord who cannot lie taunt us with any possibility that is irrevocably out of our reach? With God's helping grace, Moroni promised, we can become "holy, without spot." (Moroni 10:33.) (*Notwithstanding*, p. 28.)

There are no shortcuts to celestialness. But once the basic strategic commitments are made, the tactical problems are solvable. (*My Family*, p. 4.)

The gospel suggests to us ultimate perfection, but eternal progression rests on the assumption of gradual but regular improvement in our lives. In the city of Enoch the near perfection of this people occurred "in process of time" over many, many years. This is also the case with us. (*Deposition*, p. 71.)

Lest we be too intimidated about the plan of salvation's eventual emphasis on our becoming perfect, as the Father and Jesus are, it is well to keep in mind that the word *perfect* emphasizes that one can become "finished" and "fully developed" (see Matthew 5:48; 3 Nephi 12:48; 27:27; Ephesians 4:13). It thus emphasizes the "completeness" and wholeness essential to full happiness, including, of course, the glorious resurrection and joyous exaltation. However, instead of resulting in a democratic sameness among all resurrected people in each and every respect, God's plan clearly accepts that there will be variations of attainment. These will reflect how well we lived in mortality and to what extent we developed our individual possibilities. (*Faith*, pp. 44–45.)

Though imperfect, an improving person can actually know that the course of his life is generally acceptable to the Lord despite there being much distance yet to be covered. (*Men and Women*, p. 23.)

We may . . . see the imperfections in leaders in the Church. How we react to these manifestations of mortality is the key to *our* salvation—not *theirs*! (*Experience*, p. 112.)

The more the adversary can get us to react to each other's imperfections, the more he can deflect us from perfect principles. (*We Talk of Christ*, p. 33.)

There is a difference between stumbling along the pathway to perfection even as we display our humanness, and wandering about aimlessly in a desert of despair and disbelief. (*Not My Will*, p. 127.)

PERMISSIVENESS

A society which finally permits *anything* will eventually lose everything! (*Ensign*, May 1995, p. 67.)

Unless checked, permissiveness, by the end of its journey, will cause humanity to stare in mute disbelief at its awful consequences. (*Ensign*, May 1996, p. 68.)

The decade of the 1960s in America was one in which too many adults, insecure and uncertain, not only gave way to the permissive pressures of some in the "rising generation" [see 3 Nephi 1:29–30] but then actually adopted the lower lifestyle so promoted. (*Precious Things*, pp. 71–72.)

Kindness never takes the form of permissiveness. (*As I Am*, p. 86.)

PERSEVERANCE

When armies have been routed, it has often been because of combinations of false rumors and the feeling that everyone else has deserted his post, so "Why not me?" It's hard on those who stay at their post but tragic for those who desert or defect. So much of the serious work of salvation consists of reaching those lost battalions who have hung on even though surrounded. (*Deposition*, p. 90.)

Even yesterday's spiritual experience . . . does not guarantee us against tomorrow's relapse. Persistence thus matters greatly. (*Endure*, p. 122.)

PERSPECTIVE

One day all our temporary designations, locations, and vocations will shrink in their significance when bathed in the candlepower of Kolob's brighter and perfect day. Meanwhile, however, spiritual perspective is precious. ("Out of the Best Faculty," p. 33.)

An economic depression would be grim, but it would not change the reality of immortality. The inevitability of the Second Coming is not affected by the unpredictability of the stock market. Political despots make this world very ugly, but they cannot touch that better world to come. A case of cancer does not cancel the promises of the temple endowment. Thus the things of which we can be most certain are also those things which matter most. (*Notwithstanding*, p. 57.)

Looking through the lens of gospel perspective, we see more clearly what life is really all about. In considering, for instance, the great reconciliation of Jacob and Esau with their caravans in the desert, none of us would be much interested in reviewing the invoices of the gifts offered or exchanged. It was their reconciliation that mattered! ("Out of the Best Faculty," p. 48.)

Even something as small as a man's thumb, when held very near the eye, can blind him to the very large sun. Yet the sun is still there. Blindness is brought upon the man by himself. When we draw other things too close, placing them first, we obscure our vision of heaven. (*Heart*, p. 19.)

What is most to be focused on—the fact that Peter walked briefly on the water or that he did not continue? Has any other mortal so walked, even that briefly? (*Ensign*, May 1982, p. 38.)

In those moments when we feel the pain which is a necessary part of the plan of happiness, we can remember that there was an ancient time when that plan was first unveiled. Then the perceptive among us voted not secretly, but audibly—by shouting for joy! (See Job 38:7.) Let us not go back on those feelings now—for we saw more clearly then what we are experiencing now! (*Ensign*, November 1982, p. 68.)

As to scale, what occurred in the gardens of Eden and Gethsemane is of enormous significance to all mankind, but it was inversely proportioned to the tiny plots of earth on which those eternity-shaping dramas were played out! (*Ensign*, November 1984, p. 8.)

One-dimensional man with only a one-dimensional view of the world will surely focus upon the cares of the world, yielding to the things of the moment. (*Ensign*, November 1985, p. 17.)

Messes of pottage (Genesis 25:29–34) respond to the "now" in us, whereas only the submissive heart and mind sees eternity's considerations. (*Not My Will*, p. 60.)

The worldly appetites are, in a sense, like secularism's manna, a day-to-day thing, seldom preserved overnight. Instead, prophets urge the long view of the individual's eternal self-interest. (*Not My Will*, p. 61.)

If we have a sense of proportion here and now, our portion hereafter will be significantly larger. (*As I Am*, p. 102.)

This life's temporal lens distorts. The things of the moment are grossly magnified, and the things of eternity are blurred or diminished. (*Endure*, p. 26.)

Never let the needs of now crowd out the considerations of eternity. (*Ensign*, May 1976, p. 26.)

How can we expect to enjoy eternally that which we neglect in mortality? (*Endure*, p. 39)

The remedies for people who stumble because they feel unvalued, unloved, unused, unheeded, and unappreciated include coming to know about God's love and coming to see the disappointments of the day in the context of the blessings of eternity and God's plan of happiness. It is vital for one to know that life's real difficulties are "but for a small moment" and thereby to trust in God's timing (see D&C 122:4; 2 Corinthians 4:17). (*Flood*, p. 87.)

We misread and misuse life—except with this plain and precious perspective of the gospel, which puts the things of the world in their lesser places. Then, on that essentially unchanging mortal stage, we can see things for what they really are, such as the demanding cadence called for by the cares of the world. Like birds and animals performing some inborn ritual, amusing to everyone but the participants, these maneuverings of materialism would be comedy if they were not tragedy. So would the posturings as to power and the thirsty seeking of the praise of the world. The ploys are so transparent when seen in the gospel's light. (*Ensign*, November 1986, p. 54.)

Without enduring the in-your-face, personal experiences in the here and now of this life, how useful will we be to Him in the there and then as He continues the "one eternal round" of His grand work and glory (see 1 Nephi 10:19; Moses 1:39)? Thus how could immortality be fully appreciated without an earnest sense of proportion and perspective. (*Endure*, p. 7.)

A mere hundred years from now today's seeming deprivations and tribulations will not matter *unless we let them matter too much now!* A thousand years from now, for instance, today's serious physical ailment will be but a fleeting memory. A million years from now, those who today worry and are anguished because they are unmarried will, if they are faithful, have smiles of satisfaction on their faces in the midst of a vast convocation of their posterity. (*Prove,* p. 28.)

Unfortunately, the morning after does not occur the day before. (*Notwithstanding,* p. 77.)

Knowing the truth about those things that really matter frees us from our inhibiting and finite perspective in the same way that turning the light on in an otherwise darkened room can keep us from stubbing toes and breaking furniture. (*Smallest Part,* p. 6.)

Eternal perspective does not say to us to be inattentive to things like the dollar crises, floods, poverty, law and order, and borders— for these contemporary challenges represent, in fact, some of the interpersonal moral issues and challenges to our agency and to our ability to apply the gospel by assisting others. (*Smallest Part,* p. 28.)

Perspective would have helped those who worked on the tower of Babel, no doubt an exciting undertaking for a time. Because it was so fatally flawed, we can't be sure who was the more lightheaded— the hod carriers (as the tower's altitude increased) or the architects who designed it! (*Deposition,* p. 81.)

Without the perspective of a purposeful mortality and also of long-standing, even premortal, covenants, Israel's wanderings make of Sinai a senseless sojourn. However, Israel's wandering is actually a type for our mortal state and God's plans for us. (*Flood,* p. 38.)

As in the case of the episode of the golden calf, the view from the desert floor is very different from that atop Mount Sinai. Perspective makes such an enormous difference. (*Flood*, p. 65.)

People who look beyond the mark are clearly not without sight. They can see, but it is what they choose to look at (or for) that causes a lack of vision. It might be likened to anxiously watching a traffic light two intersections away and missing an oncoming truck in our own intersection; or a basketball player taking his eyes off the basket and missing an easy layup because he glances at a hot-dog vendor in the stands; or the blindness of the British fortifying Singapore prior to World War II with mighty guns firing only seaward as the Japanese came by land; or those who were too busy staring in search of a political liberator and missed the Messiah. (*Really Are*, p. 54.)

The Martha-like things chosen are not always the bad part—merely lesser choices. The Savior did not say that the cares of the world were not cares. But this world will pass away, and its cares with it. The things really worth caring about will still be around to be cared about forever. The other things are like last week's firewood, useful to warm a needed meal, which, in turn, helped to sustain the body. But to what end? Only His gospel gives us ultimate reasons. Without such perspective, we would be like astronomers who have never seen the stars. (*Prove*, p. 30.)

PESSIMISM

Neither provincialism nor pessimism permits a person to see himself, life, or the universe as these things "really are" and "as they really will be" (Jacob 4:13). (*Small Moment*, p. 102.)

Life, or any particular situation, if viewed only through the peephole of pessimism, presents a puzzling or discouraging picture indeed. Instead of wonder, awe, and pattern, which the Christian sees, the disciples of despair disclaim any knowledge of a "big picture" of life in which "all things denote there is a God." . . . The degree of divine disclosure—from peephole to a picture window view of things—is up to us. (*Smallest Part*, p. 12.)

Naive optimism and pervasive pessimism are both to be avoided. (*Deposition*, p. 98.)

PLAN OF SALVATION

How can we truly understand who we are unless we know who we were and what we have the power to become? How can there be real identity without real history? How can one understand his tiny, individual plot without knowing, even a little, about Father's grand, galactic plans? (*Ensign*, May 1986, p. 35.)

Without an understanding of the plan of salvation, including our premortal existence and the judgment and the resurrection, trying to make sense of this life by itself would be like seeing only the second act of a three-act play, while wondering—does it make any sense; who is the director; what is the purpose of it all? We cannot fully understand this act without the others, and particularly the trials and suffering in this second act. Failure, therefore, to understand God's plan of salvation can needlessly diminish faith in Him and in His purposes. (Talk given January 8, 1996.)

The very word *plan* confirms God's paternal purpose, a realization so desperately needed by the confused and despairing on the world's stage. (*Ensign*, May 1984, p. 21.)

Conversationally, we reference God's great design almost too casually at times; we even sketch its rude outlines on chalkboards and paper as if it were the floor plan for an addition to one's house. However, when we really take time to ponder the Plan, it is breathtaking and overpowering! Indeed, I, for one, cannot decide which creates in me the most awe—its very vastness or its intricate, individualized detail. ("'Thanks Be to God.'")

The Lord's plan of salvation is not a set of floor plans for a new house that we as clients can modify or reject. The Architect is not our employee, but our Host, even the Lord of Hosts; He is not only our Landlord, He is also our Lord! (*As I Am*, p. 9.)

This plan constitutes the mother lode of meaning and can cradle us, conceptually, amid any concern. Its truths and perspectives permit us to distinguish between a great book and mere want ads, between vengeance and justice, rage and righteous indignation, and pleasure and happiness. (*Ensign*, May 1984, p. 22.)

Even with all of its interior consistency . . . the plan cannot bring true happiness to anyone whose life is grossly inconsistent with its standards. It cannot fully enfold him who is too worried about being taken in. It has no place of honor for one too concerned with losing his place in the secular synagogue. (See John 12:42–43.) (*Ensign*, May 1984, p. 22.)

The plan always points the way, but does not always smooth the way, since individual development requires an "opposition in all things." (2 Nephi 2:11.) (*Ensign*, May 1984, p. 22.)

Truly, of all the errors mortals could make, God's plan of salvation is the wrong thing to be wrong about! No error could be more enormous or more everlasting in its consequences! (*Ensign*, May 1984, p. 22.)

God's plan . . . is not something to be deduced by logic alone, nor is human experience deep enough or long enough to inform us adequately. It requires revelation from God. (*Ensign*, November 1986, p. 53.)

It does no violence even to our frail human logic to observe that there cannot be a grand plan of salvation for all mankind, unless there is also a plan for each individual. The salvational sum will reflect all its parts. ("Meeting the Challenges of Today," p. 153.)

If we criticize God or are unduly miffed over sufferings and tribulation, we are really criticizing the Planner for implementing the very plan we once approved, premortally (see Job 38:4, 7). Granted, we don't now remember the actual approval. But not remembering is actually part of the plan! (*Believe*, p. 10.)

Knowledge of certain *future* things could affect the way in which we use our agency *now*. Thus, the future would overhang and impose itself unduly upon the present. This would be counterproductive so far as the developmental purposes of the plan of salvation are concerned. (*We Talk of Christ*, p. 127.)

Having so very long ago set in motion His plan of salvation, God will not revise the structure or the schedule of this second estate just because you and I have a bad day. (*Prove*, p. 11.)

Having faith in the Father's macro plan of salvation includes making allowance for His micro plans as well. (*Faith*, p. 38.)

Where would we be if, instead of focusing on bringing "to pass the immortality and eternal life of man," God were distracted by self-centeredness? In fact, God has described what His work is, and does nothing save it be for the benefit of man (see Moses 1:39; 2

Nephi 26:24). Where would we be, too, if our Father in Heaven experienced people fatigue and we were merely His annoying posterity who kept Him from doing what He really wanted to do? (*Faith*, pp. 38–39.)

Upon arriving at the foreseen geographical destination, President Brigham Young confirmed, "This is the place!" Of God's plan of salvation with its developmental destination, it can be confirmed, "This is the process!" (*Endure*, p. 126.)

We can and will be tried tactically, but this can occur without our calling into question the whole strategy of God's plan of salvation. (*Endure*, p. 127.)

Political Correctness

The more what is politically correct seeks to replace what God has declared correct, the more ineffective approaches to human problems there will be. (*Ensign*, May 1996, p. 68.)

One can cater to mortal constituencies but lose the support of the one Elector who matters! (*Prove*, p. 5.)

The trendy, self-congratulating multitudes [in the great and spacious building] were "politically correct" as they unmeekly mocked and pointed at those who clung to the gospel's iron rod. A few whose hands had once grasped the iron rod ended up in the great and spacious building pointing fingers of scorn at former friends. Strange as it seems, the scriptures do not indicate that these individuals let go of the iron rod for any objective reason, or because they were in truth intellectually persuaded by the view of those in the great and spacious building. They were simply ashamed and embarrassed to be separated from the worldy multitudes, whose contempt they would not endure. (*On Becoming a Disciple-Scholar*, p. 18.)

PORNOGRAPHY

The spreading oil slick of pornography . . . carries with it terrible consequences such as bizarre and oppressive sexual behavior, child and spouse abuse, and ultimately a loss of the capacity to love. Unfortunately there is no "superfund" available to underwrite the cleanup of this destructive ooze. In fact, the funding flows in just the opposite direction, as that ancient cartel of lust and greed has significant sway once again. Meanwhile those coated in the awful ooze of pornography are effectively beached, and on filthy shores. Spiritually speaking, they can never take wing again until the ooze is finally cleaned off—"every whit"! (*Believe*, p. 99.)

Pornography especially victimizes women and children. Why then the inordinate preoccupation with its protection? Pornography is better protected than citizens on the streets! (*Ensign*, May 1993, p. 77.)

It is clear in our time that lust and greed, that ancient alliance, have re-formed and commercialized around pornography, trying to clothe themselves in the First Amendment and making it difficult to deal with them. (*We Talk of Christ*, p. 98.)

POSSESSIONS

Mortal property rights have often been either non-existent, revoked, or easily lost, but this is not so with regard to a partly earned, partly grace-provided title to one of the many mansions in Heavenly Father's abode. (*Flood*, p. 53.)

We are often overly concerned . . . with our acquiring or holding turf when, in fact, we are urged instead to let go of the things of the world. Any possessiveness for the things of this world is a wasted effort, for it is obviously on a collision course with reality. One's claims to turf will have no legal status in the kingdom of heaven anyway. It is, for example, our degree of attained meekness or patience—not our title to property or position—that will "rise with us in the resurrection" and will live on. (*As I Am*, p. 63.)

Our personal possessions and our material blessings are really not ours, so what we sometimes regard as a sacrifice was given to us, anyway. (*Believe*, p. 4.)

POTENTIAL

The Lord loves each of us too much to merely let us go on being what we now are, for he knows what we have the possibility to become! ("'In Him All Things Hold Together,'" p. 107.)

Jesus knows the sheep of His fold not only for *what they now are* but also for *what they have the power to become*. (*As I Am*, p. 78.)

When a sudden, stabbing light exposes the gap between what we are and what we think we are, can we, like Peter, let that light be a healing laser? (*Men and Women*, p. 66.)

PRAISE

"Deserved specific praise" is the ingredient of fellowship, of commending Christians. ("Insights from My Life," p. 191.)

Whether in the work place, around the fireplace, or in community service—we can all do something else which is simple but powerful. Isaiah spoke of providing the "garment of praise." (Isaiah 61:3.) Of course, there are times in rendering humanitarian service when we need to give an actual, physical cloak, but, most often, those with whom most of us work need material clothing less than the "garment of praise." ("Successful Leadership in Organizations, Communities and Families.")

Those who have enough bread may still shiver for recognition and yearn for the succor of deserved commendation. ("King Benjamin's Sermon: A Manual for Discipleship.")

Those who are breathless from going the second mile need deserved praise just as the fallen need to be lifted up. (*Ensign*, November 1976, p. 14.)

We should . . . without being artificial, regularly give deserved, specific praise. One of the reasons for doing this is that we are all so very conscious of our shortcomings that it takes a persistent pattern of appreciation to finally penetrate. We are so certain, sometimes, we do not really have a particular skill or attribute that we severely discount praise. One of the reasons we need regular praise from "outside auditors" is to offset the low level of self-acknowledgment most of us have. Flattery is a form of hypocrisy to be avoided, but in overreacting to it, some close the door to commendation. (*Experience*, p. 78.)

Let us in our ministry be nondiscriminatory in the giving of commendation. True, he who is downspirited needs to be lifted up. True, those who are fledglings in the faith may need extra encouragement and deserved, specific praise. But meanwhile, let us not forget the often unnoticed, faithful veterans, lest, like the son who stayed loyally at home and saw the banquet and benefactions given to the prodigal son, the faithful wonder if they are truly appreciated. Let us not assume that another has no need of commendation. Let us give it even if the other does not seem to need it, for we need to give commendation in any event. (*Experience*, p. 89.)

We are not wise enough to know when the need for deserved commendation ceases, if it ever does. But it is significant that our Father commended his Son so openly! Surely on our finite mortal scale of action we cannot dispense with the giving of deserved commendation as a regular part of our style of helping and communicating! (*Smallest Part*, p. 72.)

Commending communications ought to flow from us without too much concern with "the balance of trade." (*Experience*, p. 79.)

The metabolism of meekness requires very little praise or commendation, of which there is usually such a shortage anyway. Otherwise, the sponge of selfishness quickly soaks up everything in sight, including praise intended for others. (*Meek*, p. 6.)

So often we can serve by bathing the wounded and bruised egos of others in the warm waters of deserved commendation. (*Experience*, p. 55.)

Let us never unwittingly turn others in the direction of the praise of the world merely because they are so starved for the praise of the righteous! (*Experience*, pp. 89–90.)

We must not retire into our vault and count the coins of commendation. The rule should be humble appreciation for deserved praise, but not to savor praise. (*Press Forward*, p. 75.)

Cuddling compliments is as dangerous as fondling failures, for neither gives us a true picture of ourselves. (*Press Forward*, p. 75.)

PRAYER

Prayer is that point where the agency of man meets the omniscience of God, and it is where time melts as it touches eternity. (*Experience*, p. 100.)

We cannot, for the purposes of real prayer, hurriedly dress our words and attitudes in tuxedos when our shabby life is in rags. More than we realize, being honest with God in our prayers helps us to be more honest with ourselves. (*Experience*, p. 96.)

Our glimpse of Gethsemane should teach us that all prayers are petitions! (*Ensign*, May 1976, p. 26.)

Genuine faith makes increasing allowance for . . . individual tutorials. In view of these tutorials, God cannot . . . respond affirmatively to all of our petitions with an unbroken chain of "yeses."
This would assume that all of our petitions are for that "which is
right" and are spiritually "expedient." (3 Nephi 18:20; D&C 18:18;
88:64–65.) No petition is so wise! Paul even acknowledged that
we sometimes "know not what we should pray for as we ought."
(Romans 8:26; see also D&C 46:30.) (*Ensign*, May 1991, p. 90.)

Unlike us, God has no restrictive office hours. (*Ensign*, November
1991, p. 31.)

We may at times, if we are not careful, try to pray away pain or
what seems like an impending tragedy, but which is, in reality, an
opportunity. We must do as Jesus did in that respect—also preface
our prayers by saying, "If it be possible," let the trial pass from us—
by saying, "Nevertheless, not as I will, but as thou wilt," and bow-
ing in a sense of serenity to our Father in Heaven's wisdom, because at times God will not be able to let us pass by a trial or a
challenge. If we were allowed to bypass certain trials, everything
that had gone on up to that moment in our lives would be wiped
out. It is because he loves us that at times he will not intercede as
we may wish him to. That, too, we learn from Gethsemane and
from Calvary. ("But for a Small Moment," p. 445.)

Petitioning in prayer has taught me that the vault of heaven, with
all its blessings, is to be opened only by a combination lock: one
tumbler falls when there is faith, a second when there is personal
righteousness, and the third and final tumbler falls only when what
is sought is (in God's judgment, not ours) "right" for us. Sometimes
we pound on the vault door for something we want very much, in
faith, in reasonable righteousness, and wonder why the door does
not open. We would be very spoiled children if that vault door
opened any more easily than it does now. I can tell, looking back,

that God truly loves me by the petitions that, in his perfect wisdom and love, he has refused to grant me. Our rejected petitions tell us not only much about ourselves, but also much about our flawless Father. ("Insights from My Life," p. 200.)

We are often not only too slow to get on our knees but too quick to rise from them, as if prayer involved physical calisthenics. (*Deposition*, p. 20.)

Some have difficulty with the reality that prayers are petitions even though God knows all and loves all anyway. True, we are not informing God, but we are informing ourselves by reverently working through our real concerns and our real priorities and by listening to the Spirit. For us merely to say, ritualistically, "Thy will be done" would not be real petitionary prayer. This would involve no genuine working through of our own feelings. There would be no experience in agonizing, in choosing, and also in submitting. (*Believe*, p. 178.)

One can pray and yet not really pray. Prayers can be routinized and made very superficial. When this happens, there is very little communication and very little growth. Yet, given the times in which we live, improving our prayers should be one of our deepest desires if we are genuinely serious about growing spiritually. (*Experience*, p. 91.)

So very much of pure prayer seems to be the process of first discovering, rather than requesting, the will of our Father in heaven and then aligning ourselves therewith. (*Experience*, p. 93.)

Neither the pure City of Enoch nor pure prayers are arrived at in a day! (*Experience*, p. 95.)

Prayer . . . that is too conscious of itself is not yet really praying. What is needed by us all are feelings of adoration that produce a mental posture of contemplation with more meditation and less premeditation. (*Experience*, p. 96.)

We sometimes find ourselves praying for others when we should be doing things for them. Prayers are not to be a substitute for service, but a spur thereto. (*Experience*, p. 97.)

How often have you and I in our provincialism prayed to see ahead and, mercifully, been refused, lest our view of the present be blurred? How many times have we been blessed by *not* having our prayers answered, at least according to the specifications set forth in our petitions? (*Prove*, p. 8.)

PREMORTALITY

We will not be strangers in the City of God. We were there before, when the morning stars sang together and the sons of God shouted for joy at the prospects of this stern but necessary mortal existence. (See Job 38:4–7.) What we sang then was doubtless an anthem of praise far greater than the "Hallelujah Chorus," more glorious than Moses' and Israel's song after crossing the Red Sea. (See Exodus 15:1–2.) (*Ensign*, May 1986, p. 36.)

Some of our present circumstances may reflect previous agreements, now forgotten, but once freely made. (*Ensign*, May 1984, p. 22.)

One day we will understand fully how complete our commitment was in our first estate in accepting the very conditions of challenge in our second estate about which we sometimes complain in this school of stress. Our collective and personal premortal promises will then be laid clearly before us. ("Taking Up the Cross," p. 253.)

In some of those precious and personal moments of deep discovery, there will be a sudden surge of recognition of an immortal insight, a doctrinal déjà vu. We will sometimes experience a flash from the mirror of memory that beckons us forward toward a far horizon. . . . And when of great truths we can come to say "I know," that powerful spiritual witness may also carry with it the sense of our having known before. With rediscovery, what we are really saying is, "I know—again!" No wonder that, so often, real teaching is mere reminding. ("Meeting the Challenges of Today," p. 156.)

Genes and environment by themselves will never provide an adequate explanation for human differences because there is a third factor in the equation of this life: all that occurred before we came here. The Gospel makes it clear that we came to earth trailing traits from our lengthy and extensive experience in the premortal existence. (*Choose*, p. 37.)

To what degree we were permitted, before coming here, to see all the outcomes and the risks of mortality, such as war and poverty, we presently know not. A *just* God surely would have let us understand sufficiently about that upon which we are soon to embark. However, with whatever measure of understanding we then had, some "shouted for joy," a stirring reaction that ought to tell us enough in terms of our perceptions then, when we had some added perspective. (*As I Am*, p. 107.)

Blessed with our knowledge of premortal experience, life is largely what we choose to make of it and of our inborn talents. (*Flood*, p. 47.)

Happily, for what we know of this precious doctrine [of premortality] we are not dependent on research—but on *revelation! (Small Moment,* p. 81.)

PRESENT

The past of each of us is now inflexible. We need to concentrate on what has been called "the holy present," for now is sacred; we never really live in the future. The holy gift of life always takes the form of now. (*Ensign,* November 1974, p. 13.)

[A] trap to be avoided . . . is the tendency we have—rather humanly, rather understandably—to get ourselves caught in peering through the prism of the present and then distorting our perspective about things. Time is of this world; it is not of eternity. We can, if we are not careful, feel the pressures of time and see things in a distorted way. How important it is that we see things as much as possible through the lens of the gospel with its eternal perspectives. ("But for a Small Moment," pp. 453–54.)

Significantly, those who look forward to a next and better world are usually "anxiously engaged" in improving this one, for they "always abound in good works" (D&C 58:27; Alma 7:24). (*Ensign,* November 1994, p. 35.)

We should not let the gray mists of the moment obscure the bright promises and prospects of eternity. (*As I Am,* p. 99.)

PRIDE

Do not pride and wickedness go hand-in-hand? For as surely as the proud elevate themselves in their own eyes, their neighbors disappear from view. The proud not only fail to look up to God, but the proud look down, if they look at all, on their neighbors. (*Look Back*, p. 8.)

Pride keeps repentance from even starting or continuing. Some fail because they are more concerned with the preservation of their public image than with having Christ's image in their countenances! (Alma 5:14.) Pride prefers cheap repentance, paid for with shallow sorrow. (*Ensign*, November 1991, p. 31.)

Just as meekness is in all our virtues, so is pride in all our sins. ("'Meek and Lowly,'" p. 57.)

Do not let yesterday hold tomorrow hostage! Walk away from your investment in the penny stock of pride; it never pays dividends. (*Ensign*, May 1982, p. 39.)

The Father, ever anxious that all be free to choose, gave Lucifer opportunity to campaign. "Behold, here am I, send me, I will be thy son, and I will redeem all mankind, that one soul shall not be lost, and surely I will do it, wherefore give me thine honor" (Moses 4:1; see also Abraham 3:27; Isaiah 6:8). Note the ego dripping from only three lines: two *me*'s and four *I*'s. Those vertical pronouns are usually accompanied by unbending knees. (*Ensign*, November 1987, p. 32.)

Though on an infinitely smaller scale, when each man insists on walking in his own way, he is but mirroring our ego-saturated brother in the premortal world who wanted things his own way. In some twisted contemporary thinking there is likewise a connection between glory and "my way." In any case, to go on insisting on "*my* way" instead of *the* way is to remain unrescued and unhappy. (*Press Forward*, p. 46.)

Cutting truth does hurt, but its lancing can drain the pustules of pride. (*Ensign*, November 1989, p. 82.)

The men and women of Christ magnify their callings without magnifying themselves. Whereas the natural man says "Worship me" and "Give me thine power," the men and women of Christ seek to exercise power by long-suffering and unfeigned love. (See Moses 1:12; 4:3; D&C 121:41.) (*Ensign*, November 1990, p. 16.)

A person's small puffs of pride are best blown away by the breeze of brotherhood; left alone, these become enlarged and dark thunderclouds which drench all round about. (*Heart*, p. 15.)

Bruising as the tumble off the peak of pride is, it may be necessary. Even then, one must be careful not to let despair continue the descent into the swamp of self-pity. (*Meek*, p. 58.)

The perils of "puffery" are especially real when combined with iniquity. . . . Those who are puffed up need constantly to be reinflated, hence the tendency of some to "play to the galleries," including by way of criticism of the kingdom. (*Meek*, p. 85.)

In their resentment, those who worry that someone will "rule over" them rationalize their resistance to repentance. They resist because they are already well along in self-pleasing. Ironically, even as they fret about being ruled over, they are actually being ruled over by an aristocracy of appetites or by the stern sovereignty of selfishness. (*Not My Will*, p. 65.)

It is possible to have illegitimate pride in a legitimate role or in a deserved reputation. Such pride must go, too, for we are servants of Him who lived His unique life as a person of "no reputation" (Philippians 2:7). (*Not My Will*, p. 93.)

PROBLEMS

Just as some people lose the same twenty pounds of weight every year, so some of us are always solving the same problem—over and over again. How weary one can get just running in place! (*Prove*, p. 111.)

PROCRASTINATION

Indeed, one of the most cruel games anyone can play with self is the "not yet" game—hoping to sin just a bit more before ceasing; to enjoy the praise of the world a little longer before turning away from the applause; to win just once more in the wearing sweepstakes of materialism; to be chaste, but not yet; to be good neighbors, but not now. (*Ensign*, November 1974, p. 13.)

One can play upon the harpstrings of hesitations and reservations just so long, and then one faces that special moment—a moment when what has been sensed, mutely, suddenly finds voice and cries out with tears, "Lord, I believe; help thou mine unbelief." (Mark 9:24.) (*Ensign*, November 1974, p. 13.)

PROFANITY

[God] does not want us . . . to take His name in vain, but this is because of what happens to us when we do. Our profanity cannot diminish His Godhood, His love, His omnipotence, or His omniscience. But our profanity does damage us and can damage us profoundly. (*Sermons*, p. 85.)

PROGRAMS

Often in the confusion of means and ends, we fail to see that programs and activities are helps, not ends in themselves, so far as developing the eternal attributes and everlasting skills are concerned. The character that can be developed by Scouting will be there in the next world, long after one has any need to make fire without matches. (*Prove*, p. 111.)

Let us not mistake program scaffolding for substance. (*Ensign*, November 1982, p. 68.)

Programs such as the Church's current recreation programs are aids and helps. These clearly provide needed fellowship, physical exercise, cultural development, opportunities for missionary work, and moments of needed recognition for individuals. However, Abraham and those about him apparently did not have an athletic program. We have it now and it is helpful. (*Notwithstanding*, p. 19.)

Some programs and practices in the Church today are important aids but have not been constant necessities in every other age. Discerning disciples understand this. (*Notwithstanding*, p. 20.)

The Church is not a democracy that responds to its constituents. We do not make demands of the Lord. Of course, the Church and its leaders at all levels should be sensitive to conditions in the Church—if for no other reason than the keeping of the second commandment—but, most of all, as shepherds of the flock. But, as we have so sadly learned in recent secular and political history, a preferential program is seldom the "cure" for a basic need. (*Notwithstanding*, p. 53.)

The Church seeks to avoid the mistakes of some secular governments that establish a program for every need and a department for every constituency. What is needed is more good families and neighbors and fewer programs. (*Prove*, p. 65.)

A few in the Church are needlessly laden with programmed hyperactivity. They unwisely and unnecessarily exceed their strength and means, running faster than they are able (see D&C 10:4; Mosiah 4:27). Their fatiguing, Martha-like anxiety should yield more often to a Mary-like sense of proportion about what matters most; then the good part will not be taken from them (see Luke 10:41–42). (*Men and Women*, p. 3.)

Progression

The scriptures are like a developmental display window through which we can see gradual growth—along with this vital lesson: it is direction first, *then* velocity! (*Ensign*, November 1976, p. 13.)

Thoughtless haste and spurts of service are not what is desired, for such naiveté is like the businessman who confuses volume with profit. (*Notwithstanding*, p. 3.)

The scriptural advice, "Do not run faster or labor more than you have strength" (D&C 10:4) suggests paced progress, much as God used seven creative periods in preparing man and this earth. There is a difference, therefore, between being "anxiously engaged" and being over-anxious. (Ensign, November 1976, pp. 12–13.)

Following celestial road signs while in telestial traffic jams is not easy, especially when our destination involves not just moving next door—or even across town. (Ensign, November 1976, p. 12.)

Men finally climbed Mount Everest, not by standing at its base in consuming awe but by shouldering their packs and by placing one foot in front of another. Feet are made to move forward—not backward! (Ensign, November 1976, p. 14.)

It does little good to speak and write brilliantly about a concept such as "eternal progression" if we are unconcerned with daily improvement. (Excellent, p. 30.)

Given our weaknesses . . . paced progress is essential, much as God used six measured and orderly creative periods (followed by respite) in preparing man and this earth. There is a difference, therefore, between being steadily and effectively or "anxiously" engaged, on the one hand, and, on the other hand, being frantically engaged one moment and being passive and detached the next. (Notwithstanding, p. 3.)

Pace is so essential to personal progress lest we magnify our weaknesses instead of our callings. (Notwithstanding, p. 7.)

We need not be perpetual motion machines—merely forward motion machines. (Prove, p. 112.)

PROPHETS

It is exceedingly important for members of the Church to get experience following the prophets in little things, so that they can follow in large matters. By following the prophets in fair weather we become familiar with their cadence, so that we can follow them in stormy times too, for then both our reflexes and our experience will need to combine to help us; the stresses will be so very real. (*Experience*, p. 102.)

Our relationship to living prophets is *not* one in which their sayings are a smorgasbord from which we may take only that which pleases us. We are to partake of all that is placed before us, including the spinach, and to leave a clean plate! (*Really Are*, p. 74.)

Throughout scriptural history, we see recurring efforts to demean prophets in order to dismiss them—to label them in order to diminish them. Mostly, however, they are simply ignored by their contemporaries and by secular history. (*Ensign*, November 1984, p. 10.)

No wonder the prophets are repetitious in their warnings. After all, if one were permitted only a few surviving lines to family, friends, and posterity, those might be headlines. (*Ensign*, November 1986, p. 54.)

In the months and years ahead, events will require of each member [of the Church] that he or she decide whether or not he or she will follow the First Presidency. Members will find it more difficult to halt longer between two opinions (see 1 Kings 18:21). . . . Not being ashamed of the gospel of Jesus Christ includes not being ashamed of the prophets of Jesus Christ. ("Meeting the Challenges of Today," p. 149.)

The true believer is growing in his patience, including being patient in following the living prophets. He knows that trying to get ahead of the Brethren is a sure way of falling behind. ("'True Believers in Christ,'" p. 138.)

Prophets are not just for following in the Sinai or on a westward journey. ("Grounded, Rooted, Established, and Settled," p. 16.)

We have obligations to the Lord's prophets, past and present, which include being fair, posthumously or presently, concerning their words. The "choice seer," Joseph, reminded the Church in an epistle (December 1838) from jail that, "our light speeches from time to time . . . have nothing to do with the fixed principle of our hearts." . . . Should we not distinguish between the utterances of the moment and considered opinions? Do not all of us wish for that same understanding on the part of our friends, hoping they, "with the breath of kindness," will "blow the chaff away?" ("'A Choice Seer,'" p. 120.)

The tendency to rely on too small a sample and to use the lazy shorthand way of assessing prophets is present today, as if driving repeatedly through a university campus were knowing a university. But that which is familiar is not necessarily always understood. (*Sermons*, p. 40.)

The absence of a commanding physical presence—or, in modern political terms, the absence of charisma—can cause people to disregard or dismiss one actually sent of God, even though the substance of the individual or his message is exceedingly important. A pseudo-sophisticated society is especially likely to dismiss someone who does not have impeccable educational credentials. Impressive as Peter and John were, they were still labeled unlearned and ignorant men. [See Acts 4:13.] (*Sermons*, p. 45.)

The lifespans of planets, as well as prophets, are known to God. (*Experience*, p. 13.)

We can scarcely be in tune with God if we are not in harmony with His prophets. We are not likely to hear God's instructions to us as we pray if we neglect the counsel of His leaders. (*Experience*, p. 100.)

Among the requirements that God has laid upon us is to pay heed to His living prophets. In our dispensation this has been described as "following the Brethren." It is a dimension of obedience that has been difficult for some in every dispensation. It will be particularly hard in ours, the final dispensation. (*Experience*, p. 101.)

To use the supposed errors of others, including those of the Brethren, as an excuse for our lessened devotion is a most grave error! All of us are in the process of becoming—including prophets and General Authorities. (*Experience*, p. 105.)

There will be times when we follow the prophets even as they are in the very act of obedience themselves; they will not, in fact, always be able to explain to us why they are doing what they are doing—much as Adam offered sacrifices without a full understanding of what underlay that special ritual. (Moses 5:6.) (*Experience*, p. 115.)

The living prophets, if to some they seem monotonous, are simply reporting what they know from the living God. The fact that it is essentially the same message from dispensation to dispensation merely confirms the truth of such utterances. . . . We may grow tired of hearing that the earth is round, but our boredom will not change its shape. (*Really Are*, pp. 38–39.)

If we believe in the living prophet, our sustaining faith will not die with a particular prophet but will be transferred to his successor. (*Really Are*, p. 71.)

The living prophet will always be in touch with eternity and, in a sense, will therefore stand outside time as he reflects God's will to a people who may be too much caught up in the fashion or problems of any particular age. (*Really Are*, p. 76.)

The living prophets are not perfect men, but they live close to Him who is perfect. (*Really Are*, p. 77.)

Prophets are alerted to tiny trends that bode ill for mankind. Prophets, therefore, are the Lord's early-warning system: they both detect and decry at his direction. What may seem to be a premature expression of prophetic concern is actually the early discovery of a difficulty that will later plague the people. (*Really Are*, pp. 77–78.)

It is not enough . . . to define the living prophet as merely the current prophet who is alive today, though that is correct enough. The living prophets were all close enough to God (before they came here) to be chosen by him then, and they will be close to him in the eternities. Moreover, while their livingness includes such precious perpetuity, even in this fleeting frame of time called mortality, these men live with a richness and in a depth that desensitized sinners do not and cannot know. (*Really Are*, pp. 80–81.)

More divine data has been given to some prophets than others, but the "bottom line" is not the comparative candlepower given to each of the Lord's prophets; rather, it is how, each time the light of heaven is focused, it shines upon the same basic truths! (*Really Are*, p. 100.)

RATIONALIZING

Occasionally we see those who do something bad justify it on the grounds that thereby they can thereafter do some good: "If I can just make this deal or gain this office, think of the position I will be in to do much good." This rationalizing might be called looking beyond Lucifer's shoulder—on to imagined possibilities. It is a very different thing from saying, "Get thee behind me!" (See Matthew 16:23.) (*Men and Women*, p. 130.)

REALISTS

The true religionist is actually the ultimate realist, for he has a fully realistic view of man and the universe; he traffics in truths that are culminating and everlasting; he does not focus on facts that fade with changing circumstances or data that dissolve under pressures of time and circumstance. (*Really Are*, p. 1.)

REGRET

Recycling regrets [doesn't] change reality. Pawing through the past is not productive. . . . Too much attention to what might have been actually gets in the way of what still can be. ("Insights from My Life," p. 189.)

Since we all make mistakes, it is crucial that we not remain immobilized thereby. Otherwise we will find ourselves caught in a ritual of regret, as memory serves up "instant replays." (*Believe*, pp. 137–38.)

Relationships

We [should] admit that if we were to die today, we would be genuinely and deeply missed. Perhaps parliaments would not praise us, but no human circle is so small that it does not touch another, and another. (*Ensign*, November 1976, p. 14.)

Our impact is less likely to emanate from the pulpit—more often it will occur in one-to-one relationships, or in small groups where we can have an impact on an individual. (*Excellent*, p. 74.)

We have an *obligation* to work out impasses as well as trespasses in interpersonal relationships. (*Press Forward*, p. 88.)

Taking the initiative and consulting in private are good not only for resolving trespasses in human relationships [see Matthew 18:15], but impasses, too. The withholding of key communications can be even more serious than withholding one's material substance. Food and raiment can sometimes be supplied by others, but the needed spiritual substance is often not available elsewhere. (*Experience*, p. 74.)

If one tends to regard others as functions and not as everlasting individual entities, he will seek as few lasting and obligating relationships as possible. Doing this, ironically, ensures less and less happiness and even further deterioration in the total human environment. Yet, today, more and more people seek to travel through life selfishly, as unencumbered and uncommitted as possible. (*We Talk of Christ*, p. 74.)

Calmness conserves energy as well as relationships. (*Endure*, p. 115.)

RELATIVISM

At times only a small, satanic breeze, now the winds of relativism have reached gale proportions. Over a period of several decades relativism has eroded ethics, public and personal, has worn down the will of many, has contributed to a slackening sense of duty, civic and personal. The old mountains of individual morality have been worn down. This erosion has left mankind in a sand-dune society, in a desert of disbelief, where there are no landmarks, no north, no east, no west, and no south. There is only the dust of despair! (*Deposition*, pp. 79–80.)

As the Church spreads across the earth, so does Satan's dominion. Prophesied for our day are such things as wars, commotions, and distress of nations. These are not all geophysical. Perhaps even more destructive is the ethical relativism that denies any spiritual order and rejects divine and fixed principles of right and wrong. This we see reflected in a wholesale decline in moral standards and in the rapidly escalating incidence of cruelty, crime and corruption. (*Endure*, p. 18.)

Without utilizing fixed principles, confused mortals will find things very hard to fix. (*Endure*, p. 15.)

Relativism may be the disbeliever's defense, but it is the devil's offense. It involves the denial of the existence of absolute truths and, therefore, of an absolute truth giver, God. (*Deposition*, p. 79.)

Reflect, for instance, on how inoperative the Ten Commandments are in many lives. Today, *killing, stealing,* and bearing *false witness* still carry some social stigma and legal sanction, but sanction is effectively gone regarding sexual immmorality, the Sabbath day, honoring fathers and mothers, and the taking of the name of the Lord in vain. Some of this decline represents the bitter harvest of ethical relativism, the philosophy of choice of many, reflecting no fixed, divine truths but merely the mores of the moment. No wonder Ortega Y. Gasset wisely warned, "If truth does not exist, relativism cannot take itself seriously." (*Ensign*, May 1994, p. 88.)

To assert that there is some way other than adherence to the divine standard that has come down to us through the centuries in our Judeo-Christian heritage is to introduce the inevitable rationalization that relativism always brings: If infidelity is not really wrong per se, then why cannot every individual walk "in his own way," determining that which pleases him or her and that which gives sensual pleasure—even if it be child molestation or masochism? A nonmoral ground is no ground at all! A pervert will be unimpressed by ethical relativism's norms. Besides, inner slackness finally dooms outer enforcement, for enforcement officials are not only dwarfed by the enormity of their tasks, but also become less effective as the definition of crime becomes less and less legally and behaviorally clear. One has only to pause and wonder about what the role of a vice squad would have been in Sodom and Gomorrah! (*Notwithstanding*, p. 96.)

RELEVANCE

By living and sharing the gospel of Jesus Christ, we are doing the most relevant thing we can do by way of helping. (There are civic and other chores to be done, of course.) Day in and day out, the gospel is the one thing that is most relevant, and we are to be of good cheer. (*Deposition*, p. 98.)

There is such a thing as irrelevant relevance; for example, a tendency to be topical, to read only newspapers rather than books, to deal with tactical truths rather than strategic truths. The unsteady follower who caroms from current cause to current cause will end up being a social cipher and very lonely much of the time. (*Choose*, p. 68.)

To be sure, we cannot, while here, entirely avoid contact with the obsolescent and the irrelevant; it is all around us. But one can be around irrelevancy without becoming attached to it. Certainly we should not become preoccupied with obsolete things, yet we need not have a discontent with the paraphernalia of this probationary estate. Yet to mistake mortal props for the real drama that is underway is a grave error to be avoided. (*Prove*, p. 12.)

RELIGION

It is clear that the dispersion, diffusion, and distortion of gospel truths has left fragments of the faith in various religions and cultures throughout the world. Many see in this an attempt by man to make his own god and religion in the absence of real ones. Rather than such similarities being evidence against the existence of God, however, these refracted truths bear witness of the initial wholeness which existed in the beginning with Adam. (*Flood*, p. 20.)

RENEWAL

We forget to pace ourselves at times. Rest and renewal permit us to go farther faster in this mortal marathon. (*Prove*, p. 109.)

Sometimes being worn down is our own fault for not providing space and time for ourselves for spiritual renewal, an area that to the adversary is "off limits." We need the equivalent of designated nonsmoking areas to secure us from secondhand sensuality, inappropriate humor, twisted film, and bad music. (*Not My Will*, p. 75.)

REPENTANCE

Real repentance involves not a mechanical checklist, but a checkreining of the natural self. (*Ensign*, November 1991, p. 30.)

True contrition brings full capitulation. One simply surrenders, caring only about what God thinks, not what "they" think, while meekly offering, "O God, . . . make thyself known unto me, and I will give away all my sins to know thee." (Alma 22:18.) Giving away all our sins is the only way we can come to know God. (*Ensign*, November 1991, p. 32.)

God asks us now to give up only those things which, if clung to, will destroy us! (*Ensign*, November 1974, p. 13.)

Cleansing circumstances are to be welcomed even if the scrubbing is painful. (*Flood*, p. 94.)

That program of progress—repentance—beckons us to betterness. (*Ensign*, May 1976, p. 26.)

For us mistake-prone mortals, this plan of mercy provides for recognition and redress of error and for the resumption of interrupted individual development. (*Ensign*, May 1984, p. 22.)

When you and I make unwise decisions, if we have frail faith we not only demand to be rescued but we want to be rescued privately, painlessly, quickly—or at least to be beaten only "with a few stripes." (2 Nephi 28:8.) Brothers and sisters, how can we really feel forgiven until we first feel responsible? How can we learn from our own experiences unless these lessons are owned up to? (*Ensign*, May 1991, p. 91.)

Repentance is a rescuing, not a dour doctrine. It is available to the gross sinner as well as to the already-good individual striving for incremental improvement. (*Ensign*, November 1991, p. 30.)

Repentance requires both turning away from evil and turning to God. . . . Initially, this turning reflects progress from telestial to terrestrial behavior, and later on to celestial behavior. As the sins of the telestial world are left behind, the focus falls ever more steadily upon the sins of omission, which often keep us from full consecration. (*Ensign*, November 1991, p. 30.)

False remorse . . . is like "fondling our failings." In ritual regret, we mourn our mistakes but without mending them. (*Ensign*, November 1991, p. 31.)

Jesus suffered for our sins; He knows perfectly what constructive sorrow we should be experiencing in order to be cleansed. His justice will insist on such needed and cleansing sorrow, for nothing less will do. Because His love of us is true charity, He will not spare us, since to exempt us would be to deny us. It is better that there be sorrow now so that later on there can be a fullness of joy. (*As I Am*, p. 18.)

[God] is ever encouraging us to regroup and try again. And there are no restrictive office hours for receiving returning prodigals—night and day He awaits us! (*Men and Women*, p. 28.)

It is strange that when one is remodeling a portion of his house, he expects visitors to be tolerant of improvements that are so obviously underway. Yet while one is remodeling his character, we often feel obligated to call attention to the messy signs of remodeling, or feel called upon to remember aloud things as they were. Forgetting is such a necessary part of forgiving. (*Experience*, p. 113.)

The past must not hold the future hostage; otherwise, what of the sons of Mosiah? Or Saul of Tarsus? Or many of us? (*Press Forward*, p. 91.)

If we really have sufficient faith to enjoy "faith unto repentance" (Alma 34:17), this in itself dramatically lightens our life loads. Even so, how long it takes us to heave off the heavy burdens of hypocrisy! Perhaps the saddest consequence of little faith is little repentance. The burden of believing seems so heavy, when it is actually the wearying weight of our own sins that we feel. (*Faith*, p. 29.)

REPROOF

Correction when it comes often has a cutting edge, and normally there is no anesthetic. Hearts which are so set upon wrong or worldly ways must first be broken, and this cannot be done with-out pain. And so it is that speaking the truth in love matters so very much! (*Experience*, p. 86.)

To withhold deserved reproof, and the reasons therefore, may be to withhold a warning that is urgently needed. Reproof is often a last railing before an erring individual goes over the edge of the cliff. ("Insights from My Life," p. 192.)

Letting others simply go erringly on may be easy—but it is not love. . . . At times we must run the risk of having our love and concern for other people seen by them as hostility. (*Excellent*, pp. 79–80.)

If we seek to administer reproof properly, we must also be willing to listen and to respond after we have issued our reproof. The re-ceiver will often need some time to test the accuracy of our reproof and the implications of that reproof. He needs to reassure himself that we care for him, that he is still safely within our circle of con-cern. (*Excellent*, p. 94.)

Jesus' fearlessness . . . was accompanied by gentleness. When He healed ten lepers and only one returned to thank Him, He then asked, "But where are the nine?" [Luke 17:17.] There was no point in His lecturing the one—as we so often do, giving the right lesson to the wrong audience—instead of the other nine. After all, the one did return! (*As I Am*, p. 84.)

The correct manner and motivation for reproof are indicated in Doctrine and Covenants 121:43. In practice, however, when we undertake to reprove we frequently are prompted not by the Holy Ghost but by ego. Moreover, we often fail to reprove "betimes," meaning speedily and *early on*. Time can harden feelings as surely as the sun bakes wet clay. (*Flood*, p. 113.)

Most of us don't like to be cut to the center [see 1 Nephi 16:2], and when the gospel standards cut us it hurts. The tendency is to deal with the pain by rejecting further surgery. (*Power*, p. 49.)

Nor should we neglect the power of *gentle* reproof. Sometimes we need not declaim the actions of others so much as remind them of who they are and what they should be. (*Experience*, p. 88.)

RESTORATION

The finished mosaic of the history of the Restoration will be larger and more varied as more pieces of tile emerge, adjusting a sequence here or enlarging there a sector of our understanding. The fundamental outline is in place now, however. But history deals with imperfect people in process of time, whose imperfections produce refractions as the pure light of the gospel plays upon them. There may even be a few pieces of tile which, for the moment, do not seem to fit. . . . The final mosaic of the Restoration will be resplendent, reflecting divine design and the same centerpiece—the Father's plan of salvation and exaltation and the atonement of His Son, Jesus Christ. (*Ensign*, November 1984, p. 11.)

The Restoration provides clarification. As prophesied, the rising sun of the Restoration melts away the icy stumbling blocks of false doctrines frozen in place over the centuries (1 Nephi 14:1). (*Not My Will*, p. 39.)

Clearly, the Book of Mormon was needed as an added witness in these the decades of deep doubt. Clearly, the theophany at Palmyra puts to rout all the chatter about the historicity of Jesus; it ended all the theological and historical fuzziness about the nature of the Godhead, while dramatically confirming the reality of the resurrection. ("'All Hell Is Moved,'" p. 178.)

What the Restoration brings clearly into our view discloses a many-splendored Savior, not simply a Socrates in Samaria or a Plato in Palestine. (*Not My Will*, p. 43.)

For those who truly desire to live not by bread alone, but by every word which proceeds forth from the Lord, there will be no famine. In fact, the harvest of the Restoration is "running over." (*Not My Will*, p. 47.)

As you and I dash about the wonder-filled landscape of the Restoration, exclaiming and observing, it should not surprise us that our first impressions are less than definitive. Little wonder that some of us mistake a cluster of trees for the whole forest or that, in some of our joyful exclamations, there are some unintended exaggerations. Roving amid the tall timber of truth, the pervasive scent of pine is inevitably upon us. Our pockets are bulging with souvenir rocks and cones. And we are filled with childish glee. There is no way to survey it all—in one tour or several. Besides, further familiarization will only increase our wonder. After all, One not given to hyperbole used the word *marvelous* to describe the Restoration! (*Ensign*, November 1987, p. 33.)

RESURRECTION

The gift of immortality to all mankind through the reality of the Resurrection is so powerful a promise that our rejoicing in these great and generous gifts should drown out any sorrow, assuage any grief, conquer any mood, dissolve any despair, and tame any tragedy. Those who now see life as pointless will one day point with adoration to the performance of the Man of Galilee in those crowded moments of time known as Gethsemane and Calvary. Those who presently say life is meaningless will yet applaud the Atonement which saves us from meaninglessness. Christ's victory over death ended the human predicament. Now there are only personal predicaments, and from these too we may be rescued by following the teachings of him who rescued us from general extinction. ("'All Hell Is Moved,'" p. 181.)

Granted, there is not full correlation among the four Gospels about the events and participants at the empty garden tomb. (See Matthew 28:1–8; Mark 16:1–8; Luke 24:19; John 20:1–10.) Yet the important thing is that the tomb was empty, because Jesus had been resurrected! Essence, not tactical detail! (*Ensign*, November 1984, p. 11.)

All men ultimately die, but the accumulated "luggage" they take with them into the next great adventure is so different. Should we who see differences in babies so soon after their birth not expect variety in each human snowflake after the resurrection? (*My Family*, p. 96.)

If we ponder just what it is that will rise with us in the resurrection, it seems clear that our intelligence will rise with us, meaning not simply our IQ but also our capacity to receive and apply truth. Our talents, attributes, and skills will rise with us; certainly also our capacity to learn, our degree of self-discipline, and our capacity to work. Our precise form of work here may have no counterpart there, but the capacity to work will never be obsolete. (*Prove*, p. 45.)

REVELATION

Many sects—without the reinforcing rods of revelation—have been badly shaken by theological tremors; the resulting ecclesiastical erosion has been so rapid it is measured in years, not centuries. (*Ensign*, May 1976, p. 26.)

In the economy of heaven, God does not send thunder if a still, small voice is enough, or a prophet if a priest can do the job. (*Deposition*, p. 29.)

He [Jesus Christ] lives today, mercifully granting unto all nations as much light as they can bear. . . . And who better than the Light of the World can decide the degree of divine disclosure—whether it is to be flashlights or floodlights. (*Ensign*, November 1981, pp. 9–10.)

Whenever the words of heaven are filtered through mortal minds, tongues, and vocabularies there is some diminution. (*Ensign*, November 1983, p. 55.)

As the Lord communicates with the meek and submissive, fewer decibels are required, and more nuances are received. (*Ensign*, May 1985, p. 71.)

When the Lord gives us "line upon line" and "precept upon precept" about Himself and His plans, many ignore these great gifts. Instead of lines, some demand paragraphs and even pages. When God provides "here a little, and there a little" (Isaiah 28:10), some want a lot—now! (*Ensign*, November 1987, p. 31.)

Let us be wary about accommodating revealed theology to conventional wisdom. (*Ensign*, November 1993, p. 20.)

God gives to us the gospel, by which we get *direction*, *motivation*, and *illumination*. But there appears to be no point . . . in God's constantly illuminating the trail beyond where my eyes of faith can now see. ("Insights from My Life," p. 190.)

We cannot determine by using radio telescopes . . . that there is a plan of salvation operating in the universe, helpful as radio telescopes are for astrophysical purposes. Salvational truths are obtainable only by revelation. (*Flood*, p. 18.)

There are important gradations as between types of blessings. One type—very real and much appreciated—is tied to temporal and passing conditions. We might call these operational revelations— how to build an ark, or how to illuminate barges, for example. These are remarkable blessings which respond to urgent needs, but they cannot compare to the illuminating revelations from Jesus concerning what we must do to be more like Him. That type of blessing is tied to the eternal conditions. Both types are needed. Both are to be remembered. (*Flood*, p. 54.)

Divine disclosure is metered in "process of time" at a pace largely dependent upon our readiness to receive. (*Meek*, p. 91.)

We have a notable lack of capacity to appreciate things that, like water out of a fire hydrant, come in a rush. Hence the Lord meters out divine disclosure according to what is deserved and usable. (*Meek*, p. 91.)

What reason concludes are impassable mountains, revelation shows to be rolling hills over which we can pass if we press forward.

Sitting and staring at the slopes can make them into stern Sierras. (*Press Forward*, p. 43.)

Continuing revelation is like the timely unfolding of a huge tapestry. Those of us who live out our lives seeing mostly one segment of that tapestry must not mistake what we see for the whole of the tapestry. It is the same with the unfolding of the kingdom. (*Really Are*, p. 40.)

REVERENCE

We can and should have more reverence in our chapels and foyers, but isn't it good that the increase in the decibel level when we are together occurs because of good feelings rather than bad ones? (*Press Forward*, p. 103.)

RIGHTEOUSNESS

Righteousness preserves and sharpens the tastebuds of the soul, while selfishness first scalds and then destroys them. (*Experience*, p. 65.)

Righteousness is not a matter of role, nor is goodness a matter of gender. (*Ensign*, May 1978, p. 10.)

Before the ultimate victory of the forces of righteousness, some skirmishes will be lost. Even these, however, must leave a record so that the choices before the people are clear and let others do as they will in the face of prophetic counsel. There will also be times, happily, when a minor defeat seems probable, that others will step forward, having been rallied to rightness by what we do. We will know the joy, on occasion, of having awakened a slumbering majority of the decent people of all races and creeds—a majority which was, till then, unconscious of itself. ("Meeting the Challenges of Today," p. 151.)

Eight were rescued in the time of Noah, but finally only three from Sodom (in view of Lot's wife's fate). While the precise mathematical proportions of the critical mass of good people necessary to save a society is not known to us, it cannot be doubted that without that critical mass, societies decline rapidly and significant changes come, in one form or another, and sometimes suddenly! (*Look Back*, p. 26.)

Any response but righteousness is risky. (*Deposition*, p. 13.)

Eternal things are always done in the process of time. Men are ripened in righteousness as the grain is ripened. Each process requires rich soil and the sunlight of heaven. Time is measured only to impatient men. Direction is initially more important than speed. Who would really want momentum anyway, if he were on a wrong course? (*Heart*, p. 35.)

Righteousness increases the uniqueness of our presence, but sin sinks us into sameness. (*Heart*, p. 35.)

Evil people exist. The in-betweeners merely survive. But those who have really lived will be those who have lived righteously, because they will have lived righteously and served selflessly in a time of stunning contrasts. They will have managed to keep clean in a dirty world. And being free, they will be happy in otherwise sad times, and all their experiences will be for their good. (*Experience*, p. 65.)

SACRIFICE

Real, personal sacrifice never was placing an animal on the altar. Instead, it is a willingness to put the animal in us upon the altar and letting it be consumed! (*Ensign*, May 1995, p. 68.)

When we have *truly* given what we have, it is like paying a full tithe; it is, in that respect, *all* that was asked. The widow who cast in her two mites was neither self-conscious nor searching for mortal approval. (*Deposition*, p. 30.)

By putting everything we have on the altar of the Lord and not waiting for Him to give us a receipt, we show our submissiveness. Otherwise our giving may become linked with expecting recognition or with soliciting proof of the Lord's appreciation. (*Not My Will*, p. 96.)

Since the natural man is too attached to his possessions anyway, the plan requires that we must have experience in giving possessions away—in sharing and even losing them—in order to give us experience with the principle of sacrifice without worrying about getting credit or receiving recognition as we worship Him who made the "great and last sacrifice" (Alma 34:10). (*Faith*, p. 42.)

The submission of one's will is placing on God's altar the only uniquely personal thing one has to place there. The many other things we "give" are actually the things He has already given or loaned to us. (*Endure*, p. 54.)

SAINTS

Those who are (or who will become) Saints reach breaking points without breaking. (*Deposition*, p. 52.)

May we be different in order to make a difference in the world. (*Ensign*, November 1974, p. 13.)

When the Saints are spotlighted, it will not always be for us to take curtsies and bows; sometimes the spotlights will be search-lights. Because of the distinctiveness of the Restoration, we will be held to higher standards. ("'All Hell Is Moved,'" p. 176.)

Saints do not have sad or woeful countenances. They are much more interesting than sinners. Sinners are so much the same in their sadness. Sometimes their very flamboyance betrays their sense of sameness. (*Deposition*, p. 52.)

It is exceedingly important that Latter-day Saints avoid both a bunker and an onlooker mentality. (*Deposition*, p. 85.)

Some people resent the Latter-day Saints because what we believe is so stunning and mind-expanding. Certainly our individual hypocrisies and shortcomings are made more glaring by all the bold and demanding doctrines in which we believe. Our theologi-cal certitude is also sometimes seen as smugness. It certainly helps if absolute truth is possessed by those who are, in turn, especially loving and behaving. (*Believe*, p. 62.)

SCHOLARSHIP

LDS scholars can and should speak in the tongue of scholarship, but without coming to prefer it and without losing the mother tongue of faith. (*Deposition*, p. 16.)

SCIENCE

It would be unwise, of course, for the Church to tie itself to the provisional truths of science at any point in science's unfolding history. Ultimately, scientific truth will align with divinely revealed truth; meanwhile we can applaud genuine scientific advances, noting them without depending overly much upon them. (*Men and Women*, pp. 91–92.)

SCORN

Members [of the Church] will be cleverly mocked and scorned by those in the "great and spacious building," representing the pride of the world (1 Nephi 8:26; 11:36). No matter, for ere long, He who was raised on the third day will raze that spacious but third-class hotel! (*Ensign*, May 1987, p. 71.)

So let us have patience and faith as did Lehi who saw pointing fingers of scorn directed at those who grasped the iron rod, which rod, ironically, some of those same fingers once grasped (see 1 Nephi

8:27, 33). But, said Lehi, "we heeded them not." So it should be with us! Brothers and sisters, being pointed in the right direction we do not need to worry about being pointed at! (*Ensign*, November 1993, p. 20.)

Why—really why—do the disbelievers who line that [great and] spacious building [see 1 Nephi 8:26–27, 33] watch so intently what the believers are doing? Surely there must be other things for the scorners to do—perhaps in that building's bowling alley—unless, deep within their seeming disinterest, there is interest. ("Meeting the Challenges of Today," p. 151.)

It is not easy to be a rescuer of one's fellowmen, especially when those to be rescued make fun of the rescuers. Sometimes the hand to be grasped is not outstretched at all, but features a pointing finger of scorn! (*Deposition*, p. 32.)

We see a few around us who simply can't stand to be separated from the "politically correct" multitudes in the great and spacious building. The "finger of scorn" has its own way of separating the faithful from those who have little or no faith (see 1 Nephi 8:33). (*Faith*, p. 99.)

Scriptures

For "the man of Christ," the words of scriptures are like parachute flares above the trenches of life, illuminating the landscape only briefly, but long enough for him to see the enemy clearly and to make his way along the path he must take—and to help others so to do. (*Deposition*, p. 95.)

One reason to "search the scriptures" is to discover these luxuriant meadows of meaning, these green pastures that can nourish us in our individual times of need. (*Not My Will*, p. 30.)

Only by searching the scriptures, not using them occasionally as quote books, can we begin to understand the implications as well as the declarations of the gospel. (*Ensign*, May 1986, p. 34.)

Traversing these truths requires more than a casual stroll up sloping foothills; they take us instead up the breathtaking ridges of reality to an Everest of understanding. On a clear day, we can see forever! (*Ensign*, May 1986, p. 34.)

Searching the scriptures includes facing the wintry doctrines therein. We are not to brush by a truth any more than we are to brush by a person. Of course, what is desired in this searching of the scriptures is comprehension, not genuflection or ritualistic reading; insight, not incantation; and penetration, not coverage. And if we tremble occasionally when we stand in the presence of a prophecy yet to be fulfilled, it should not surprise us. ("Thanksgiving for the Holy Scriptures.")

We possess these precious truths! Now they must come to possess us! (*Ensign*, May 1986, p. 35.)

The holy scriptures represent mankind's spiritual memory. And when man's connection with scripture is severed, mortals are tragically deprived of an awareness of spiritual history. Thereby, when shorn of true identity, mortals keep their legs intact, but each walks in his own way. (*Ensign*, November 1986, p. 52.)

One day we will have a third book of scripture to go with the record of the Jews, the Bible, and the record of the Nephites, the

Book of Mormon. All three will be testaments of Jesus! This third book will be the record of the Lost Tribes of Israel, whom Jesus also visited. (2 Nephi 29:13.) In the distant future, three volumes of scripture bound in white may well lie on the altars of hundreds of temples. (Talk given January 8, 1995.)

Later on, there will also be many other nourishing and inspiring scriptures. However, we must first feast worthily upon that which we already have! (*Ensign*, November 1986, p. 52.)

Without this precious, spiritual perspective, the human family is seldom more than one generation away from deep doubt and even disbelief. (*Ensign*, November 1986, p. 52.)

Some try to get by with knowing only the headlines of the gospel, not really talking much of Christ or rejoicing in Christ, and esteeming lightly His books of scripture which contain and explain His covenants (see 2 Nephi 25:26). (*Ensign*, May 1987, p. 70.)

The scriptures not only witness the truth about Christ and his relevance for mankind, but are, in a sense, like a songbook. There are many melodies that need to be sung and heard, and adult favorites are not necessarily those that attract or are relevant for the young. Only through personal involvement with the scriptures can we find the particular scriptural songs to meet our needs. We cannot depend entirely on group study of the Gospel to fill all our individual requirements. We must—ourselves—open the songbook and hear the music. The answers are there and the music of the Gospel, like its physical counterpart, suffers from too much filtering without high fidelity. (*Choose*, pp. 52–53.)

May we emulate the feelings for the scriptures held by Tyndale and Paul? Tyndale was imprisoned for translating holy scripture, and Paul was martyred for providing and testifying of holy scripture.

The parallels are powerful: Heroic Tyndale, from a cold, dark dungeon where he stayed for 16 months and from which he would soon go to be strangled and then burned, sent a letter begging for "a warmer cap . . . a warmer coat also . . . also a piece of cloth to patch my leggings . . . but above all my Hebrew Bible." Heroic Paul, aging Apostle—in Rome waiting to be brought before Nero a second time and then to be martyred, deserted by friends—asked Timothy to bring his "cloke," "the books," and "especially the parchments." (2 Timothy 4:13.) ("Thanksgiving for the Holy Scriptures.")

The scriptures are doors with immense truths behind them, divine insights of major proportions; there is an eternal curriculum— things God would have all men and women upon the face of the earth learn for their happiness. (*Choose*, p. 53.)

We must search the scriptures regularly. Unstudied, unapplied, dormant doctrines will seem to shrink in importance and relevance, for this is the atrophy that precedes indifference or apostasy. (*Choose*, p. 66.)

It is so easy to scan rather than search the holy scriptures, and to nibble at them rather than to feast upon them! (*Precious Things*, p. 3.)

It is my opinion that all the scriptures, including the Book of Mormon, will remain in the realm of faith. Science will not be able to prove or disprove holy writ. However, enough plausible evidence will come forth to prevent scoffers from having a field day, but not enough to remove the requirement of faith. (*Precious Things*, p. 4.)

Today we carry convenient quadruple combinations of the scriptures, but one day, since more scriptures are coming, we may need to pull little red wagons brim with books. Of course, computers may replace wagons. (*Flood*, p. 18.)

The greater the circumference of our collective spirituality, the larger the pulpit of memory from which the Holy Ghost can stir us. We are far more likely to "come off conqueror" in our holy present if we are truly familiar with mankind's spiritual past. (*Sermons*, p. 9.)

For those athirst for the living waters, searching the holy scriptures will cause those books to release their nourishing juices and will invigorate us for the long journey of discipleship. (*Men and Women*, p. 7.)

Various verses contain stinging one-liners for unfaithful "two-timers." They provide instructive case studies for egoists who have "a case" on themselves! Similarly, the scriptures contain sobering words for those who are intoxicated by riches, power, or the praise of men. (*Believe*, p. 185.)

The scriptures can give us needed rock-like steadiness, especially in this latter-day, topsy-turvy world in which "all things are in commotion" (D&C 45:26; 88:91). (*Believe*, p. 185.)

Given the divine design of the "other books," [Book of Mormon, Doctrine & Covenants, Pearl of Great Price] believers in and students of them regard the correlative relationships between ancient and modern scriptures as unsurprising. They are the expected latticework of the Lord, and the multiple interweavings and abundant cross-supports among them are part of a natural pattern for scriptures that were to converge doctrinally and grow together "fitly framed." (*Small Moment*, p. 42.)

Because the waters of life everlasting all come from the same divine well, it should not be surprising that conceptual similarities appear between the various books of scripture, both at the lofty levels having to do with Christ's mission, etc., and at other conceptual levels. (*Power*, p. 42.)

One would not forgo partaking of the sacrament because he is trying to lose weight, yet some neglect the scriptures because they are too busy minding the pressing cares of the world. (*Really Are*, p. 5.)

Obviously the prophets and apostles of different dispensations have written or spoken on these truths without consulting with each other to correlate what they were saying. They were correlated by that powerful and perfect correlator, the Holy Ghost. (*Really Are*, p. 97.)

The disciple, through the living scriptures, hears the strains of immortal music played by prophets, a symphony of seers. (*Really Are*, p. 109.)

Ordinary books contain comparative crumbs, whereas the bread of life provides a feast! ("The Children of Christ," p. 83.)

SECOND COMING

Soon, He who was once mockingly dressed in purple will come again, attired in red apparel, reminding us whose blood redeemed us. All will then acknowledge the completeness of His justice and His mercy and will see how human indifference to God—not God's indifference to humanity—accounts for so much misery and suffering. Then we will see the true story of mankind—and not through glass darkly. The great military battles will appear as mere bonfires that blazed briefly, and the mortal accounts of the human experience will be mere graffiti on the walls of time. (*As I Am*, p. 120.)

When He comes again, unlike coming to the signifying meekness of the manger, He will come in overwhelming majesty and power. In at least one appearance, He will come in red apparel to remind us that He shed His blood for us. (D&C 133:48; Isaiah 63:1.) Among the astounding, accompanying events, stars will fall from the heavens, as Christ will declare, "I have trodden the wine-press alone, and none was with me." (D&C 133:50.) What will we and those who witness these marvelous events speak of, then and later? Not the falling stars! Instead, we will speak of Jesus' "loving-kindness." For how long will we so exclaim? "Forever and ever." (D&C 133:52.) The more we come to know of Jesus and the Atonement, the more we shall praise and adore Him "forever and ever." ("Jesus: Lord of Loving-Kindness and of the Far-flung Vineyard.")

The chiliast, one who believes in a second coming of Christ that will usher in a millennial reign, has special challenges in reading signs. First, he is urged to notice lest he be caught unawares. Second, he must be aware of how many false readings and alarms there have been in bygone days, even by the faithful. For instance, has any age had more "wonders in the sky" than ours, with satellites and journeys to the moon? Has any generation seen such ominous "vapors of smoke" as ours with its mushroom clouds over the pathetic pyres of Hiroshima and Nagasaki? Yet there is "more to come." Our task is to react and to notice without overreacting, to let life go forward without slipping into the heedlessness of those in the days of Noah. (*Power,* p. 20.)

How quickly and easily the few are misled! Such members may know superficially of the doctrines of the kingdom, but their root system is shallow. Though able to provide doctrinal recitation, they seem not to know either the implications or interconnections of those doctrines. For instance, instead of wisely noticing the warning leaves on the fig tree, a few proceed to fixate on the specific timing of Jesus' second coming. Yet the Savior clearly stated, "But of that day and hour knoweth no man, no, not the angels of

heaven, but my Father only" (Matthew 23:36). Clearly, since even
the angels in heaven—an otherwise reasonably well-informed
group—do not know, we should be wary of mortals obsessed with
calendaring. So often modern gnostics who in one exotic way or
another pretend to be "in the know" are, in fact, spiritually "out of
touch"! Meanwhile, mature members will take time both to smell
the flowers and to watch the leaves on the fig tree to see when
"summer is nigh" (Matthew 24:32–33). (*Faith*, p. 94.)

We are to ponder signs without becoming paranoid, and to be
aware without frantically keeping score between current events
and scriptural expectations. The wise chiliast will use his or her
energy in serving God and man instead of fretting and will resist
secularism's heavy sedation. (*Endure*, p. 12.)

SECULARISM

Secular remedies resemble an alarmed passenger traveling on the
wrong train who tries to compensate by running up the aisle in the
opposite direction! (*Ensign*, November 1994, p. 35.)

Secularism, too, has its own "priests" and is jealous over its own
"orthodoxy." Those who choose not to follow Him are sometimes
quick to say "Follow me." They enjoy being a light, and the accompanying recognition and reward are not unpleasant. (*Precious
Things*, p. 87.)

Secularism, unsurprisingly, has allied itself with relativism, and it is
busy practicing what it preaches in what I would call an *alliance* of
dalliance. ("'Build up My Church,' 'Establish the [Lord's] Righteousness.'")

We shall see in our time a maximum if indirect effort made to establish irreligon as the state religion. It is actually a new form of paganism that uses the carefully preserved and cultivated freedoms of Western civilization to shrink freedom even as it rejects the value essence of our rich Judeo-Christian heritage. . . . Irreligion as the state religion would be the worst of all combinations. Its orthodoxy would be insistent and its inquisitors inevitable. Its paid ministry would be numerous beyond belief. Its Caesars would be insufferably condescending. Its majorities—when faced with clear alternatives—would make the Barabbas choice, as did a mob centuries ago when Pilate confronted them with the need to decide. ("Meeting the Challenges of Today," p. 149.)

Ironically, as some people become harder, they use softer words to describe dark deeds. This, too, is part of being sedated by secularism. Needless abortion, for instance, is a "reproductive health procedure,". . . . "Illegitimacy" gives way to the wholly sanitized words "non-marital birth" or "alternative parenting." (*Ensign*, May 1996, p. 68.)

Great men can, and have, come out of economic poverty, but much less often out of an emotional ghetto. Thus while secularism sincerely seeks to tear down brick and mortar ghettos, it leaves the human debris of doctrinal deprivation in its wake and creates "a herd morality." (*Smallest Part*, p. 37.)

So many secular solutions are really soothing slogans; there is no real substance to them. (*Deposition*, p. 23.)

Sincere, secular solutions to one problem often create an equally difficult problem in its place. (*Choose*, p. 69.)

Any secular system without sufficient human goodness and righteousness will, sooner or later, fail. We must not mistake mere scaffolding for substance. (*As I Am*, p. 16.)

Secular solutions that ignore the family often become not only counterproductive but also dangerous. (*My Family*, p. 8.)

It is most unfortunate that in the surge toward secularism those who have ignored the teachings of God about the purpose of life and this planet have been so heedless; the Christian's response involves more than merely replacing the doctrinal divots on the fairway that the secularists have torn up. (*My Family*, p. 33.)

Secularism, the setting in which most Christians will live out their lives, is both a diversion from and a perversion of life's true purpose. Hence the disappointment in the secular search for the meaning of life. Hence the drooping of the human spirit in which the conscience can come to be regarded as an intruder. Indeed, ennui, boredom, and humdrum hedonism are descriptive of those thus afflicted. (*Sermons*, p. 70.)

A secular society is the most likely cultural candidate to be especially surprised by a Jesus who comes "as a thief in the night." A society indifferent, even hostile, to things spiritual will be truly astonished. (*Believe*, p. 171.)

Is not secularism often sincere? Yes, but suppose someone had installed suggestion boxes on the last day on the job at the construction site of the Tower of Babel! Would his sincerity have mattered much? (*Prove*, p. 95.)

Secular solutions tend to be rehabilitative rather than preventive. (*Not My Will*, p. 84.)

Without fixed principles and a steady spiritual focus for life we will be diverted by the cares of the world and intimidated by boldly striding secularism. It is very easy to underestimate the pervasiveness and preoccupations of secularism. Merely surviving, then striving for advantage, getting and spending; then being anesthetized by relentless routine, and sensing, as the secularist does, the finality of death—all these combine to ensure the grim dominance of the cares of the world. (*Endure*, pp. 13–14.)

We should avoid being deeply disappointed or surprised when the modern innkeepers or the establishments of the world have no room for Christ's servants or cannot "give place for a portion" of Christ's word (Alma 32:27). For us too, better a spiritual manger than a stay in those secular inns of the intellect which are so exclusionary of spiritual things. (*The Christmas Scene*, p. 11.)

Self-Control

True law enforcement depends on the policing of one's self. If the sentry of self fails, there are simply not enough other policemen to restrain those who will not restrain themselves, and beating the system will become the system. (*Ensign*, May 1975, p. 101.)

On occasion the biting of the tongue can be as important as the gift of tongues. (*Ensign*, November 1990, p. 16.)

To have the faith to deny oneself certain of life's questionable pleasures is to affirm oneself, an attitude involving a healthy self-respect that is proper for the submissive. One's intrinsic, eternal worth is not to be traded for the things of the moment. (*Not My Will*, p. 61.)

Self-Esteem

If another person only had in his storehouse of deserved self-esteem what you had put there, what would he have to draw upon and to sustain him? (*Smallest Part*, p. 59.)

We [should] make quiet but more honest inventories of our strengths, since, in this connection, most of us are dishonest book-keepers and need confirming "outside auditors." (*Ensign*, November 1976, p. 14.)

We cannot build up the kingdom steadily if we are consantly tearing ourselves down. (*Not My Will*, p. 12.)

Self-contempt is of Satan; there is none of it in heaven. (*Deposition*, p. 30.)

Since self-esteem controls ultimately our ability to love God, to love others, and to love life, nothing is more central than our need to build justifiable self-esteem. (*Excellent*, p. 90.)

Our self-esteem need not be shattered by failure, if a kind of resilience and bounce can be developed early in life. "Picking ourselves up off the floor" can best be learned where there is "friendly" floor; where the risks are not so great, and love and support are there to assist us. In the home there can be praise which can balance off our occasional failures. (*Excellent*, p. 122.)

Some among us mistakenly see the size and response of their audiences as the sole verification of their worth! Yet those fickle galleries to which we sometimes play have a way of being rotated and emptied. They will surely be empty on Judgment Day; everyone will be somewhere else—on their knees. (*Men and Women*, p. 64.)

SELF-IMAGE

We are sometimes so anxious about our personal images, when it is His image we should have in our countenances. (See Alma 5:14.) (*Ensign*, November 1988, p. 31.)

SELF-IMPROVEMENT

We [should] distinguish more clearly between divine discontent and the devil's dissonance, between dissatisfaction with self and disdain for self. We need the first and must shun the second, remembering that when conscience calls to us from the next ridge, it is not solely to scold but also to beckon. (*Ensign*, November 1976, p. 14.)

Let us participate in the rigorous calisthenics of daily improvement, and not just in the classroom rhetoric of eternal progression! (*Ensign*, November 1980, p. 15.)

The imperfections of others never release us from the need to work on our own shortcomings. (*Ensign*, May 1982, p. 39.)

If sudden, stabbing light exposes the gap between what we are and what we think we are, can we, like Peter, let that light be a healing laser? (*Ensign*, May 1989, p. 64.)

We must care about self-improvement, for this is appropriate in a church that teaches that we shall be together a million years from now—and longer! We have a real stake in each other's improvement and an even greater stake centuries from now. (*Choose*, p. 13.)

Can't one rest a little while longer before starting a quiet new campaign of self-improvement? No, because being "valiant" in our testimony of Jesus includes precious few recesses and no vacations! (See D&C 76:79.) The school day in the mortal classroom is so very brief at best. (*Faith*, p. 116.)

SELFISHNESS

Selfishness is much more than an ordinary problem because it activates all the cardinal sins! It is the detonator in the breaking of the Ten Commandments. (*Ensign*, November 1990, p. 14.)

In all its various expressions, selfishness is really self-destruction in slow motion. (*Ensign*, November 1990, p. 16.)

The distance between constant self-pleasing and self-worship is shorter than we think. Stubborn selfishness is, actually, rebellion against God. (*Ensign*, November 1980, p. 14.)

The selfish individual . . . seeks to please not God, but himself. He will even break a covenant in order to fix an appetite. (*Ensign*, November 1980, p. 14.)

The selfish individual has a passion for the vertical pronoun *I*. Significantly, the vertical pronoun *I* has no knees to bend, while the first letter in the pronoun *we* does. (*Ensign*, November 1980, p. 14.)

Myopic selfishness magnifies a mess of pottage into a banquet and makes thirty pieces of silver look like a treasure trove. (*Ensign*, November 1990, p. 15.)

Each spasm of selfishness narrows the universe that much more by shutting down our awareness of others and by making us more and more alone. (*Ensign*, November 1990, p. 16.)

Most of the time, the sponge of selfishness quickly soaks up everything in sight, including praise intended for others. ("'Meek and Lowly,'" p. 55.)

Just as fire requires oxygen, so generosity and mutuality require significant unselfishness. We are accustomed to reading about the challenges of spiraling violence and spiraling inflation, and these are very real; but spiraling selfishness is at the very center of all the other spiraling challenges of today. (*My Family*, p. 33.)

Selfishness, which comes in many costumes, is particularly cruel, not only because it gives priority to pleasure, but because it usually means one person's pleasure comes at the expense of another person's pain. Its most fundamental characteristic, however, is that one possessed of selfishness sees others as mere functions or objects to be used—or to be ignored—and not as humans to be helped, to be loved, or to be listened to. (*My Family*, p. 34.)

Selfishness views life in such a way that one should get all the gusto he can out of life; selfishness is the social equivalent of heedless strip-mining. (*My Family*, p. 34.)

Those who are selfish are not free at all, because their only choice is to yield to their appetites. (*My Family*, p. 36.)

The selfish person is somewhat in the position of the drug addict; he is always in fresh need of a fix. (*My Family*, p. 40.)

Selfishness need not be gross in order to call the cadence in our lives. It merely needs to deflect us from thinking about an act of service to thinking about needing a new pair of shoes; or from making a nurturing phone call to watching a soap opera. (*Men and Women*, p. 104.)

The steady secretions of selfishness will continue to reencrust us until we put off the natural man and woman—firmly and finally! (*Believe*, p. 47.)

Selfishness is a near-religion for some. Its theology is "me," its here-after is "now," and its rituals consist of sensation! (*Experience*, p. 58.)

Selfish people are forever taking their own temperature, asking themselves, "Am I happy?" (*Experience*, p. 60.)

The quality of our love and concern for our fellowmen can often be measured in seemingly little ways. For instance, if we are so task-oriented that we murmur at a busy intersection because a siren-wailing ambulance comes through that intersection on "our" green light, then we have forgotten the needs of another, putting our convenience ahead of his necessity. (*Press Forward*, p. 106.)

A narcissistic society in which each person is too busy looking out for "number one" can build no brotherhood; it will finally be shattered against its own selfishness. Had God's Firstborn looked out for Himself first, there would have been no Gethsemane or Calvary—and no immortality! (*Prove*, p. 92.)

Selfishness is a form of self-worship, and we have been told, "Thou shalt have *no* other Gods before me" (Exodus 20:3). (*Not My Will*, p. 8.)

Our physical as well as our familial environment is likewise threatened by selfishness. But some worry only about holes in the ozone layer, while the fabric of many families who lack the lamp [see Proverbs 6:23] resembles Swiss cheese. (*Ensign*, May 1995, p. 68.)

SELF-PITY

Self-pity is that sludge in which sin sprouts so easily. (*Ensign*, November 1991, p. 32.)

A constructive critic truly cares for that which he criticizes, including himself, whereas self-pity is the most condescending form of pity; it soon cannibalizes all other concerns. (*Ensign*, November 1976, p. 13.)

Even while Jesus was literally providing salvation for all mankind, the perfect Shepherd simultaneously reached out to individuals. When you and I suffer we sometimes tend to pass it along. Or, if overcome with self-pity, we simply ignore others, saying, in effect, "I've got all I can handle with my own problems." (*Faith*, p. 25.)

SENSUALITY

Those so drained by sensuality do, in fact, seek to compensate for their loneliness by sensations. However, in the arithmetic of appetite, anything multiplied by zero still totals zero! (*Ensign*, February 1986, p. 19.)

Carnality is always such a profound contraction of life; it destroys even that which it pretends to focus upon! (*Experience*, p. 53.)

Truly, "the spirit indeed is willing, but the flesh is weak" (Matthew 26:41). While we must beware of excusing ourselves too much, we do need to make some allowance for that fundamental fact. Spiritual stimuli, for instance, can be choked out by the steady stimuli of the world. Thirst, hunger, fatigue—all can magnify the attractiveness of a mess of pottage. (*Men and Women*, pp. 104–5.)

SERVICE

I know the celestial criteria measure service, not status; the use of our talents, not the relative size of our talent inventories. (*Ensign*, May 1974, p. 112.)

We need some institutionalization, even in the kingdom. Random goodness is, by itself, not enough to resist the march of evil. . . . I am grateful that God has so organized us and that he has given us specific things to do. Otherwise, we would be like the lonely sharpshooters trying to slow the advancing army of evil. ("Insights from My Life," p. 197.)

We, more than others, should carry jumper and tow cables not only in our cars, but also in our hearts, by which means we can send the needed boost or charge of encouragement or the added momentum to mortal neighbors. (*Experience*, p. 56.)

Unless we grasp them firmly and quickly, many of the proffered opportunities to serve have a short shelf life and are perishable. Golden moments come and go. (*Endure*, p. 113.)

[I express] appreciation for your sustaining vote which was not vindication but an invitation—an invitation for me to be and to do better. (*Ensign*, May 1974, p. 112.)

On the straight, narrow path, which leads to our little Calvarys, one does not hear a serious traveler exclaiming, "Look, no hands!" (*Ensign*, May 1990, p. 34.)

Do you and I understand that the significance of our service does not depend upon its scale? (*Ensign*, May 1989, p. 63.)

Sometimes . . . in our search for status, [we] get confused about the relationship of status to righteousness. It is not the expanse of the ecclesiastical epaulets we wear on our shoulders, but our willingness to put our shoulder to the wheel that counts! ("It's Service, Not Status, That Counts," p. 6.)

Most people would gladly serve mankind if somehow they could get it over with once, preferably with applause and recognition. ("But for a Small Moment," p. 446.)

We may feel underused, underwhelmed, and underappreciated, even as we ironically ignore unused opportunities for service which are all about us. ("'True Believers in Christ,'" p. 136.)

Sometimes we are tested not only by the requirement that we place certain things on the altar of sacrifice and service, but also by the trial of circumstances that seem to prevent us from placing a portion of self on the altar. ("It's Service, Not Status, That Counts," p. 6.)

The Lord's work is not usually performed on a luxuriant landscape, but, said Jacob, in "the poorest spot in all the land of [the] vineyard" (see Jacob 5:21, 70). The world's Caesars pay little heed to such workers. ("'Meek and Lowly,'" p. 55.)

We so often depersonalize our assistance to others that we might be called "checkbook Christians." We pay our taxes and offerings and unintentionally move away from the personal acts of brotherhood. (*Choose*, pp. 63–64.)

We are the clinical material God has given us to work on in this estate. He lets us practice on each other. That means failure, pain, frustration, and deep disappointment as well as success. (*Deposition*, p. 36.)

We can't lead, or draw, others to the Lord unless we stand closer to Him than they do! (*Deposition*, p. 36.)

Sometimes the gears of proffered help do not mesh with the gears of received help. But even so, we should not shift into neutral; we ought to go on trying. (*Experience*, pp. 81–82.)

To withdraw into our private sanctuaries not only deprives others of our love, our talents, and our service, but it also deprives us of chances to serve, to love, and to be loved. (*Excellent*, p. 89.)

Of a truth, those who can easily bend their knees in prayer do not feel they are stooping when they bend to help a neighbor in need. (*Heart*, p. 14.)

Frequently, we busily search for group service projects, which are surely needed and commendable, when quiet, personal service is also urgently needed. Sometimes the completing of an occasional group service project ironically salves our consciences when, in fact, we are constantly surrounded by a multitude of opportunities for individual service. (*Experience*, p. 55.)

We should strive to render significant, though often quiet, service, instead of superficial service and rushed relationships. (*Experience*, p. 56.)

There are so many times when genuine human service means giving graciously our little grain of sand, placing it reverently to build the beach of brotherhood. We get no receipt, and our little grain of sand carries no brand; its identity is lost, except to the Lord. (*Experience*, p. 63.)

There are . . . times when one of the greatest acts of service we can perform is to stop something. The emotional chain of reaction and overreaction can come at us like electric voltage; it is very tempting to simply pass along. But we must say, "Let it stop with me." Brave but battered French soldiers in World War I finally held against an invading enemy at a place called Verdun, where the solemn password was "They shall not pass." At times we too should be stern, sweet sentries willing to expose ourselves to misunderstanding and pain in order to keep undesirable things from spreading any farther. (*Experience*, p. 64.)

We must lose our life *for His sake*—not just any cause. There are those carefully masqueraded versions of service to others that are really ego exercises coated with a thin layer of public interest. One sees it all the time, especially when some politicians have some temporary glee as their selfish interests appear to be visibly aligned with the public good; they almost enjoy it too much, suggesting it is not a regular experience. (*Experience*, p. 69.)

Christ didn't wait to mount the cross to sacrifice Himself until He was guaranteed that all people would appreciate and accept His gift and His message. (*Press Forward*, p. 6.)

Those who were able in life to give place for gospel things will have, thereby, found a place in the next world that will provide for them even more opportunities for service; while those who were shrunken by selfishness in this life, jettisoning inconvenient babies and aging parents, will have a chance, perhaps first-hand, to face those who were so dispatched or disregarded. (*Really Are*, p. 115.)

SHORTCOMINGS

Let us . . . not be too long-suffering with our own shortcomings. (*Ensign*, November 1980, p. 15.)

Only Jesus was perfect in all things, including love and meekness. Even the greatest of mortal prophets fall short of Christ's high and perfect standards. Thus, as members of the Church, if we can see the life of discipleship, whether for ourselves or for the prophets, as a combination of *proving*, *reproving*, and *improving*, we will be much better off. (*Ensign*, November 1984, p. 10.)

Part of the marvel and the wonder of God's "marvelous work and a wonder" will be how perfect Divinity mercifully used us—imperfect humanity. (*Ensign*, November 1984, p. 11.)

SIGN-SEEKING

Craving a sign is actually an inversion of the teacher-pupil relationship: The pupil demands of a Divine teacher that he perpetually produce proof—when it is the pupil who must produce! (*Choose*, p. 65.)

SIN

God's counsel aligns us and conjoins us with the great realities of the universe; whereas sin empties, isolates, and separates us, confining us to the solitary cell of selfishness. Hence the lonely crowd in hell. (*Ensign*, May 1985, p. 71.)

Why do some of our youth risk engaging in ritual prodigalism, intending to spend a season rebelling and acting out in Babylon and succumbing to that devilishly democratic "everybody does it"? Crowds cannot make right what God has declared to be wrong. Though planning to return later, many such stragglers find that alcohol, drugs, and pornography will not let go easily. Babylon does not give exit permits gladly. It is an ironic implementation of that ancient boast: "One soul shall not be lost." (Moses 4:1.) (*Ensign*, November 1988, p. 33.)

Sin . . . brings sameness; it shrinks us to addictive appetites and insubordinate impulses. For a brief surging, selfish moment, sin may create the illusion of individuality, but only as in the grunting, galloping Gadarene swine! (See Matthew 8:28–32.) (*Ensign*, November 1991, p. 30.)

The raucousness and the shouting of sin, the Cain-like glorying in it, is also the sound of pain trying to erase itself. ("Insights from My Life," p. 199.)

It is so much more difficult for us to carry the cross when our back is already bent with the burdens of bad behavior. ("Taking Up the Cross," p. 259.)

There is no sin that is truly private, for ere long what is done privately will be justified and promoted publicly. A man cannot, for long, be good when the sun is high in the sky but then be bad as night comes, for such a one is divided against himself. (*Look Back,* pp. 11–12.)

[We must] sharpen our sensing of the sulfurous sins about us today which threaten us . . . with deterioration and cataclysm, as more and more people worship at the altar of appetite and also seek to force the orthodoxy of relativism on others. The forces of evil now march to a louder and louder cadence called "in consequence of evils and designs which do and will exist in the hearts of conspiring men in the last days. . . . " (D&C 89:4.) (*Look Back,* pp. 27–28.)

The sewage of sin is so devastating as it rolls downstream in life. (*Choose,* p. 14.)

Iniquity is perspective-shrinking, since it increasingly diminishes one's perception of redemptive reality. (*Flood,* p. 8.)

Sin is a special form of insanity. It reflects a kind of blackout in which we either lack or lose perspective about the consequences of our thoughts, words, and actions. (*Choose,* p. 15.)

Sin, and time not well spent, can erode even bright spiritual experiences unless we are constantly active and growing. (*Choose,* p. 64.)

Of all the stumbling blocks, personal sins are clearly the largest and most retarding. Before we can receive all that God has for us, we must first make room by giving away our sins. (*Flood,* p. 91.)

Even when we repent, we still cannot recycle the time lost nor do retroactively the good deeds that might have been. (*Notwithstanding,* pp. 26–27.)

So far as our real self-interests are concerned, sin is irrational even when measured merely in the dimension of time. It is insanity when viewed by the eyes of eternity. Of course, the adversary's trick is to make that which hurts us seem pleasing and that which is ugly seem attractive. Such huckstering requires real cleverness—but, most of all, credulous consumers. Discerning consumerism is currently much urged in the marketplace of goods, but it is regarded as out of place in the bazaar of behavior! (*Notwithstanding*, p. 74.)

Those who are so parochial as to think that what is unseen cannot be unethical neglect the reality that there are always at least His two piercing eyes watching. (*Press Forward*, p. 9.)

No wonder we despair when we sin, because we act against our own interests and against who we really are. When we are imprisoned by iniquity, we turn the cell lock on ourselves. (*Really Are*, p. 8.)

Sinners consistently mistake a passing mood for a basic need. (*Prove*, p. 25.)

When sin scalds the tastebuds of the soul . . . we lose our appetite for true sweetness. (*Prove*, p. 73.)

To cease sinning is to begin living. (*Not My Will*, p. 61.)

While sins are individual, their accumulations have macro consequences. (*Not My Will*, p. 81.)

It is our giving heed to temptations by dallying over them and by anticipating, savoring, and recycling them that gets us into trouble. Jesus' character is such that He was consistently decisive and dismissive as to temptation and sin. There is no equivocation in Him regarding evil. He and His Father can make no allowance for sin (see D&C 1:31)—because of the terrible toll sin exacts from the happiness of all those they love. (*Faith*, pp. 23–24.)

We mortals . . . tend to tolerate our own little clusters of sin. We rationalize that we can dismiss these whenever we really want to. The trouble is that these "squatters," too, come to have "rights." By means of their persistent presence, they take over more than we ever intended; whereas to give no heed means to give no foothold, however small. To delay their eviction is, in effect, to "heed" and accommodate the temptation. (*Faith*, p. 24.)

Gross sins arise ominously and steadily out of the swamp of self-indulgence and self-pity. But the smaller sins breed there, too, like insects in the mud, including the coarsening of language. (*Ensign*, May 1995, p. 67.)

Once the telestial sins are left behind and henceforth avoided, the focus falls ever more upon the sins of omission. These omissions signify a lack of qualifying fully for the celestial kingdom. Only greater consecration can correct these omissions, which have consequences just as real as do the sins of commission. (*Ensign*, November 1995, p. 23.)

SINGLE WOMEN

We have special admiration for the unsung but unsullied single women among whom are some of the noblest daughters of God. These sisters know that God loves them individually and distinctly. They make wise career choices even though they cannot now have the most choice career. Though in their second estate they do not have their first desire, they still overcome the world.

These sisters who cannot now enrich the institution of their own marriage so often enrich other institutions in society. They do not withhold their blessings simply because some blessings are now withheld from them. (*Ensign*, May 1978, p. 11.)

The sense of deprivation that can occur in the life of a single woman in her forties who feels she has no prospects of marriage is real. Yet some deprivations are but delayed blessings, which, if endured well, constitute the readying of reservoirs into which a generous God will pour "all that he hath." Indeed, it will be the Malachi measure: "There shall not be room enough to receive it." (Malachi 3:10.) (*Prove*, pp. 28–29.)

SKEPTICISM

Skeptics are not only smug, but are pathetically provincial and insular. Skeptics come to believe strongly in skepticism, and they are very orthodox. Far from being liberating, skepticism leads men into cruel, conceptual cul de sacs. (*Deposition*, p. 77.)

Faith proceeds on to promised knowledge. It develops us and it delivers us to new data. Skepticism starts with some unprovable declarations and ends there too. (*Deposition*, p. 18.)

If you look closely, you will be able to see many so-called skeptics who keep one eye on the dikes of disbelief and who seem to have a small rowboat nearby. (*Deposition*, p. 86.)

Those who demand a "voiceprint" of the "voice of the Lord" probably would not like His doctrines anyway (see John 6:66). The things of the Spirit are to be "sought by faith"; they are not to be seen through slit-eyed skepticism. (*Not My Will*, p. 32.)

Social Causes

The Church and its members can and should cooperate in seeing that the community chores are done without letting others use or exploit us—without unconsciously finding ourselves marching to the cadence of a cause which is called by other voices for other purposes. (*Power*, p. 22.)

Society

Only reform and self-restraint, institutional and individual, can finally rescue society! Only a sufficient number of sin-resistant souls can change the marketplace. As Church members, we should be part of that sin-resistant counterculture. Instead, too many members are sliding down the slope, though perhaps at a slower pace. (*Ensign*, May 1993, p. 77.)

Is our society beyond the point of return? One lesson of Nineveh is that we must not give up. (*Endure*, p. 19.)

Solutions

The wrong kind of help—however well motivated or lavishly administered—can be harmful. One does not run about indiscriminately with a jackhammer in times of earthquake, though a jackhammer might be needed in some situations. (*Deposition*, p. 70.)

Pat solutions are usually shortcuts which really don't take us any place but which seem to. One early, easy, and wrong answer was given by a status-ful individual who was very, very anxious to be the leader, when he said ages ago: "I will redeem all mankind that one soul shall not be lost." (*Excellent*, p. 47.)

Sophistry

The sophist, who is often a carrier of cleverness, is really an intellectual guerrilla, a forlorn man without a country who draws his delight and satisfaction from the process of verbal combat and encounter itself; he does not seek resolution, but disruption. He has no homeland and, therefore, seeks always to fight his battles on the homefront of the believer. The sophist has nothing to defend. He takes no real risks because he believes in nothing. Perhaps, in a strange and twisted way, he wants to create anomy and drift by using the sword of speciousness to cut other men away from the eternal things that anchor them. (*Choose*, p. 31.)

Spirit World

Death does not suddenly bestow upon the disbeliever full awareness of all reality, thereby obviating the need for any faith. Instead, what follows death is a continuum of the basic structure in mortality—until the Judgment Day, when every knee shall bow and every tongue confess that Jesus is the Christ (see Romans 14:11; Philippians 2:10; D&C 76:110). Until then, we "walk by faith, not by sight" (2 Corinthians 5:7). How will God ensure this condition in the spirit world? We do not know. Yet He has certainly so handled the second estate in relation to the first estate, hasn't He? The memories of the first estate are not accessible in the second estate. The spirit world will be so arranged that there will be no legitimate complaints later over the justice and mercy of God (see Mosiah 27:31; Alma 12:15). (*Believe*, p. 94.)

SPIRITUAL EXPERIENCES

President Marion G. Romney observed that we would have more spiritual experiences if we did not talk about them so much! As if having them were more important than benefitting from them, some lust after spiritual experiences rather than desiring the substance of such experiences: "Ask not, that ye may consume it on your lusts, . . . but that ye will serve the true and living God" (Mormon 9:28). Perhaps, in recounting their spiritual experiences, some may unconsciously wish to demonstrate their ascendancy; just as some academics, in a sort of intellectual imperialism, enjoy the knowing more than they enjoy utilizing what is known. This illustrates the old problem of the desire for preeminence, which can take so many forms. (*Believe*, pp. 69–70.)

Even a touching spiritual moment can be so quickly lost in the bustle of an afternoon's traffic jam, in the cares of tonight's phone calls, or because of the pressures brought by tomorrow's mail. (*We Talk of Christ*, p. 112.)

SPIRITUAL GROWTH

The calisthenics of spiritual growth involve isometrics, the pitting of the emerging self against the stern resistance of the old self. (*Ensign*, November 1983, p. 55.)

Spiritual housework is done room by room and corner by corner. In some seasons of our lives, this is supplemented by inspirationally induced bursts of spring cleaning. (*Men and Women*, p. 27.)

While events often induce submissiveness, one's development need not be dramatic or tied to a single moment; it can occur steadily in seemingly ordinary, daily settings. If we are meek, a rich and needed insight can be contained in reproof. A new calling can beckon us away from comfortable routine and from competencies already acquired. One may be stripped of accustomed luxury in order that the malignant mole of materialism be removed. (*Ensign*, May 1985, p. 72.)

Spiritual refinement is not only to make the gross more pure but to further refine the already fine! Hence, said Peter, we should not think a "fiery trial" to be "some strange thing." (1 Peter 4:12.) (*Ensign*, May 1991, p. 90.)

Alma asked some members of the Church how they felt now—at the moment—about spiritual things. (Alma 5:26.) He was simply underscoring the recurring reality of lapsed literacy in spiritual things, a condition for the disciple as much to be feared as arthritis in acrobats. (*Deposition*, p. 78.)

The developmental dimensions of discipleship and the rigorous calisthenics essential to continuing Christian commitment insure us against premature access to power. Our Father also shields us from Icarian insights—dazzling sunbursts of celestial sense which we cannot comprehend. Otherwise, like Icarus, we might fly too high and too close to the sun on wings which premature proximity melts, sending us crashing back to earth. (*Choose*, pp. 29–30.)

Perhaps . . . what seems stern, even harsh, as a required experience is merely the necessary crust around the sweetbread of spiritual progress. (*As I Am*, p. 46.)

Only a few come to this mortal experience with substantial saintliness already developed. Rather, our individual best is presently but the bud of possibility. Even so, these buds of possibility—the early stages of divine attributes—are unmistakably there. While unfolding and enlarging over time, these key qualities should also "grow together," producing full felicity. (*Flood*, p. 42.)

Our spiritual development is to be achieved amid differentially dispensed measures of time. For some of the unwell and aged, unwanted time can be like taffy to be shaken free of. Others are required to endure the sudden karate chop of changed circumstances. (*Not My Will*, p. 122.)

SPIRITUAL STIRRINGS

Some do not own up even to the small spiritual stirrings within them; they are not . . . intellectually honest. When in the later Judgment there is access to the seismographs of the soul, I predict there will be some very interesting recordings that can be introduced as evidence. Agrippa had such a moment. Probably Pilate also. We are often in the presence of a good and powerful person, or truth. Sometimes it is not until later that we remember our hearts burned within us, but the record will so show. (*Deposition*, p. 18.)

STANDARDS

What we are seeing now in so many situations is a more rigorous setting of standards for commercial relationships, but also a simultaneous, cheek-by-jowl retreat from standard setting in personal behavior. This is somewhat like building more lifeboats and de-emphasizing swimming lessons. (*Deposition*, p. 22.)

The Church sets standards for us in many areas, but many of the standards of personal performance must be set by us. An unwillingness to set standards or goals for ourselves, of course, can result in a Mormon malaise, going nowhere—but doing it very anxiously. (*Deposition*, pp. 71–72.)

In a society in which "anything goes," its members will learn too late that everything has gone! (*Smallest Part*, p. 22.)

The Church is pulling away from the world at a rate that would be noticeable even if the world were standing still in its standards. This is because the world is pulling away even from the standards it once held. Thus the Church and the world are parting company like two speeding cars going in opposite directions. (*Deposition*, p. 63.)

Mortals who lose their bearings then proceed to lose their souls. (*Press Forward*, p. 27.)

Secular standards so often constitute a naive Maginot-Line morality that is quickly outflanked by the reality of what occurs when men and women try to live without God in the world. (*Prove*, p. 92.)

STATUS

Some followers [of the Prophet Joseph Smith] became disaffected, but later returned—including once-statusful men like Oliver Cowdery, Martin Harris, and Thomas B. Marsh. Yet these men voted with their feet to rejoin and reconcile with the kingdom. The true doctrines drew them back, however, and the only status sought or conferred was membership, once again, in the Lord's church. (*Ensign*, November 1984, p. 10.)

In heaven, Christ's lofty name was determined to be the only name on earth offering salvation to all mankind. (See Acts 4:12; 2 Nephi 25:20; see also Abraham 3:27.) Yet the Mortal Messiah willingly lived so modestly, even as a person "of no reputation." (Philippians 2:7.) (*Ensign*, May 1989, p. 63.)

For those of us who are too concerned about status or being last in line or losing our place, we need to read again those words about how the "last shall be first" and "the first shall be last." (Matthew 19:30.) (*Precious Things*, p. 54.)

A "Who's Who" is not needed in a church that teaches us all our real identity and in which there is, significantly, a democracy of dress in the holy temples. (*Notwithstanding*, p. 84.)

STEREOTYPING

The world has been led to lazy stereotypes of prophets as being wild and fanatic people to be ignored. Such stereotyping is the work of him who has also encouraged art that portrays an effeminate Jesus. Lucifer just cannot bring himself to present things as they really are, for the truth is not in him. (*Really Are*, pp. 78–79.)

Stereotyping reflects both intellectual laziness and lovelessness. The straight and narrow path leads us to a wide horizon of discovering and knowing people, but stereotyping confines us into the solitude of a conceptual cul-de-sac. (*Endure*, p. 96.)

STEWARDSHIP

How we view ourselves, others, and the universe really does shape everything else! Our view of such strategic matters determines, among many other things, whether while on this planet we will act as concerned stewards or merely as transient pleasure-seekers and alien exploiters. A genuine world religion requires a world (not a worldly) view—better still, a gospel with a galactic view! (*Flood*, p. 10.)

STILL, SMALL VOICE

Whatever the decibels of decadence, these need not overwhelm the still, small voice! Some of the best sermons we will ever hear will be thus prompted from the pulpit of memory—to an audience of one! (*Ensign*, May 1993, p. 77.)

Imperviousness to the promptings of the still small voice of God will also mean that we have ears but cannot hear, not only the promptings of God but also the pleas of men. (*Choose*, pp. 59–60.)

STRAIT AND NARROW PATH

At the risk of detracting from the usual imagery associated with the straight and narrow path, pressing forward seems more like striding in the surf than walking on dry land. If we don't press forward in water, we are quickly taken in another direction. (*Press Forward*, p. 39.)

There are times when the only way the strait and narrow path can be followed is on one's knees! (*Ensign*, May 1982, p. 38.)

Christ's doctrines pertaining to the plan of salvation stand like sentinel scriptures to mark and light the way. His gospel guardrails line the strait and narrow path to steady us, nudge us, and even jar us for the sake of our spiritual safety! (*Ensign*, May 1984, p. 22.)

Of course God is forgiving! But He knows the intents of our hearts. He also knows what good we might have done while AWOL. In any case, what others do is no excuse for the disciple from whom much is required. (See Alma 39:4.) Besides, on the straight and narrow path there are simply no corners to be cut. (See D&C 82:3.) (*Ensign*, November 1988, p. 33.)

There is a real risk that members of the Church—particularly the young—may perceive the "strait and narrow way" too narrowly. References to this concept appear many times in the scriptures, essentially as a description of a clearly marked corridor to salvation and exaltation—a path of high adventure for the brave. It is not for the intolerant. It is not an ecclesiastical country club situated on a narrow theological terrace. (*Choose*, pp. 17–18.)

The "way" is as wide as infinity in terms of its focus on love and truth. It confines us simply by marking those peril points along the path of life that only a fool would ignore, and fools are never really free; they are not brave—they are ignorant. (*Choose*, p. 18.)

To risk leaving the straight and narrow way is to risk sliding into sensuality or tumbling into terror—so much so that divine reminders are appropriate. (*Choose*, p. 21.)

Far from the smugness which some wrongly see in the straight and narrow path; far from the Jonah-like pattern of viewing mankind in its misery safely from the hillside; far from disengaging us from service to the multitude—the Gospel of Jesus Christ calls us to help others and hurry home where a divine parent is expecting us. (*Choose*, pp. 21–22.)

There is not one strait and narrow path for the officers—the chosen—and another for the enlisted men. We are all to experience life "according to the flesh"; there is no other way, for it is the way to immortality and eternal life. (*Sermons*, p. 26.)

As we look about us we perceive that unfortunately some Church members are in the "broad" way; most are scattered all along the straight and narrow path. The enlightened are moving forward steadily toward becoming men and women of Christ (see 3 Nephi 27:27; Helaman 3:29–30). Others are moving, but only irregularly. Some are dawdling. Still others are milling round the exits and entrances. A few have turned back or been turned aside. . . . Others are moving but, having pursued the wrong azimuth, find themselves caught in various cul-de-sacs. In order to resume the journey they must back up in full view of other climbers. These are among the moments when some find out whether they are "ashamed" of the gospel of Jesus Christ, including its grand principle of repentance. (*Men and Women*, pp. 1, 3.)

Perhaps the tilt to the telestial occurs because many feel less compromised when they are led carefully down the paved, gently descending, wide way, on which there is no exhilaration, whereas in climbing up the straight and narrow way, one seems to notice every chuckhole and all the loose gravel. (*Experience*, p. 2.)

The straight and narrow way stretches before us. It is not a freeway or an escalator; it is not even a gentle slope upward. There are no turnoffs and few scenic views or pauses for one to catch his breath. (*Press Forward*, p. xi.)

Lest the initiate think he is hemmed in because of the straightness and narrowness of the way, that analogy pertains to doctrines and behavior, for there is a wide world with remarkable room for creativity in our service to others and in the application of our God-given talents. (*Press Forward*, p. 33.)

Pressing forward without looking back too much is recommended for the same wise reasons some are told not to look down when climbing, lest the heights dizzy them. All of us are acrophobes so far as the ascending straight and narrow is concerned. (*Press Forward*, p. 87.)

Those who insist on walking in their own way will find that all such paths, however individualistic in appearance, will converge at that wide way and broad gate—where there will be a tremendous traffic jam. (*Not My Will*, p. 12.)

Our posture on the straight and narrow path is not to be one of resigned, rounded shoulders accompanied by downcast eyes. God's invitation to "come home" and Jesus' to "come, follow me" are not invitations to a contraction of one's soul; rather they are invitations to expansion and enrichment in both the here and now and the there and then. (*Faith*, p. 119.)

SUBMISSIVENESS

There can be no conditions attached to unconditional surrender to God. Unconditional surrender means we cannot keep our obsessions, possessions, or cheering constituencies. (*Not My Will*, p. 92.)

We express our desires out of an imperfect perception, and upon learning the Father's desires, we yield to His eternal perspective and purposes. It is the only surrender that is also a victory! (*As I Am*, pp. 47–48.)

To be submissive "even as a child doth submit to his Father" is a hard saying, but it is more than poetry; it reminds us of our true genealogy and our true possibility. (*As I Am*, p. 95.)

Spiritual submissiveness is so much more than bended knee or bowed head. (*Ensign*, May 1985, p. 70.)

Spiritual submissiveness means . . . community and communion as the mind and the heart become settled. We then spend much less time deciding, and much more time serving; otherwise, the more hesitation, the less inspiration. (*Ensign*, May 1985, p. 71.)

Most forms of holding back are rooted in pride or are prompted by the mistaken notion that somehow we are diminished by submission to God. Actually, the greater the submission, the greater the expansion! (*On Becoming a Disciple-Scholar*, p. 22.)

Subjection to God is really emancipation. (*Ensign*, May 1985, p. 71.)

Some are so proud they never learn of obedience and spiritual submissiveness. They will have very arthritic knees on the day when every knee shall bend. There will be no gallery then to play to; all will be participants! (*Ensign*, May 1987, p. 70.)

Why do we resist and resent life's developmental and obedience tests? By declaring, "I will walk in my own way and do that which is right in my own eyes," we reject the curriculum of the mortal school in which we are irrevocably enrolled. (See Judges 21:25; D&C 1:16.) There is only one exit gate leading unto eternal life. Unhappily, only a few find it—but not because God is exclusionary, but because they exclude God from their lives. Even God cannot bring to pass a reconciliation involving only one party. (*Ensign*, November 1988, p. 33.)

Our submissiveness to the Lord must be real, not the equivalent of obeying the speed limit only as long as the highway patrolman is there in his pace car. (*Prove*, p. 7.)

SUCCESS

We should be genuinely glad when others succeed; if we cannot at first cheer, then let us at least not sneer. (*Press Forward*, p. 37.)

Since time is so precious a commodity, we must not be dismayed when the time permitted to savor success seems so small on occasion. High moments are soon followed by fresh challenges. It could scarcely be otherwise, for none of us would for long want to be banqueting over our blessings while others stood without, waiting for the touch of our lives and talents. (*Press Forward*, p. 125.)

SUFFERING

Righteous sorrow and suffering carve cavities in the soul that will become later reservoirs of joy. (*Meek*, p. 11.)

There are many who suffer so much more than the rest of us: some go agonizingly; some go quickly; some are healed; some are given more time; some seem to linger. There are variations in our trials but no immunities. Thus, the scriptures cite the fiery furnace and fiery trials. (Daniel 3:6–26; 1 Peter 4:12.) Those who emerge successfully from their varied and fiery furnaces have experienced the grace of the Lord which He says is sufficient. (Ether 12:27.) Even so, such emerging individuals do not rush to line up in front of another fiery furnace in order to get an extra turn! However, since the mortal school is of such short duration, our tutoring Lord can be the Schoolmaster of the compressed curriculum. (*Ensign*, May 1997, pp. 11–12.)

Suffering is the sweat of salvation. (*Choose*, p. 42.)

[The true believer] is ready to follow the Lord into soul-stretching experiences even if it means enrolling [in] the schooling of suffering and paying his tuition. ("'True Believers in Christ,'" p. 138.)

Only the Lord can compare crosses! ("Taking Up the Cross," p. 255.)

We may genuinely wonder if any good can come out of a particular situation of suffering. Whether the sufferer is actually growing and developing in some needed way may not be apparent to us. We may wonder whether the suffering of another person provides an opportunity for the rest of us for expressions of service, prayer, empathy, and attentiveness that we need to develop further. (*Believe*, p. 108.)

In life, the sandpaper of circumstances often smooths our crustiness and patiently polishes our rough edges. There is nothing pleasant about it, however. And the Lord will go to great lengths in order to teach us a particular lesson and to help us to overcome a particular weakness, especially if there is no other way. In such circumstances, it is quite useless for us mortals to try to do our own sums when it comes to suffering. We can't make it all add up because clearly we do not have all the numbers. Furthermore, none of us knows much about the algebra of affliction. (*Notwithstanding*, pp. 67–68.)

With regard to human suffering . . . there is no way in which the misery caused by misused agency could be removed without removing agency. (*Not My Will*, p. 71.)

Since the Most Innocent suffered the most, our own cries of "Why?" cannot match His. But we can utter the same, submissive word, "nevertheless . . . " (Matthew 26:39). (*Ensign*, November 1995, p. 24.)

The more one's will is . . . "swallowed up," the more his afflictions, rather than necessarily being removed, will be "swallowed up in the joy of Christ" (Alma 31:38). (*Ensign*, November 1995, p. 24.)

TALK SHOWS

Instead of being communicating neighbors, we are flooded with talk shows, some of which feature not real conversation but exhibitionism and verbal voyeurism among virtual strangers. (*Ensign*, May 1993, p. 77.)

The recurring irony of some talk shows is [that they] often feature those who bare their inmost souls to strangers but cannot converse effectively with spouse or children! (*Endure*, p. 92.)

TEACHING

Let all gospel instruction in the home or classroom be a genuine experience in learning—not merely doctrinal Ping-Pong. (*Ensign*, November 1980, p. 15.)

Jesus loved people enough to teach them specific things. He did not merely live among people as so many of us do, for co-existence is not real brotherhood. Teaching is a significant form of service, just as is witnessing to one's neighbor. (*Experience*, p. 68.)

We live and teach amid a wide variety of individual personalities, experiences, cultures, languages, interests, and needs. Only the Spirit can compensate fully for such differences. "The sword of the Spirit" is the penetrating "word of God" (Ephesians 6:17). Thus holy scripture and the words of living prophets occupy a privileged position and they also perform a special task. Teaching by the Spirit employs what the Prophet Joseph Smith called "the language of inspiration." (*Believe*, p. 39.)

When we speak about teaching by the Spirit it is not about a mystical process which removes responsibility from the missionary or teacher for prayerful and pondering preparation. Teaching by the Spirit is not the lazy equivalent of going on "automatic pilot." We still need a carefully worked out "flight plan." Studying out something in one's own mind is, in itself, an invitation to the

Spirit in our preparations as well as in our presentations. We must not err, like Oliver Cowdery, by taking no thought except to ask God for His Spirit (D&C 9:7). The Lord is especially willing to take the lead of an already informed mind in which things have been "studied out." Additionally, if we already care about those to be taught, the Lord can inspire us with any customized counsel or emphasis which may be needed. (*Believe*, pp. 40–41.)

Somewhere between the extreme of "cat's cradle" classrooms and the other extreme of hypertense, activist teachers (who do not undestand the role of contemplation, reflection, and worship and who would empty the classrooms of the Church and have us all march off heedlessly to become involved) there is a golden mean wherein teaching is outcome oriented, in which teaching makes fresh demands of us with our consent—a kind of teaching which brings life and lessons together. Such teaching generates faith which moves us to productive action in behalf of others because the gospel is true. And we continue to know that it is true because we constantly witness it working! (*Power*, pp. 7–8.)

Instruction . . . must be of a high quality. Attendees must feel the Spirit as they are taught. These individuals need the bread of life, not crumbs from the table. After all, the father of the prodigal son prepared a feast for the returnee—he did not merely warm up some leftovers! (*Ensign,* May 1982, p. 37.)

The failure to connect the teaching of the gospel with real life can make gospel discussion a kind of intellectual "cat's cradle," to be reshaped and passed back and forth. (*Power*, p. 7.)

Since we can only speak the smallest part of what we feel, anyway, we should see to it that the "smallest part" is taught by the Spirit. (*Believe*, p. 45.)

TELEVISION

We are lathered with soap operas in need of nothing so much as soap—for the scrubbing of themselves! Some seriously maintain that media violence and sleaze leave consumers untouched. But revenue is received from commercials precisely because of their influence. Either we deserve reforms, or sponsors deserve refunds! (*Ensign*, May 1993, p. 77.)

TEMPLES

Temple attendance is not a guarantee that we will become better, but it provides a powerful and pointed invitation to become better. The ways of the world receive constant reinforcement—should not the ways of heaven? (*Not My Will*, p. 133.)

Temples are designed not only to endow and to seal us but also to refine us. (*Flood*, pp. 125–26.)

While the temple is a place of service, work done there is not a substitute for Christian service in the outside world. It can be a powerful spur thereto, however, by reminding us of the need for sacrifice—not the giving of just our means but also of ourselves. (*Not My Will*, p. 133.)

Temple work is not an escape from the world but a reinforcing of our need to better the world while preparing ourselves for another and far better world. Thus, being in the Lord's house can help us to be different from the world in order to make more difference in the world. (*Not My Will*, p. 133.)

Through a democracy of dress, temple attendance reminds us that God is no respecter of persons (Acts 10:34). The symbolic purity of white likewise reminds us that God is to have a pure people (D&C 100:16). (*Not My Will*, p. 135.)

TEMPTATION

Jesus noticed the tremendous temptations that came to him, but He did not process and reprocess them. Instead, He rejected them promptly. If we entertain temptations, soon they begin entertaining us! Turning these unwanted lodgers away at the doorstep of the mind is one way of giving "no heed." Besides, these would-be lodgers are actually barbarians who, if admitted, can be evicted only with great trauma. (*Ensign*, May 1987, p. 71.)

So much will depend. . . upon our developing and using righteous reflexes. Reprocessing the same temptation, again and again, is unnecessary and unwise. (*Ensign*, February 1986, p. 19.)

The tempter's triad of tools, identified by Jesus as temptation, persecution, and tribulation, will be relentlessly used. (See Matthew 12:21; Luke 8:13.) (*Ensign*, November 1982, p. 68.)

Cycling and recycling the same temptation (instead of rejecting such blandishments out of hand) is not only to risk one's soul, again and again, but is to bring on fatigue, so that the Adversary may be able to do indirectly what we will not let him do directly. (*Smallest Part*, p. 51.)

Succumbing to temptation is not the result of one's being grossly overprogrammed, but of grossly undervaluing oneself! (*Notwithstanding*, p. 79.)

A disciple . . . would avoid being in an earthly environment that perpetually presses him to compromise. . . . Joseph . . . finally fled out of the presence of Potiphar's wife. Even then, he didn't escape unrighteous judgment, but he refused to become bitter because he had been falsely accused. Chances are that some of us would do well to flee (more often than we do) those settings in which Satan can so incessantly work upon us. By refusing to escape, we can place ourselves in circumstances where temptations could become more than we can bear. It is our obligation to get out of such circumstances. (*Deposition*, p. 67.)

Going to "Lucifer's Lounge" is not only risky for us, but may also mislead, divert, or discourage another weaker colleague. It is up to us to use our agency to make certain that we are not tempted above that which we are able to bear. (*Deposition*, p. 67.)

In coping with temptation we can usually interrupt the temptation by a change of thought, scenery, or circumstance. Alcoholics on the road to reform don't hang around bars. (*Deposition*, p. 67.)

Our temptations, small or large, seem to match the moment. The evil one also avoids using that which is most apt to be deflected by us. (*As I Am*, p. 72.)

Brooding over temptations can produce self-pity and a false sense of nobility. Prolonged consideration of a temptation only increases the risks—but it does not increase our options: the two options and the consequences remain the same regardless of our dallying. Moreover, protracted consideration of a temptation does not increase the justification to succumb—only our rationalization. (*As I Am*, p. 73.)

Just as personal goodness in mortality consists of accumulating service rather than a single act, so temptation is not a one-time thing
either. The points of our personal vulnerability, as Satan cunningly
observes them, will be exploited. Lucifer will quote scripture if it
helps, or cite supposed opportunities for us to do good. He will
offer chances for self-indulgence and even provide the preparatory
self-pity—whatever might induce rationalization on our part. (*As I
Am*, p. 76.)

There are simply too many bleached bones lying about the landscape which serve as haunting reminders of the importance of flee-
ing from the terrain of temptation. (*My Family*, p. 116.)

Those confronted by *large* temptations *usually* got there by "setting
themselves up" in *small* ways. Their dalliance has already caused
them to look the other way as some guerrillas are let into the
palace grounds of the soul. (*Notwithstanding*, pp. 77–78.)

Unlike Jesus, sometimes we first provide access for temptations.
By paying even small heed to a temptation, we thus forget that
temptations are like a poison gas—they spread through the time
and space available to them. Once inside and unrebuked, they are
not easily evicted. (*Prove*, p. 44.)

TEN COMMANDMENTS

Without the Decalogue there is decadence. (*Ensign*, November
1980, p. 14.)

Of the Ten Commandments, *as originally given*, eight were stated as
"thou shalt nots" and two required affirmation. (See Exodus 20,

Deuteronomy 5, but also Leviticus 19:18.) Jesus' later statement cast the two great commandments as grand affirmatives (see Matthew 22:34–40). Our duties involve implementing ways of keeping the two great commandments because they require us to "do" rather than to merely "abstain." Abstentions do not necessarily move us on to affirmative actions, and our duties constitute the "thou shalts," in the gospel of Jesus Christ. ("'True Believers in Christ,'" pp. 135–36.)

Human misery is nothing more than the flip side of the Ten Commandments. Most of the news we read or watch on television represents, in one way or another, the breeching of God's commandments, departures from the "great plan of our God." Different consequences emerge so quickly from different lifestyles. (*We Talk of Christ*, pp. 73–74.)

TESTIMONY

Let us be articulate, for while our defense of the kingdom may not stir all hearers, the absence of thoughtful response may cause fledglings among the faithful to falter. What we assert may not be accepted, but unasserted convictions soon become deserted convictions. ("'All Hell Is Moved,'" p. 179.)

My tongue cannot tell all I know. (*Ensign*, May 1976, p. 26.)

When we first cross the border of belief and enter the territory of testimony, that is a highly significant moment. We come through, as it were, a port of entry. The Spirit has borne witness to us that Jesus is the Christ, that God lives, that other truths related to these are accepted by us. Our later experiences do not really represent the recrossing of that border again and again, but are reminders and reassurances of the earlier resolve. One does not need perpetual reasons for reentry. (*Deposition*, p. 51.)

TESTING

Mortality without the dimension of temptation or trial would not be a full proving; it would be a school with soft credits and no hard courses. (*Prove*, p. 45.)

Knowing that one is in the midst of a testing time does not make the test any less real. The disciple is not able to wink slyly, as if he could cope with one hand tied behind him. Instead, his teeth rattle, too. (*Deposition*, p. 52.)

We [should not] be surprised if, having passed one test well, another seems to come so quickly. Was it not so for Him? He did not get three months off after the three great temptations or a weekend at the seashore after delivering the Sermon on the Mount. He was not allowed to extend His triumphal entry into Jerusalem into a year-long celebration. Quickly, so quickly, the realities of what He next had to do bore down upon Jesus. (*As I Am*, p. 66.)

The tests given to us here are given not because God is in doubt as to the outcome, but because we need to grow in order to be able to serve with full effectiveness in the eternity to come. . . . The relentless love of our Father in Heaven is such that in His omniscience He will not allow the cutting short some of the brief experiences we are having *here*. To do so would be to deprive us of everlasting experiences and great joy *there*. What else would an omniscient and loving Father do, even if we plead otherwise? He must at times say no. (*Experience*, p. 26.)

One may be stripped of accustomed luxury so that the malignant mole of materialism may be removed. One may be scorched by humiliation, so pride can be melted away. Whatever we lack will get attention, one way or another. (*Ensign*, November 1995, p. 24.)

THANKSGIVING

Thanksgiving is historically and rightly connected with the sense of *annual* blessings of the harvest. Such annualized pauses (whether for Christmas, Easter, etc.) can cause us to ponder and reflect concerning all of that which is good. However, we should not only celebrate our *annual* Thanksgiving but gladly affirm by our attitudes and behavior the great and *continual* blessing of life itself. (Local Thanksgiving speech [untitled] November 26, 1980.)

Though we live as neighbors, we function in geographical units. It is necessary and proper that we do the latter, but it is good, on occasions such as this, to gather in love as neighbors—and as an appreciative community of believers. Thanksgiving is a time in which we can count our blessings and celebrate family life. We also stir through our individual storehouses of memories, being nourished in the autumn and winter of our lives by what was placed there in times of spring and summer. Hence, Thanksgiving is an especially poignant time of reflection for the widows and widowers who are here. Thanksgiving is a time, too, of hopeful anticipation for those few parents who have prodigals who are still away—but for the harvest of whose spiritual homecoming they ceaselessly pray. ("Patience and the Law of the Harvest.")

Among so many things deserving of our deepest gratitude in this season of Thanksgiving is the feasting fulness of the Restoration. It is like a harvest basket which, to use Jesus' metaphor, is a "good measure, pressed down, and shaken together, and running over." (Luke 6:38.) This abundant harvest spares us from hungering because of doctrinal deprivation. The lack of fulness has real consequences, especially for those who struggle, for instance, with adversity while trying to believe in a God of loving purpose. Each of the key doctrines . . . by itself, would help us. In combination, however, these doctrines can produce stronger faith by providing vital spiritual nourishment. The Restoration is not only a harvest "running over," but it also brings back vital "plain and precious things"—the balanced essentials. (1 Nephi 13:26.) ("Fulness in the Fulness of Times.")

THEOCRACY

Some dismiss the Church out of hand for not being trendy in its theology and for being authoritarian. To such I say, better a true theocracy with a little democracy than a democracy without any theology. Yes, the kingdom of God is a kingdom; there is no "one man, one vote" rule between its King and its citizens. ("'All Hell Is Moved,'" p. 177.)

THOUGHTS

In a decaying environment, the mind is the last redoubt of righteousness, and it must be preserved even amid bombardment by evil stimuli. (*Ensign*, May 1987, p. 71.)

The human mind is remarkably retentive. We must be careful of what we allow in our mind, for it will be there for a long time, reasserting itself at those very times when we may be most vulnerable. Just as harmful chemicals heedlessly dumped in a vacant lot can later prove lethal, so toxic thoughts and the mulching of the wrong memories in the vacant corner of the mind also take their toll. (*Prove*, p. 44.)

TIME

Whereas the bird is at home in the air, we are clearly not at home in time—because we belong to eternity. Time, as much as any one thing, whispers to us that we are strangers here. ("Patience," p. 220.)

How we spend our time is at least as good a measure of us as how we spend our money. An inventory of how we spend our disposable time will tell us where our treasure is. (Matthew 6:19–21.) (*Notwithstanding*, pp. 116–17.)

There are no idle hours; there are only idle people. In true righteousness there is serenity but there is an array of reminders that the "sacred present" is packed with possibilities which are slipping by us, which are going away from us each moment. ("Taking Up the Cross," p. 260.)

Good management of one's time can actually make more time available for people. On a few occasions, in kindness and in love, we can help others avoid imposing on our time inefficiently or inappropriately. Except for real crises, if we have relationships of trust, we can without fear indicate that a particular moment is not best for us, offering a genuine alternative. There are examples of situations when even the Savior made others wait—for their own good. "Instant" help is not always the best help, if it creates in others the unrealistic expectation that such mortal help is always available to them. (*Smallest Part*, p. 49.)

Longevity does not automatically produce humility. The mere passage of time does not mean the automatic passing of milestones in personal development. (*As I Am*, p. 47.)

To withhold some of oneself brings subtle consequences. There is always the irrevocable loss of misspent time. Time spent in indulging oneself cannot be spent simultaneously in other ways. We cannot engage in murmuring and use that same time for praising. We cannot engage in griping at the very time we are consoling others. (*Flood*, p. 98.)

Time, unlike some material things, cannot be recycled. (*Choose*, p. 13.)

We are often actually less generous with our time than with our money. We keep forgetting where our time comes from! (*Experience*, p. 73.)

TITHING

If . . . we were spiritually ready for the law of consecration, there would be no poor among us. (D&C 49:20.) No wonder the Church stresses the law of tithing, a law to prepare us for something higher. The world looks at the principle of tithing and sees a system of revenue; we look at it and see also a system of salvation, an anticipation of consecration. (*Deposition*, p. 87.)

TRAGEDY

Sin is the only real and lasting tragedy! (*Ensign*, May 1983, p. 11.)

[Speaking of a gymnast whose tragic tumble left her paralyzed in body, but vibrant in spirit and mind:] She fell not into paralysis but into saintliness. She becomes a witness in a wheelchair. How tall she stands, and how much she stretches the souls of others! Her deprivation is like an excavation, the readying of a reservoir into which a generous God, one day, will pour the Malachi measure of compensatory blessings, "that there shall not be room enough to receive it." (Malachi 3:10.) (*Ensign*, May 1983, p. 11.)

TRAVEL

Is it the terrain one traverses which is the true test of his life? If so, should those of us who travel in the jet age view with condescension the mileage logged by Jesus during his mortal ministry? In those days "from Dan to Beersheba" seemed so sweeping, yet it involved only a little over a hundred miles. One day our travels about this planet will seem quite provincial too when we are wafted from planet to planet. ("Grounded, Rooted, Established, and Settled," p. 18.)

TRENDS

As we consider the context in which we live, including various and vexing trends, it is ever to be borne in mind that the Church is surely not trendy, though too many of its members, alas, follow the trends of the world. (*Endure*, p. 31.)

Some trends need correcting, others accelerating. (*Press Forward*, p. 31.)

It is not only today's America that is in trouble. So are the next generations, who will live dangerously "downwind" from these contaminating conditions. (*Endure*, p. 25.)

TRUST

It is better to trust and sometimes be disappointed than to be forever mistrusting though right occasionally. This is to endorse empathy, not naivete. ("Insights from My Life," p. 199.)

Mostly, to avoid muttering, we need to trust more. So many of the things muttered about beforehand turn out to be marvelous experiences later, and we are inwardly, and deservedly, ashamed for having grumbled. (*Deposition*, p. 31.)

TRUST IN GOD

It is only by yielding to God that we can begin to realize His will for us. And if we truly trust God, why not yield to His loving omniscience? After all, He knows us and our possibilities much better than do we. (*Ensign*, May 1985, p. 72.)

What we already know about God teaches us to trust him for what we do not know fully. (*Deposition*, p. 56.)

For the faithful, what finally emerges is an understanding of "things as they really are" (Jacob 4:13), such as the reassuring realization that we are in the Lord's hands! But, brothers and sisters, we were never really anywhere else! (*Ensign*, May 1985, p. 72.)

Mormon [declared]: "And now, I *do not know all things*; but *the Lord knoweth all things* which are to come; wherefore, *he worketh in me to do according to his will.*" [Words of Mormon 1:7; italics added.] Such is the trust that we need in God's omniscience, causing us to be entreated, freely, into participating in His purposes—and without fretting. Such trust allows us to be concerned with making a good choice rather than brooding over whether or not we had a choice. Besides, if we cannot accept and trust in the Lord's declaration that He has left us "free to choose," in which of His other declarations can we then trust? Being now limited in our information and limited in our perception, it is a good time to trust God! (*As I Am*, p. 59.)

Thus it is that our faith and trust in our Heavenly Father, so far as this mortal experience is concerned, consists not simply of faith and gladness that He exists, but is also a faith and trust that, if we are humble, He will tutor us, aiding our acquisition of needed attributes and experiences while we are in mortality. We trust not only the Designer but also His design of life itself, including our portion thereof! (*Prove*, p. 12.)

Coming to "put our trust in the living God" is not the work of a day or a season. Instead, this mortal school continues to the very end, when the final school bell rings for each of us. (*Believe*, p. 33.)

TRUTH

Salvational truths combine longevity and relevancy; they contain both span and significance! Education that is only "for a season" is narrow; it pertains only to a knowledge of things as they temporarily are, like today's weather forecast or an airline schedule. Temporary facts are useful but terminal. ("The Inexhaustible Gospel," p. 146.)

We constantly need to distinguish between the truths which are useful and those which are crucial, and between truths which are important and those which are eternal. The restored gospel gives us this special sense of proportion. (*On Becoming a Disciple-Scholar*, p. 6.)

In human affairs, erroneous and unchallenged assertions sometimes assume an undeserved aura of truth. While a response to this hopelessness may not create conviction in disbelievers, it can bolster believers against the silent erosion of their own convictions. (*Ensign*, May 1983, p. 9.)

Truth, as Mount Sinai showed, transcends the importance of the terrain on which it is given. (*Ensign*, November 1984, p. 9.)

In point of value, longitudinal truth, when compared to truth which reflects reality as it exists in only a portion of one of the three great time zones—past, present, and future—is like the Bible when it is compared with the single issue of a newspaper. (*Smallest Part*, p. 5.)

Gospel truths about life and the human condition stand in stark contrast to the world's view; the world's solutions so often lead mankind into conceptual cul-de-sacs. Without gospel truths, man's efforts to reach his goals are like the northbound explorer who drove his dog sled feverishly northward on an ice pack that was flowing southward—only to find himself farther from his destination at the end of a hard day's journey than he had been at dawn! (*Smallest Part*, p. 36.)

The theology of truth about man, life, and the universe does not depend for its validity on acceptance by many, or even any. Only eight people were right about the weather in Noah's time when being right really mattered. (*Deposition*, p. 14.)

The gospel is continuing education at its best. However, the gospel isn't simply another building block to be fitted into the tower of truth; it is the tower of truth itself. (*Deposition*, p. 16.)

Truth cuts across all three time zones—our premortal state, our second state (mortality), and the eternal future that is fashioned for us. (*Deposition*, p. 48.)

Truth can be very threatening. We do not read, for instance, that the power structure in Jerusalem ever seriously searched the sermons of Jesus with a view to understanding; the *cognoscente* concerned themselves with entrapment, not enlightenment. (*Deposition*, p. 61.)

One wonders if the reaction to Jesus' first visit to Nazareth—rage—was not in some respects preferable to the deliberate disdain experienced in connection with his second visit. Satan's stratagems are apparent: If one cannot face truth, then he can merely dismiss it by stereotyping or dismissing the source. Dismiss the message because of the lowly messengers. (*As I Am*, p. 85.)

Truth does not eliminate the force of life's tragedies and frustrations, but it provides a context within which one can cope with them. (*My Family*, p. 32.)

Christ's disciples should ever realize that wandering in the under-
brush of the unimportant or in the forest of facts there are many
"who are only kept from the truth because they know not where to
find it" (D&C 123:12). In our passion for equality we sometimes
wrongly assume there is a democracy among truths. (*Believe*, p. 140.)

Intellectual embroidery is but an unreliable frill; the hardy and
homely cloth of truth is to be found in the hardy gospel of Jesus
Christ. (*Heart*, p. 29.)

Bearers of truth are often victimized by partial truths. Partial
truths can sometimes have such an influence as to make full false-
hoods green with envy. (*Meek*, p. 108.)

Trends do not change truths. (*Press Forward*, p. 3.)

A dying civilization can, of course, be annoyed by the living
Church. People who are cut to the very center by the truth, the
laser of our Lord that emanates from the living Church, will gladly
"turn away their ears from the truth, and be turned unto fables"
(2 Timothy 4:4); it is so much less painful. (*Really Are*, pp. 58–59.)

God, who does not grow weary of making all daisies alike and
whose course is one eternal round, does not tire of certain truths as
do we mortals. Nor does the repetition of a true phrase reduce its
relevancy; it vouches for its validity. (*Really Are*, p. 101.)

Universe

Wonder is added to wonder as temples and scriptures tell us of still other worlds—of a universe drenched in divine design, with, as it were, spiritual "cousins" in the cosmos. (*Ensign*, May 1986, p. 36.)

We are . . . enveloped in a planned universe, and we live on a purposeful planet; and these truths describe "things as they really are" (Jacob 4:13). No wonder the gospel is such glorious and good news! (*Ensign*, November 1986, p. 54.)

"Worlds without number" have been created (Moses 1:33; see also John 1:3; Hebrews 1:2; 22:3; D&C 93:10). These gospel truths are very significant assurances for us, situated as we are on this tiny "speck of sand" at the outer edge of a minor galaxy, the Milky Way. Without the gospel's fulness, we would appear to be living during one tick of the geological clock and in the midst of unexplained vastness. (*Ensign*, November 1987, p. 30.)

The Restoration gives us few details concerning the universe, of course, but from what we are given we know that we are not alone, and that we are in the midst of meaning and unfolding, divine purposes. Though understandably desiring to know more, we do not presently possess the capacity to absorb more. Nor do we have an adequate "security clearance." (*Endure*, p. 81.)

Valiance

[Some Church] members are "honorable" but not "valiant." They are not really aware of the gap nor of the importance of closing it (see D&C 76:75,79). These "honorable" individuals are certainly not miserable or wicked, nor are they unrighteous and unhappy. It is not what they have done, but what they have left undone that is amiss. For example, if valiant, they could touch others deeply instead of merely being remembered pleasantly. (*Ensign*, November 1995, p. 22.)

VALUES

When we stop acknowledging the existence of fixed value points in the scheme of things, we stop navigating by these points. And having stopped steering, to use a simple analogy, there is, at first, the naive, excited exclamation: "Look! No hands!" But this will be followed by the shocked realization: "Help! No brakes!" (*My Family*, p. 37.)

Do not overpack the luggage you plan to take with you when you leave this world, for we simply cannot get most mortal things by celestial customs; only the eternal things are portable. (*Ensign*, November 1974, p. 12.)

There is, as we all know, much talk about family values, but rhetoric, by itself, cannot bring reform. (*Ensign*, May 1994, p. 89.)

Where are those synagogues now in which it was once so desperately important for some to maintain their place rather than to confess publicly their belief in Jesus? (See John 12:42–43.) (*Sermons*, p. 13.)

If the big things that really matter are finally going to work out in eternity, then the little things that go wrong mortally are not cause for desperation but perhaps only for a little frustration and irritation. (*Notwithstanding*, p. 50.)

VEIL

Without the veil, we would lose that precious insulation which would constantly interfere with our mortal probation and maturation. Without the veil, our brief mortal walk in a darkening world would lose its meaning—for one would scarcely carry the flashlight of faith at noonday and in the presence of the Light of the World. Without the veil, we could not experience the gospel of work and the sweat of our brow. If we had the security of having already entered into God's rest, certain things would be unneeded; Adam and Eve did not clutch social security cards in the Garden of Eden. ("Patience," p. 219.)

The partition which produces [premortal forgetfulness] is something we call the veil—a partition the presence of which requires our patience. We define the veil as the border between mortality and eternity; it is also a film of forgetting which covers the memories of earlier experiences. This forgetfulness will be lifted one day, and on that day we will see forever—rather than "through a glass, darkly" (1 Corinthians 13:12). ("Patience," p. 219.)

We are cocooned, as it were, in order that we might truly choose. Once, long ago, we chose to come to this very setting where we could choose. It was an irrevocable choice. And the veil is the guarantor that our ancient choice will be honored. ("Patience," p. 220.)

Fortunately, the veil keeps the first, second, and third estates separate, hence our sense of separateness. The veil insures the avoidance of having things "compound in one"—to our everlasting detriment. (2 Nephi 2:11.) (*Experience*, p. 11.)

The veil (which is both the film of forgetting and the border between mortality and eternity) will, one day, be shown to have been a succoring screen for us earthlings. Were it possible to breach it on the wrong terms, we would see and experience, before we are ready, things that would moot much of the value in this mortal experience. (*Experience*, p. 11.)

The veil of death stands, not to forever shut us out but as a reminder of God's tutoring and patient love for us. Brushing against it can produce a feeling of "Not Yet," but also faint whispers of anticipation. Then there is the still later and glorious moment when, in the words of the hymn, those who have prevailed "by the patience of hope and the labor of love" will hear in the final judgment these glad words, "Well and faithfully done; enter into my joy and sit down on my throne." (*Hymns*, no. 217.) ("Patience and the Law of the Harvest.")

WAR

The almost unceasingness of wars is but the fulfilling echo of prophecy. Who knows better than the Lord that wars originate in the hearts and minds of man? . . . Can we presume to lecture the Lord on war? Or dare to use war as an argument against His existence or His Lordship? Do we need to warn Him about how the earth can be destroyed by fire? (*As I Am*, p. 105.)

WARNINGS

The Paul Reveres in our lives may have voices too shrill, use bad grammar, ride a poor horse, and may pick the oddest hours to warn us. But the test of warnings is their accuracy, not their diplomacy. The disciple's commitment to truth must be to truth, without an inordinate concern for the method of delivery. (*Press Forward*, p. 69.)

If in these times there seem to be more warnings than in other ages, it is because this is not a time when there can be many words. When someone is about to step into the path of an oncoming truck, the individual giving the warning does not take time to explain the make, model, and color of the truck that is coming or indeed to mention the velocity. He simply shouts! There is often no time to do more regarding some of the trends in our society. (*Press Forward*, p. 113.)

Little wonder that the prophets are so repetitious in their warnings, some almost shrill at times. After all, if one were permitted only a few final lines—words to be transmitted to family, friends, and posterity—they might very reasonably take the form of headlines or a shouted summation to those not stirred by the still, small voice. (*Not My Will*, p. 78.)

Voices of warning are meant to be heard, not just raised. (*Ensign*, November 1994, p. 36.)

WEAKNESSES

By playing upon the weaknesses of men, the adversary can easily persuade many that these weaknesses are so congenital that they cannot (indeed, need not) be overcome. (*As I Am*, p. 87.)

WEALTH

Large bank accounts [can not] fill the empty vault of the soul. (*Experience*, p. 61.)

WICKEDNESS

The laughter of the licentious, which was so much a part of Sodom, is not a sign of real joy, for sensuality is sadness. The peculiar hypocrisy of the sinner is that he pretends he is happy when truly his heart is pierced with deep wounds, for wickedness never was happiness. Oh, how relentlessly the wicked seek company with others, for in departing from their God, their loneliness is an awful and a solemn loneliness. (*Look Back*, p. 24.)

Truly, not only do seeds and species produce after their own kind, but wickedness begets wickedness. (*Look Back*, p. 6.)

A little mud sliding down a hill can soon become a flood of filth. (*Look Back*, p. 15.)

The deluge in Noah's time was a disaster after which mankind began all over again. In the case of Sodom, there were three survivors, but the destruction of culture and place was total; there was no Phoenix-like re-emergence; until this day one sees in that place only barrenness and unfertility. Where once the ungodly ate, drank, and made merry, now there is perpetual silence. But it is a special silence that shouts to those who have ears to hear! (*Look Back*, p. 26.)

WISDOM

A man cannot be truly "learned" if he deliberately seeks to ignore the wisdom not only of the ages, but of the eternities. If during his mortal journey he drinks only worldly water, he will find that his deepest thirsts are unslaked and inextinguishable. We can obtain "living water" from only one stream. (*Choose*, pp. 53–54.)

The wise learn from their past, but the stubborn, by their lack of understanding, err endlessly. (*Look Back*, p. 4.)

Being "learned" (by simply indiscriminately stockpiling a silo of truths) is not necessarily the same thing as being wise, for wisdom is the useable distillation of data—not merely its collection and storage. (*Smallest Part*, p. 4.)

WOMEN

The daughters of the world may grow more shrill, more hard, more selfish, and less motherly—but the faithful daughters of Zion will be ladies of light; they will be elect because they have elected to follow in the footsteps of the faithful women of God who have existed in all dispensations of time. That we know less than we would like of these marvelous women of God should fill us with anticipation for the day when there will be a fulness of their record before us, a part of all that God will yet reveal. Service less reported is service still. Contributions are never really measured in column inches of coverage in newspapers or even in the scriptures. Indeed, their deferred recognition only mirrors faintly the quiet queenliness of One we shall meet and greet when we leave "this frail existence." (*Press Forward*, pp. 80–81.)

I have never sung Eliza R. Snow's lyrics of 1845 in the anthem of appreciation, "O My Father," without being touched by its reverence for womanhood, which is light years ahead of some current, cosmetic attempts to dignify womanhood. (*Deposition*, p. 82.)

We men know the women of God as wives, mothers, sisters, daughters, associates, and friends. You seem to tame us and to gentle us, and, yes, to teach and to inspire us. For you, we have admiration as well as affection, because righteousness is not a matter of role, nor goodness a matter of gender. In the work of the Kingdom, men and women are not without each other, but do not envy each other, lest by reversals and renunciations of role we make a wasteland of both womanhood and manhood. (*Ensign*, May 1978, p. 10.)

[Men] know that we can go no place that matters without you, nor would we have it otherwise. When we kneel to pray, we kneel together. When we kneel at the altar of the holy temple, we kneel together. When we approach the final gate where Jesus Himself is the gatekeeper, we will, if faithful, pass through that gate together. (*Ensign*, May 1978, p. 11.)

Just as certain men were foreordained from before the foundations of the world, so were certain women appointed to certain tasks. Divine design—not chance—brought Mary forward to be the mother of Jesus. The boy prophet, Joseph Smith, was blessed not only with a great father, but also with a superb mother, Lucy Mack, who influenced a whole dispensation. . . . A widow with her mite taught us how to tithe. . . . The divine maternal instincts of an Egyptian woman retrieved Moses from the bullrushes, thereby shaping history. . . . Does it not tell us much about the instrinsic intelligence of women to read of the crucifixion scene at Calvary, "And many women were there beholding afar off." (Matthew 27:35.) Their presence was a prayer; their lingering was like a litany. And who came first to the empty tomb of the risen Christ? Two women. Who was the first mortal to see the resurrected Savior? Mary of Magdala. Special spiritual sensitivity keeps the women of God hoping long after many others have ceased. (*Ensign*, May 1978, p. 10.)

So often the service of women seems instinctive, while that of men seems more labored. (*Ensign*, May 1978, p. 10.)

WORD OF WISDOM

The Word of Wisdom, whose validity has been demonstrated amply by science—at least in some of its specifics—has too often been lauded solely as a health code, which, while true, often leaves out the relevancy of this doctrine in terms of the awful arithmetic of alcoholism, for instance. If, as many of the young generation maintain, violence and death are the ultimate obscenity, alcohol is obscene in terms of the death and maiming it causes on the high-ways, the child beatings, and the terrible tragedies in the homes where it visits its full afflictions. (*Power*, p. 55.)

WORK

We ignore the fact that work is a spiritual necessity at the peril of our souls. (*Choose*, p. 54.)

The principle of work is also fundamental to spiritual ecology. We shall come to know that work is a spiritual necessity, even if the time comes when it is not an economic necessity. (*Power*, p. 2.)

If we ponder just what it is that will rise with us in the resurrection, it seems clear that our intelligence will rise with us, meaning not simply our IQ, but also our capacity to receive and apply truth. Our talents, attributes, and skills will rise with us; certainly also our capacity to learn, our degree of self-discipline, and our capacity to work. Our precise form of work here may have no counterpart there, but the capacity to work will never be obsolete. (*Prove*, p. 12.)

WORLD

To be too quick to adjust to the ways of this world is to be malad-justed for the next. (*Really Are*, p. 3.)

By letting go of the world, we gain the grasp of an outstretched hand that belongs to Him who was once offered the world. Satan now tries to persuade us through his blandishments that what he offered Jesus (and was turned down) is still a bargain. We, too, must spurn Satan, that loser who knows nothing of real success and who wants to mutualize his misery. (*Press Forward*, p. 2.)

The more quickly we loosen our grip on the things of the world, the more firmly we can take hold of the things of eternity. ("'Build Up My Church,' 'Establish the [Lord's] Righteousness.'")

My beloved young friends, you are the vanguard of the righteous spirits to be infused into the Church in the last days. Back beyond time, it was so determined, and you were prepared—before the foundations of the world—to help save others in the latter-day world. You cannot keep that resplendent rendezvous if you become like the world! Make your righteous marks on the world instead of being spotted by the world. (*Ensign*, February 1986, p. 20.)

And when we tear ourselves free from the entanglements of the world, are we promised a religion of repose or an Eden of ease? No! We are promised tears and trials and toil! But we are also promised final triumph, the mere contemplation of which tingles one's soul. (*Ensign*, November 1974, p. 13.)

Knowing that we live in eternity, how can we conclude that, because of the fleeting pleasures and pressures of the world, we have no time for children? Furthermore, may not the many wounded strewn along life's way justifiably expect us eternals not to be in too much of a hurry? (*Flood*, p. 44.)

Perhaps one of the reasons people try desperately at times to effect a "merger" is that they still want either the praise of the world or the ways of the world. They think, somehow, to have them both when, in fact, the essence of the gospel of Jesus Christ is that we must clearly *choose* some things and *reject* others. Mortal philosophies can be mixed and merged with each other almost at will, because they are not totally dissimilar, but we can't weld the Lord's way to the world's ways. (*Experience*, pp. 108–9.)

By even appearing to throw in with the world, we throw off those who may just be making their first tentative moves toward faith and spiritual stability. (*Deposition*, pp. 24–25.)

The world's way is the equivalent of using Band-Aids for arthritis. (*As I Am*, p. 106.)

Some mean to keep their place in the synagogue, even if it means losing their place in heaven! (*As I Am*, p. 113.)

When we speak of letting go of the world, this does not mean forgoing its sunsets, its beautiful music, nor, best of all, its people. The "world" is a way of life that takes us away from, not toward, God. Away from, not toward, happiness. Away from sense to nonsense. (*Press Forward*, p. 1.)

Worldly emancipation carried to excess is typical of telestial trends that usually lack any inner controls. Only the Lord's way balances our need for liberty and belonging. If we cling to the world, we will have neither! (*Press Forward*, p. 17.)

The only way to avoid being overcome by the cares of the world . . . is to stop caring so much for the world. (*Press Forward*, p. 20.)

WORLDLINESS

Our hope, unless it is strong, can be at the mercy of our moods and can be badgered and bullied by events and by the contempt of the world, which we will experience in rather large doses in the irreligious last part of the last dispensation. Part of the contempt of the world comes because the worldly do not understand the things of the Spirit and regard such as foolishness and stupidity. Therefore, attacks on the Church are not always rebuttable *in worldly terms*. There are those who are multilingual but cannot communicate in the mother tongue of faith. Sometimes the best response is a certain silence, such as that of the Master before Pilate. (*Notwithstanding*, p. 45.)

Not losing behavioral uniqueness or theological thrust is a challenge both for the institution of the Church and for the individuals in it, but never more so than now, when these restored values are in the path of the killer tides in various cultures. Indeed, the surf has already begun to pound. . . . As wave after worldly wave breaks over the rising generation in the Church, there will be casualties. Some waves will be huge, one-time waves; others will be repeater waves, striking again and again. Drugs, pornography, promiscuity, alcoholism, homosexuality, ersatz emancipation movements, divorce, and statism (in which citizens surrender to the state, saying "save us from ourselves") are among such waves. (*Press Forward*, p. 60.)

Each generation is consumed with building sand castles which the tides of time soon wash away, clearing the beach just in time for the next "tourists" to start the whole process anew. (*Sermons*, p. 16.)

Casual members are usually "anxiously engaged" with the cares and the things of the world. . . . Some of these otherwise honorable members mistakenly regard the Church as an institution, but not as a kingdom. They know the doctrines of the kingdom, but more as a matter of recitation than of real comprehension. (*Ensign*, November 1992, p. 66.)

It will take no faith to renounce worldly things when these are among the ashes of a melted planet (3 Nephi 26:3; D&C 43:32; Ether 4:9). (*Not My Will*, p. 12.)

The Father's plan . . . was set up to bring us all the way "home." Upon entering the third estate, however, we will never know the welcoming embrace of the celestial gate's keeper if in this second estate we embrace the things of the world (see 2 Nephi 9:41; Mormon 5:11; 6:17). (*Faith*, p. 47.)

If settled [see Colossians 1:23; 2:7; 2 Peter 1:12], we will not be "tossed to and fro," whether by rumors, by false doctrines, or by the behavioral and intellectual fashions of the world. Nor will we get caught up in the "talk show" mentality, spending our time like ancient Athenians "in nothing else, but either to tell, or to hear some new thing" (Acts 17:21). Why be concerned with the passing preferences of the world anyway? "For the fashion of this world passeth away" (1 Corinthians 7:31). (*Ensign*, May 1987, p. 70.)

Nations continue their costly and obsessive work on the Maginot Line of materialism, looking to it for satisfaction and safety even as they are being outflanked by racing columns of consequences. (*Not My Will*, p. 79.)

If one "mind[s] the things of the flesh" (Romans 8:5), he cannot "have the mind of Christ" (1 Corinthians 2:16), because his thought patterns are "far from" Jesus, as are the desires or the "intents of his heart" (Mosiah 5:13). (*Ensign*, November 1995, p. 22.)

WORSHIP

The ultimate adoration is emulation, which helps us to become like those we worship. (*Flood*, p. 36.)

Verbal veneration by itself is like tipping one's hat and nodding with a smile—instead of falling upon one's knees. (*As I Am*, p. 36.)

The world encourages us to pay attention to secular Caesars. The gospel tells us, however, that these Caesars come and go in an hour of pomp and show. It is God whom we should worship, and His Son, Jesus Christ. (*Not My Will*, p. 137.)

Part of worshipping God is to appreciate the blessed and happy things even as we pass through the noxious and obnoxious things. True, life's recesses and reveries do not last for long, but they are there, as a foretaste. The many blessings to be counted far outnumber the trials which press upon us. (*Faith*, p. 119.)

YOUTH

Our youth are sometimes buffeted daily in Babylon beyond what we who are older know. They need at least a rudimentary understanding of the plan of salvation, especially in their tender times of growing up. For them, in a moment of needed response, the smile of one friend is like a standing ovation. A compliment can part the curtain on their unappreciated possibilities. Unfortunately, however, our youth can almost be terrorized by the disapproval of their peers. It is as if their group's "thumbs down" were the equivalent of a Roman emperor dispatching with finality gladiators in the Colosseum. (*Faith*, p. 36.)

Emancipation from adult control is often replaced by peer-run "prisons." (*Choose*, p. 7.)

Can the Fall—with the resultant necessity of work "by the sweat of the brow"—be taught without the youth having validating experiences with work? The latter is hard to achieve, especially for some advantaged youth in some urban settings. But we ignore the principle of work at our developmental peril. (*Faith*, p. 117.)

The wave of anti-establishment feelings (or at least of very low confidence in national institutions and our historical ways of doing society's business) among some of the young in America and the way they act it out (ranging from passivity to hostility) will not wash over the youth of the Church completely; but some will be sprayed by the surf, and this could dampen their ardor. (*Choose*, p. 3.)

ZION

Zion . . . is where the pure in heart dwell and where there is joy of countenance. By contrast, in hell there are no smiles! (*Heart*, p. 37.)

Since there are no instant Christians, to withhold what we can do to accelerate the process of the perfection of Zion until Zion is nearly perfected is to misconstrue mortality. To withhold all (or even much) of our fellowship, our talents, or our tithing until the Church and its people meet our "high" standard is like trying to book passage on Noah's ark without driving a nail in a plank. We simply walk on board and ask to be shown to our stateroom and inquire as we enter the stateroom about what time dinner is served at the Captain's table! We must sign on for the voyage with all our imperfections, and commit to help each other. (*Press Forward*, pp. 5–6.)

NEAL A. MAXWELL'S
SPEECHES AND WRITINGS CITED

General Conference Addresses (in chronological order)

"Response to a Call," *Ensign*, May 1974, p. 112.

"Why Not Now?" *Ensign*, November 1974, pp. 12–13.

"The Man of Christ," *Ensign*, May 1975, pp. 101–2.

" 'Jesus of Nazareth, Savior and King,' " *Ensign*, May 1976, pp. 26–27.

"Notwithstanding My Weakness," *Ensign*, November 1976, pp. 12–14.

"The Women of God," *Ensign*, May 1978, pp. 10–11.

"The Net Gathers of Every Kind," *Ensign*, November 1980, pp. 14–15.

" 'O, Divine Redeemer,' " *Ensign*, November 1981, pp. 8–10.

" 'A Brother Offended,' " *Ensign*, May 1982, pp. 37–39.

" 'Be of Good Cheer,' " *Ensign*, November 1982, pp. 66–68.

" 'Shine As Lights in the World,' " *Ensign*, May 1983, pp. 9–11.

"Joseph, the Seer," *Ensign*, November 1983, pp. 54–56.

"The Great Plan of the Eternal God," *Ensign*, May 1984, pp. 21–23.

" 'Out of Obscurity,' " *Ensign*, November 1984, pp. 8–11.

" 'Willing to Submit,' " *Ensign*, May 1985, pp. 70–73.

"Premortality, a Glorious Reality," *Ensign*, November 1985, pp. 15–18.

" 'Called and Prepared from the Foundation of the World,' " *Ensign*, May 1986, pp. 34–36.

" 'God Will Yet Reveal,' " *Ensign*, November 1986, pp. 52–59.

" 'Overcome . . . Even As I Also Overcame,' " *Ensign*, May 1987, pp. 70–72.

" 'Yet Thou Art There,' " *Ensign*, November 1987, pp. 30–33.

" 'For I Will Lead You Along,' " *Ensign*, May 1988, pp. 7–9.

" 'Answer Me,' " *Ensign*, November 1988, pp. 31–33.

"Irony: The Crust on the Bread of Adversity," *Ensign*, May 1989, pp. 62–64.

" 'Murmur Not,' " *Ensign*, November 1989, pp. 82–85.

" 'Endure It Well,' " *Ensign*, May 1990, pp. 33–35.

"Put Off the Natural Man, and Come Off Conqueror," *Ensign*, November 1990, pp. 14–16.

" 'Lest Ye Be Wearied and Faint in Your Minds,' " *Ensign*, May 1991, pp. 88–91.

"Repentance," *Ensign*, November 1991, pp. 30–32.

" 'My Servant Joseph,' " *Ensign*, May 1992, pp. 37–39.

"'Settle This in Your Hearts,'" *Ensign*, November 1992, pp. 65–67.

"'Behold, the Enemy Is Combined,'" *Ensign*, May 1993, pp. 76–79.

"'From the Beginning,'" *Ensign*, November 1993, pp. 18–20.

"'Take Especial Care of Your Family,'" *Ensign*, May 1994, pp. 88–91.

"'Brightness of Hope,'" *Ensign*, November 1994, pp. 34–36.

"'Deny Yourselves of All Ungodliness,'" *Ensign*, May 1995, pp. 66–68.

"'Swallowed Up in the Will of the Father,'" *Ensign*, November 1995, pp. 22–24.

"'Becometh As a Child,'" *Ensign*, May 1996, pp. 68–70.

"'According to the Desire of [Our] Hearts,'" *Ensign*, November 1996, pp. 21–23.

"'From Whom All Blessings Flow,'" *Ensign*, May 1997, pp. 11–12.

Brigham Young University Speeches

"'All Hell Is Moved,'" *1977 Devotional Speeches of the Year*. Provo, Utah: Brigham Young University, 1978, pp. 176–81.

"'Brim with Joy' (Alma 26:11)," *1995–96 Speeches*. BYU, 1996, pp. 141–50.

"But for a Small Moment," *Speeches of the Year 1974*. BYU, 1975, pp. 443–57.

"The Children of Christ," *1989–90 Devotional and Fireside Speeches*. BYU, 1990, pp. 79–91.

"'A Choice Seer,'" *1985–86 Devotional and Fireside Speeches*. BYU, 1986, pp. 113–21.

"Grounded, Rooted, Established, and Settled," *1981–82 Fireside and Devotional Speeches*. BYU, 1982, pp. 14–19.

"'In Him All Things Hold Together,'" *1990–91 Devotional and Fireside Speeches*. BYU, 1991, pp. 103–12.

"The Inexhaustible Gospel," *1991–92 Devotional and Fireside Speeches*. BYU, 1992, pp. 139–48.

"Insights from My Life," *1976 Devotional Speeches of the Year*. BYU, 1977, pp. 187–201.

"'Meek and Lowly,'" *1986–87 Devotional and Fireside Speeches*. BYU, 1987, pp. 52–63.

"Meeting the Challenges of Today," *1978 Devotional Speeches of the Year*. BYU, 1979, pp. 149–56.

"Out of the Best Faculty," *Brigham Young Magazine*, February 1994, pp. 30–33, 48.

"Patience," *1979 Devotional Speeches of the Year*. BYU, 1980, pp. 215–20.

"Taking Up the Cross," *1976 Devotional Speeches of the Year*. BYU, 1977, pp. 249–63.
"'True Believers in Christ,'" *1980 Devotional Speeches of the Year*. BYU, 1981, pp. 134–40.

Other Talks

"The Book of Mormon: A Marvelous Work and a Wonder," seminar for new mission presidents, June 21, 1996.
"'Build Up My Church,' 'Establish the [Lord's] Righteousness,'" local Thanksgiving speech, November 24, 1996.
"'A Choice Seer,'" local Thanksgiving speech, November 27, 1985.
Church Educational System Fireside, June 4, 1995, Marriott Center, Brigham Young University.
"Coordination of Full-Time and Stake Missionary Work," Regional Representatives Seminar, March 30, 1990.
Fourth of July Celebration, Midway, Utah, July 4, 1991.
"Fulness in the Fulness of Times," local Thanksgiving speech, November 23, 1994.
"Integrity . . . The Evidence Within," speech to Brigham Young University Law School alumni, October 9, 1992.
"Jesus: Lord of Loving-Kindness and of the Far-flung Vineyard," local Thanksgiving speech, November 27, 1991.
"King Benjamin's Sermon: A Manual for Discipleship," F.A.R.M.S. Symposium, [BYU] April 13, 1996.
"'Lord, Increase Our Faith,'" local Thanksgiving speech, November 24, 1993.
"'Meek and Lowly,'" local Thanksgiving speech, November 26, 1986.
"'O, How Great the Plan of Our God,'" Church Educational System Fireside, February 3, 1995.
"Patience and the Law of the Harvest," local Thanksgiving speech, November 21, 1979.
Remarks [untitled] given at BYU-Hawaii, January 7, 1994.
Satellite, Missionary Training [untitled remarks], delivered at Missionary Training Center, September 13, 1994.
"Successful Leadership in Organizations, Communities and Families," Marriott School of Management [BYU] fireside, June 21, 1996.
Talk given January 8, 1995.
Talk given January 13, 1995.
Talk given October 14, 1996.

"'Thanks Be to God,'" local Thanksgiving speech, November 25, 1981.
"Thanksgiving for the Fulness of the Gospel Granary," local Thanksgiving speech, November 23, 1983.
"Thanksgiving for the Holy Scriptures," local Thanksgiving speech, November 24, 1982.
Thanksgiving speech [untitled], November 26, 1980.

Books

All These Things Shall Give Thee Experience. Salt Lake City: Deseret Book Co., 1979.
"But for a Small Moment." Salt Lake City: Bookcraft, 1986.
Deposition of a Disciple. Deseret Book, 1976.
Even As I Am. Deseret Book, 1982.
"For the Power Is in Them . . ." Mormon Musings. Deseret Book, 1970.
If Thou Endure It Well. Bookcraft, 1996.
Look Back at Sodom. Deseret Book, 1975.
Lord, Increase Our Faith. Bookcraft, 1984.
Meek and Lowly. Deseret Book, 1987.
Men and Women of Christ. Bookcraft, 1991.
". . . A More Excellent Way." Deseret Book, 1967.
"Not My Will, But Thine." Bookcraft, 1988.
Notwithstanding My Weakness. Deseret Book, 1981.
Of One Heart. Deseret Book, 1975.
Plain and Precious Things. Deseret Book, 1983.
Sermons Not Spoken. Bookcraft, 1985.
The Smallest Part. Deseret Book, 1976.
That My Family Should Partake. Deseret Book, 1974.
That Ye May Believe. Bookcraft, 1992.
Things As They Really Are. Deseret Book, 1978.
A Time to Choose. Deseret Book, 1975.
We Talk of Christ, We Rejoice in Christ. Deseret Book, 1984.
We Will Prove Them Herewith. Deseret Book, 1982.
Wherefore, Ye Must Press Forward. Deseret Book, 1977.
A Wonderful Flood of Light. Bookcraft, 1990.

Pamphlet

The Christmas Scene. Salt Lake City: Bookcraft, 1994.

Ensign Articles

" 'By the Gift and Power of God,'" *Ensign*, January 1997, pp. 36–41.
" 'Cleanse Us from All Unrighteousness,'" *Ensign*, February 1986, pp. 18–20.
"It's Service, Not Status, That Counts," *Ensign*, July 1975, pp. 5–7.

Other Publications

"A Conversation with Elder Neal Maxwell," in Hugh Hewitt, *Searching for God in America*, Dallas: Word Publishing, 1996.
Neal A. Maxwell, "The Disciple Scholar," in *On Becoming a Disciple-Scholar*, Henry B. Eyring, editor. Salt Lake City: Bookcraft, 1995.
Neal A. Maxwell, "King Benjamin," in *Heroes from the Book of Mormon*. Salt Lake City: Bookcraft, 1995.

Letter

Neal A. Maxwell letter to a Church member, August 9, 1995.

Video Presentation

" 'The Gift and Power of God,'" video presentation recorded June 8, 1993.

INDEX

Boldface page numbers refer to main topics.